PRINCIPLES FOR GROWTH

Biblical Principles
For Christian Maturity

By John H. Stoll, Th.M, Ph.D.

John H. Stoll, Copyright 1996
All rights reserved
Biblical Principles for Christian Maturity,
Reviewed and Extended, 2003, 2004, 2009

Unless otherwise noted, all Scripture taken from
The Authorized King James Holy Bible

ISBN: 0-9706962-7-2

Publisher
River City Press, Inc.
15400 28th Avenue
Plymouth, MN 55447
www.rivercitypress.net
publisher@rivercitypress.net

Cover Photograph
Roger James Donald
Sacramento, CA

Cover Design
Holland-Tuve Design
Dianne and Chris Holland-Tuve
Minneapolis, MN

Graphic Layout Design
Sara Jo Johnson
Roseville, MN

Second Edition
Printed in the USA

DEDICATION IN MEMORY

To my beloved father, Dr. Ralph H. Stoll; my eleventh grade Sunday school teacher, Faye Keith; Dr. Robert Culver, my Old Testament and Hebrew language Professor; and Theology Professor Dr. Alva J. McClain who, together, instructed, nurtured, and inspired my spiritual development.

PEARLS OF WISDOM
FOR UNDERSTANDING THIS BOOK

Do not let this book of the law depart from your mouth; meditate on it day and night, so that you may be careful to do everything written in it. Then you will be prosperous and successful.

- Joshua 1:8 (NIV)

Blessed is the man whose delight is in the law of the Lord, and on His law he meditates day and night. He is like a tree planted by streams of water, which yields its fruit in season and whose leaf does not wither. Whatever he does prospers.

- Psalm 1:2,3 (NIV)

Delight yourself in the Lord, and He will give you the desires of your heart. Commit your way unto the Lord; trust also in Him, and He will bring it to pass.

- Psalm 37:4,5 (NIV)

The mind of sinful man is death, but the mind controlled by the Holy Spirit is life and peace.

- Romans 8:6 (NIV)

The Lord will make you the head, not the tail. If you pay attention to the commands of the Lord your God that I give you this day and carefully follow them, you will always be at the top, never at the bottom.

- Deuteronomy 28:13 (NIV)

Wisdom is a shelter as money is a shelter, but the advantage of knowledge is this: that wisdom preserves the life of its possessor.

- Ecclesiastes 7:12 (NIV)

TABLE OF CONTENTS

Section Two: Philosophical/Psychological Principles with Biblical Truths For Practical Living

FOREWORD

From now on, book shelves will be graced by Dr. Stoll's revision and expansion of his previous and very successful book entitled, "Biblical Principles For Christian Maturity."

The quality of maturity in the Christian's faith is of utmost importance. Pastors are often confronted by problems caused mostly by spiritual immaturity. The sure and only way to be a victor in the Christian life is to attain spiritual maturity in Christ. It should be stressed that a new believer in the Lord Jesus does not mature immediately or automatically. It is a process and could be also defined as *sanctification*, that is, becoming more like our Master, Jesus. In Romans 8:29, Paul emphasized God's will for the believer as being, "Predestined to be conformed to the image of His Son...."

In his numerous, short, easy to read chapters, Dr. Stoll discusses a great variety of subjects related to growth in Christ. In every realm of our lives we should desire growth and the kind that brings maturity. The author clearly sets forth the elements that are necessary as we travel the road that leads to maturity.

Dr. Stoll is eminently qualified to write such a book, for he has served as a pastor, professor, Bible conference speaker, counselor and author. Having known him for over half a century, I know that he has keen understanding of the subjects of spiritual growth and maturity based on II Peter 3:18, "But grow in the grace and knowledge of our Lord and Savior, Jesus Christ." The better we know Him, the more mature we will be, and hence more pleasing to our Heavenly Father.

I recommend this volume very highly. It deserves to be read, carefully studied and, above all, put into practice.

P. Fred Fogle, Th.M.; Ph.D.

Tallahassee, Florida

i

INTRODUCTION

Across the pathway and into the life of every person, come people who leave an indelible impression upon that individual. Such was my life. Of the many and varied influences that have molded me, there were four men who touched my life, made an indelible impact upon it, and fashioned my character. What I am today, and for whatever quality of life I experience, I have realized over and over again, these men have made me what I am, and who I am. They were my foundation for life, and I have constructed my life upon their influence.

The majority of concepts in forming my worldview or philosophy of life came through the modeling of these men. The seminal ideas and constructs in this book—hammered out over the fifty years I have been privileged to serve Him—have grown out of the seeds implanted in me by their examples of Godly living, as well as the precepts I learned from them.

He has taken these four human instruments of His Grace, and together used them to mold me into the person I have become. Added to this, has been the consistent prodding, teaching, guiding, correcting, and helpful instruction of God's Holy Spirit. For all this I shall be eternally grateful, for truly, "The lines have fallen unto me in pleasant places." My Lord and Savior not only saved me through the influence of Godly parents, but also used these men as guides and influences in my life.

These men to whom I owe so much, and to whose memory I gratefully dedicate this book, (three have passed on to their eternal reward) include the following: first of all, my beloved father, Dr. Ralph H. Stoll, who modeled an exemplary Christian life before me, taught me the way of life, was a kind, gracious Christian gentleman, and an outstanding Bible expositor; secondly, my eleventh grade Sunday School teacher, Faye Keith, who knew how to handle teenagers in a Christlike way; thirdly, my Old Testament and Hebrew professor in seminary, Dr. Robert Culver, who gave me a love for the Old Testament and the Hebrew language; and finally, the one who fleshed out my understanding of Scripture in Theology classes in seminary, Dr. Alva J. McClain. Without them, from a human perspective, I would never

iii

have achieved what I have acquired in education—professionally or experientially.

When I started this book, I decided to write all the chapters in outline form, duplicated them and taught the contents to the men in my Bible class at the Minneapolis Athletic Club over a three year period. They became my pilot project, and their feedback helped in fleshing out the chapters as they are now written. To these men I owe a debt of gratitude for their spiritual and wise comments which gave me greater insight to the truths presented in this book. They were of tremendous help.

In II Timothy 2:2, the Apostle Paul, in speaking to his son in the faith, Timothy, stated, "And the things you have heard of me among many witnesses, the same you commit to faithful men, who shall be able to teach others also." One of the blessings and joys I have experienced through all these years, is to have been spiritually fed by great men of faith, and then, in turn, be able to convey to thousands of my students in college, the blessings and challenges of God's Holy Word. Many of my former students have gone on to serve the Lord, and it rejoices my heart to realize that God's Word is being passed along from generation to generation.

God's revelation to mankind, is found in His word, the Bible— a book devoted to principles for living, illustrated through human relationships, and thus applicable to us today for our daily guide. The chapters of this book are written from a two fold concept: first to be a guide to understanding the principles, and secondly, to show in a practical way how the principles may be applied to life's situations. So, every chapter is both Biblical and practical. It is with prayerful anticipation that this volume may be used of the Lord to instruct and guide those who read to a fuller life of experience, since Christ said in John 10:10, "I am come that you may have life, and that you may have it more abundantly." The command to the Christian is to, "Grow in grace and the knowledge of the Lord Jesus Christ" (I Peter 2:2; II Peter 3:18).

John H. Stoll, Th.M., Ph.D.
Executive Director, ASK. Inc.
Spring 2004

There is joy in serving Jesus
As I journey on my way,
Joy that fills my heart with praises,
Every hour and every day.

There is joy in serving Jesus,
Joy that triumphs over pain,
Fills my soul with heaven's music,
Till I join the glad refrain.

There is joy in serving Jesus,
As I walk alone with God;
Tis the joy of Christ, my Saviour,
Who the path of suffering trod.

There is joy in serving Jesus,
Joy amid the darkest night,
For I've learned the secret,
And I'm walking in the light.

There is joy, joy, joy in serving Jesus.
Joy that throbs within my heart;
Every moment, every hour, as I draw upon His power,
There is joy, joy, joy, that never shall depart

PREFACE

In Ecclesiastes 12:12, Solomon states, "...of making many books there is no end." With the plethora of books today, on any given subject, why should there be another one?

When I was trying to decide the research project for my doctoral dissertation at the university, I searched for an idea that would be challenging, as well as fruitful, to use in my ministry. Having been a Bible and Theology professor for over 25 years, and having taught thousands of students, I felt that, by and large, Christians were basically ignorant, not of Bible facts, but of Biblical concepts and principles and underlying purposes for which God had revealed Himself through the Scriptures. They knew names, dates, places, events, history, geography, etc., but could not fit this information into the larger picture, i.e. God's desire that the Bible be a guide for mature Christian living.

In addition to my classroom teaching, I had been privileged to minister in many churches and various denominations, held Bible conferences in churches and conference facilities, as well as conducting home Bible study classes. All of these resources of information that I had experienced led me to believe that my basic premise was valid. Therefore, I undertook to investigate it in a research project for my dissertation.

My first concern was to find a testing instrument that would evaluate what I wanted to know. Unfortunately, after careful research on a testing device, I found that there was none. I did find Bible knowledge tests, but they tested the things that I already knew that people understood about the Bible. They did not evaluate the concepts behind the facts. So, my first task was to design a Biblical conceptual evaluating instrument to provide me with the information I wished to obtain. It took a year to design and validate my testing instrument. Then I administered it to over 1300 high school seniors in 33 Christian academies. Basically these students had been raised in a Christian home, attended an evangelical church, and for the most part had gone to Christian schools. I felt that they, if any, should have many of the Biblical concepts for Christian maturity of life. At that point my basic premise stood up.

Many years have passed and I have been privileged to direct a Christian counseling clinic, with a Bible teaching element directed toward business people. I have continued to pursue my premise, believing that Christians are basically illiterate of the underlying revelation of God through His word to His children, and the real reason for the Bible. My present ministry along with my teaching career, and my research, has only confirmed what I originally perceived to be a deficiency among God's children.

Once a person has become a Christian, with a personal committal of life to the Lord Jesus Christ, and what He did for us through His death, burial, and resurrection, God's anticipation for His child is spiritual maturity. That is primary and foremost of what God desires in each of us. In I Peter 2:2, it states, "As newborn babes, crave the unadulterated milk of the word, that you may grow thereby." Then in II Peter 3:18 we have what I believe is the primary concept of God for His children, that is to, "Grow in Grace, and in the knowledge of our Lord and Savior Jesus Christ." In both passages it is in the imperative mode in the Greek, which means a command to do it.

Growing in Grace means to become more Christ-like in our character, so that we exemplify in our behaviors the fruit of the Spirit, as seen in Galatians 5:22-24. To grow in the knowledge of Christ has two aspects, intellectual knowledge of Him through the Bible, and experiential understanding through the trials and tribulations of life. When all this is put together in one's life, with an openness for the Holy Spirit to apply the basic principles of the Bible to life, then that person truly experiences the fullness of life that God intends all of His children to have. That is why Christ said in John 10:10, "I am come that you may have life, and that you may have it more abundantly."

To further enlighten the reader as to what I believe the Bible refers to as the maturation process of the Christian, let me illustrate by analogy. When one begins to learn a foreign language, he memorizes elements of that language, then he begins to formulate sentences, etc., but when he *crosses over* and begins to think in that language, he enjoys a fullness of understanding never afforded to him before. It opens up a whole new concept of understanding. So likewise, God not only wants us to know the facts of God's Word, but He desires that we know the concepts and principles primarily, so that we can put them all together and think Biblically, as God thinks. This is what is meant by I Cor. 2:14, "But the unregenerate person receives not the things of the Spirit of God…because they are spiritually discerned." God desires that His children have this discernment in life (not just to know the facts of the Bible) so that we are able to apply these principles to life itself.

This is what this book is all about. Over fifty years of teaching and ministering God's word to countless Christians, has impressed upon me the deficiencies of the knowledge of Biblical principles. Therefore, I trust that the chapters of this volume will help provide a conceptual understanding of God's truth, so that those who read it will be able to see more clearly what the revelation of God to us is really all about. When we get to heaven we will no longer need the Bible for, "We shall be like Him, for we shall see Him as He is" (I John 3:2). There will no longer be a, "looking through a glass darkly" (I Cor. 13:12), but a fullness of God Himself throughout eternity. No, the Bible is a book for the here and now, to guide us into mature living for today. Yes, there are glimpses of the future, but the fullness of that understanding awaits the revelation of it.

There are many and varied deceptions in the world, and the primary design of Satan against mankind is to keep one from an understanding of a person's separation from God due to sin, and how that separation may be overcome through a personal commitment to Jesus Christ as Lord and Savior. Once a person has made a commitment to Christ, and become a regenerated person (i.e. a child of God), then Satan uses a very subtle deception on the Christian. Since the devil can't take a person's salvation from him, for that is God's gift of eternal life, he tries to keep the Christian from becoming a spiritually mature person, so that he does not develop as God desires, nor is he able to be used of God as an *ambassador* of Him (II Cor. 5:20). The means by which Satan achieves this deception is to fill the Christian's mind with the knowledge and facts of the Bible, thereby subtly causing the Christian to believe he has Biblical understanding, and is coming to maturity. Rather, one needs to be taught the principles/concepts of Scripture, which are the elements of growth and productivity in the Christian life. I am not saying by this that Bible facts and knowledge are unimportant; I am saying that we have far too long placed an undue emphasis on facts, almost to the exclusion of principles, and been deluded unto believing we are mature Christians through knowing the facts.

As a young man in high school I found myself always behind in most subjects, for I was trying to find out the purpose or objective of what the subject was all about. What was the *big picture*? What would this subject do for me? By the time I had figured that out, and put all the various elements of the subject together so that I could figure out the purpose, I was way behind the rest of the class. I thought to myself that if ever I were to be a teacher (which I never intended as I wanted to be a chemist), I would tell the class at the very beginning—what the goals, purpose, and objectives of the subject were, and the practicality of the subject for them.

When I came to college I was quite surprised. The first thing the professor did was to pass out the syllabus for the subject, and the purpose or objective was clearly stated at the very beginning. Now it was clear. Now there was some goal or purpose in studying the given subject. All of the outline of the work that was to follow was directed to help one understand the purpose through its various parts. There was a cohesiveness there, for the sum of the parts helped one to see the whole.

So it is with Scripture. God's revelation in the Bible has distinct goals or objectives for us as His children. My purpose in writing this book is to show, through the Biblical principles, the *whole* of God's revelation and how the *bits and pieces* that we read fit into God's overall plan of redemption.

Briefly, God's original purpose in the creation was threefold, as stated in Psalms 8:4-6. In v.4 it notes that we were created for fellowship with God; in v.5, to be a reflection of God's moral character (this is what the word "image" means); and in v.6 to have dominion (be king) over the rest of creation. Had Adam and Eve not sinned, these purposes would continue to be filled eternally. But Adam and Eve turned from being God-centered to being self-centered, and God's purpose for mankind was temporarily thwarted. Thus the reason for God's redemptive purpose is to restore mankind to His original purpose in creation. This conclusion awaits future fulfillment. Everything in between is a revelation from God to us, as to how we can become reconciled to Him, and live lives in fulfillment through His guiding principles.

The primary emphasis in the Bible is the principles, God given for our spiritual growth to maturity. He conveys these principles to us, couched in illustrations of human beings in the Bible, so that we can comprehend the principles. We have focused on the illustrations (i.e. names, dates, geography, history, etc.) and many times overlooked what God is trying to help us understand about spiritual growth. These facts of the deprivation of spiritual maturity in the majority of Christians, was borne out in my research of Bible knowledge tests, the examination of over a thousand Christians, and my forty years of teaching Christians Biblical truths. I can honestly say that I believe the majority of Christians today are Biblically illiterate, not in the facts of the Bible, but in the principles and concepts for mature living, that God desires for each of us to have.

In II Peter 3:18, it states, "But grow in grace and in the knowledge of our Lord and Savior Jesus Christ." The *knowledge* that is spoken of here are the principles and concepts for mature Christian growth and development. This is further reinforced in Phil. 3:8,10. When we develop in the likeness of Jesus Christ, then the outliving of God's principles for us will be that our lives will exemplify God's grace, and we will be living examples of the "fruit of the Spirit" (Gal. 5:22-24). To "glorify" God in our lives means to become more like Him in His moral attributes, and thereby live out His likeness, which helps us personally, as well as our being a better *light* to the world (Matt. 5:16).

It is my fondest desire that those who read the pages of this book, may be open to the Holy Spirit's leading and guiding. Christ said of the Holy Spirit that, "He will guide you into all the truth, —and He will glorify me." (John 16:13,14) As growing Christians we need both the truth of God's Word, and the guidance of the Holy Spirit. I liken these two somewhat to a steam locomotive. In order to operate properly it needs both tracks upon which to run, as well as steam in its boiler. So, the Bible is the track of principles to give us guidance, and the Holy Spirit is like the steam to energize, motivate, and give understanding to the principles. In this way the maturity that God desires for every Christian is progressively being fulfilled.

There needs to be a word of caution in reading this book. One of the misconceptions that many Christians have about the Christian life is that God is primarily interested in our performance for Him. This comes from Christ's commission to His disciples to go into all the world and make disciples of all people, as well as the understanding that we are all ambassadors for Him. This is all true, but before we can carry out His command, we need to be instructed and to grow spiritually to Biblical maturity. The divine commission to go should not be so much of an external constraint from other people and the church, as it should be an inner compulsion generated out of a growing maturity that causes one to want to share his faith. The purpose of this book is to assist the Christian in his spiritual growth and journey, so that one will want to share what he is learning out of the resources of knowledge and wisdom he has gained from God's Word.

God has given to every Christian certain distinct gifts and talents, to be used for His service. The Bible and the Holy Spirit are the instruments God uses to develop and hone the gifts. The purpose God has for them, in each person's life, is found in Ephesians 4:12-14, "For the work of maturing of the saints, for the work of ministrations or helps, for the building up of the body of Christ: until we all come in the unity of the faith, and of the knowledge of the Son of God, unto a mature person, unto the measure of the stature of the fullness of Christ: that we be henceforth no more children, tossed to and fro, and carried about with every wind of false doctrine, by the deceitfulness of men, and cunning craftiness, whereby they lie in wait to deceive."

It is this author's hope that as one reads this book, with the understanding that its purpose is intended to provide a framework of Biblical principles upon which to grow, that the reader will be open to the Holy Spirit's leading in developing one's talents, so that together, as the body of Christ, we may individually and collectively fulfill God's holy purpose in our lives. Then, both the author and the reader will be fulfilled through the exercise that both accomplish.

All my life long I had panted,
For a draught from some clear spring,
That I hoped would quench the burning,
Of the thirst I felt within.

Hallelujah! I have found Him,
Whom my soul so long has craved!
Jesus satisfies my longings,
Through His blood I now am saved.

Feeding on the husks around me,
Till my strength was almost gone,
Longed my soul for something better,
Only still to hunger on.

Poor I was, and sought for riches,
Something that would satisfy,
But the dust I gathered round me,
Only mocked my soul's sad cry.

Well of water, ever springing,
Bread of life so rich and free,
Untold wealth that never faileth,
My Redeemer is to me.

Hallelujah! I have found Him,
Whom my soul so long has craved!
Jesus satisfies my longings,
Through His blood I now am saved.

Chapter 1

A THEOLOGY OF THE GRACE OF GOD

There is a need for Christians to think Biblically. That means that one needs to integrate Biblical facts with Biblical principles, so that in discerning God's will one is able to correlate everything that the Bible has to say on that point. Thus the Christian is able to assimilate with understanding what God desires His child to know, through instruction in the Word. The result is that the Christian comes to maturity in Biblical understanding, and follows the admonition to, "Grow in grace and the knowledge of our Lord and Savior Jesus Christ." Maturity in one's spiritual development is the primary goal that God has for all His children. Everything else, e.g. service/ministry, will follow as one comes to maturity. Thinking Biblically is an indication of maturation.

In order for us to properly develop according to God's word, we must begin with the *bottom line* of who God is and His relationship with us. Therefore, we need to understand a theology of God's grace.

In Romans 3:23 we read, "All have sinned and come short of the glory of God." God by *rights* could *write* us all off to eternal damnation, and still be a just God. He created mankind sinless and gave him every opportunity to follow Him. But Adam and Eve turned from being God centered to becoming self-centered, and by that first sin placed all of mankind in sin. (Rom. 5:12) BUT "God so loved the world that He gave," (John 3:16) and sent His Son, Jesus Christ, into this world to provide redemption for all from sin and reconciliation to God. (Rom. 3:24; 5:1; II Cor. 5:17-19; Titus 3:5-7) This is grace,

1

which means the favor of God upon mankind without any merit on anyone's part, love—pure and simple.

The process of God's grace is seen in Eph. 2:8,9 which states that, "By grace are you saved through faith, and that not of yourselves, it is the gift of God." Then in Titus 3:3-8 we have the most condensed and succinct overview of God's grace, "At one time we too were foolish, disobedient, deceived and enslaved by all kinds of passions and pleasures. We lived in malice and envy, being hated and hating one another. *This is the Christian's past.* But when the kindness and love of God our Savior appeared, He saved us, not because of righteous things we had done, but because of His mercy. He saved us through the washing of rebirth and renewal by the Holy Spirit, whom He poured out on us generously through Jesus Christ our Savior. *This is the Christian's present situation by God's grace.* So that, having been justified by His grace, we might become heirs having the hope of eternal life. *This is the Christian's future by God's grace.* This is a trustworthy saying. And I want you to stress these things, so that those who have trusted in God may be careful to devote themselves to doing what is good. These things are excellent and profitable for everyone." *This is God's admonition to Holy living in the Christian.*

An understanding of the Grace of God begins with John 1:17, "For the law was given by Moses, but Grace and truth came by Jesus Christ." Then in Romans 8:14 it says, "For as many are led by the Spirit of God, they are the children of God." In other words, the law of Moses was given for two reasons, first to provide the children of Israel with God's requirements for holiness so that Israel would know how to measure up to that holiness, and also to show the inability of a sinful people to be able, by their own works, to measure up. So, the law which was intended to be a guide to eternal life, in essence became a barrier to it, since none could measure up. (Rom. 7:10) The failure to measure up resulted in separation and alienation from God. (Rom. 3:19,20) Thus the failure of Israel to live up to the law is what the Old Testament teaching is all about, and the need for the prophetic teaching of the coming of Christ to accomplish for mankind what the law was unable to do.

This is why the contrast is given in John 1:17. The law did not accomplish reconciliation of Israel to God, but the grace of God, coming by Jesus Christ did. Now, all who have made a commitment to God through Jesus Christ, and indwelt by the Holy Spirit (Rom. 8:2,14-16) are children of God. Christ said in Matthew 5:17, "Think not that I am come to destroy the law or the prophets; I am come not to destroy, but to fulfill." The law was holy, and just, and good; it was mankind who fell short of what God's holiness required. Therefore, the grace of God, in the person of Jesus Christ, came to fulfill for each of us, what none of us could do, that is, measure up to God's holy requirements. This is God's grace. The child of God has been freed from the penalty of the law. (Rom. 8:2)

The problem to present day application of God's grace, is that in some instances the church has placed the Christian back under the law through legalism (i.e. the imposition of church standards of behavior, e.g. *do's and don'ts*, which may or may not have a Biblical foundation, and are externally imposed, rather than through internal constraint by the Holy Spirit). See Gal. 1:6,7; 2:20,21; I Cor. 1:30; Titus 3:3-8; Rom. 8:4; Phil. 3:9.

How then should a Christian live, if freed from the law? The answer to that is one's attitude toward the Biblical principles. It is not how much is one able to live according to the fleshly desires, but how close one can live to the guiding help of the Holy Spirit through the Word. Let me illustrate. Many years ago there was a gentleman who desired to hire a young man to drive his carriage with a team of horses. As each applicant came in he was asked one simple question, "Sir, tell me how close you can drive my team of horses to the edge of the cliff by the river road without going over." Each young man tried to explain his ability in answer to the question. Finally, one man replied, "Sir, I don't see how close I can drive without going over; I see how far away I can stay." This illustrates what God desires of His children. If we would heed the Word, and discernment of the Holy Spirit, we would not be troubled by the legalism of the church, and thereby walk in the freedom of God's grace. See Col. 2:20-3:4 NIV.

3

In order to better understand the difference between law (legalism) and grace, let us look at various contrasts:

LAW	vs.	GRACE
1. Demands righteousness from mankind.		1. God gives righteousness to all. Rom 3:21;Phil 3:9.
2. Is connected with the Old Testament & works.		2. Is connected with Christ & faith. Rom. 10:4-10.
3. Blesses the good works Exod. 19:5.		3. Saves the bad Eph. 2:1-9.
4. Demands that blessings be earned Deut. 28:1-6.		4. Is a free gift. Eph. 2:8; Rom. 4:4,5.
5. Power is by the individual Rom. 8:4.		5. Power is through the Holy Spirit. Titus 3:5; John 16:13; I Cor. 2:9-14.
6. Is the wrong path of life for the Christian. Rom. 7.		6. Is the right path of life and victory, with peace & joy for the Christian. Rom. 6; Rom. 8:5.

When we walk with the Lord, in the light of His Word,
What a glory He sheds on our way. While we do His good will,
He abides with us still, and with all who will trust and obey.

Trust and obey, for there's no other way,
To be happy in Jesus,
But to trust and obey.

But we never can prove the delights of His love,
Until all on the altar we lay;
For the favor He shows, and the joy He bestows,
Are for them who will trust and obey.

Trust and obey, for there's no other way,
To be happy in Jesus,
But to trust and obey.

—Victorious Life, Keswick, NJ

4

Chapter 2

GOD'S THREE ESSENTIALS

In a point of God's existence, He broke into time and created a world of things, i.e. the heavens, both starry and atmospheric, the earth, and mankind. Genesis 1:26 tells us that God created mankind in His "image and after His likeness," referring not to physical likeness, but according to God's moral character.

In Psalm 8:4-6 it states the threefold purpose for which God created mankind: (1) for fellowship with His creation, v.4; (2) to reflect God's moral character, v.5; and (3) to place mankind as *king* over the rest of creation, v.6. In God's eternal plan this was not only a perfect state, but would be that which would last for eternity. He also told man to fill the earth with his progeny. Into this perfect context Satan came to destroy what God had created, and through deception undermined the creation. This consisted of Satan deceiving Adam and Eve to turn from being God-centered to being self-centered.

Genesis 3:1-7 recounts for us the story of how Satan, through the instrumentality of the serpent, appealed to Adam and Eve in three ways: *the lust of the flesh*, i.e. the tree was good for food, *the lust of the eyes*, i.e. pleasant to the eyes, and *the pride of life*, i.e. desired to make one wise. They ate and thereby separated themselves from God eternally through their self-centeredness. It was not in the eating, per se, that they sinned, but in their willingness to listen and follow Satan rather than God.

5

Into this scene steps God, and in Genesis 3:8-19 we see His confrontation with Adam and Eve. In spite of their sin and consequent separation from God, He made a significant pronouncement in Genesis 3:15 that the "seed" or descendants of Adam through their sin would *bruise his heel*, meaning the sin of mankind would cause God's son, Jesus Christ, to die on a cross, but in His death, burial, and resurrection He would ultimately destroy Satan and sin, and provide reconciliation to all mankind.

Now God began the process of carrying out His pronouncement by choosing Abraham to be the father of a great nation, called Israel, through whom would come the *seed of the woman* that would destroy what Satan had caused. In Galatians 4:4, it states that "when the fullness of the time was come, God sent forth His son, Jesus Christ, made of a woman, to redeem them that were under the law of God's holiness." The first coming of Christ was to destroy the deception of Satan, (Hebrews 2:14) so that God would have a basis for reconciling mankind to Himself, and ultimately fulfill in him the threefold purpose for which He had originally created him. Today, every person who has made a personal commitment to Jesus Christ as savior for their sins, has been regenerated, reconciled, and made a child of God spiritually. (Ephesians 1:3-14) Now, we await the ultimate fulfillment of our body as well as our spirit. (Romans 8:23-25) The Christian today looks forward to the time when God will set up His eternal kingdom, over which we His children will live and reign with Him throughout eternity. Together we will enjoy the ultimate fulfillment of that threefold purpose for which He originally created us. Our knowledge of all this is found in God's revelation to mankind, the Holy Bible.

The Bible is not a book of all knowledge about everything, though it was written by an infinite, omniscient God. As such, it is a highly selective book, and it contains two basic types of information: (1) ESSENTIAL information that God has revealed to mankind, to help him live for today, and (2) RELATIVE information, which relates to and helps us understand the essentials. In itself it is fragmentary, open-ended, and God has not seen fit to reveal the completeness of it to us today but may, throughout eternity, continue to allow us to understand it.

God has given us three essentials in Scripture, and of these there is a complete record found. These essentials are for our benefit in order to live in today's world. They are needed now, and will be concluded when Christ takes the Christians to heaven, though our hope of eternity rests upon our understanding and acceptance of them now. They are: (1) THE REVELATION OF SIN: that is, to show that all have sinned before God, and have come short of measuring up to what His holiness requires. See Romans 3:10-12,18,23. The results to all are both physical and spiritual death. Romans 5:12, John 3:36, 5:24.

(2) THE REVELATION OF SALVATION: to show that Christ came into the world to provide salvation from sin, and to give regeneration and reconciliation to all who trust Him, to God. He did this through His death, burial, and resurrection. (Romans 5:6-8,5:18,3:24, II Corinthians 5:19) In the Bible, not only is the way of Salvation made plain, but the complete plan is given. The results to the believer are great: *Justification*, God's declaration of righteousness; *Sanctification*, the holiness of God conferred upon His children; and ultimate *Glorification*, the eternal life of God for us, which He guarantees to us now through the indwelling Holy Spirit, and will someday fulfill for us in heaven. (Romans 5:1,2; 8:29; Titus 3:7; Ephesians 2:4-7)

(3) THE REVELATION OF SANCTIFICATION: To show those who are justified by faith and are children of God, how they should live as Christians. (Romans 8:3,4; II Corinthians 3:18; Galatians 2:19,20; 5:25; Titus 2:12; I Peter 4:2; Ephesians 5:18 with Colossians 3:16) The Bible provides the guidelines of life, or the track upon which we should walk, and the Holy Spirit provides the power to enable us to carry out God's principles.

When one evaluates these three essentials of the Bible, it is plain to see that qualitatively they are equal, and must be followed in order. Yet, when evaluated quantitatively, it shows that the first two ways take up very little of the Bible, and the third way consumes the major portion of Scripture. It doesn't take God long to show the entrance and destruction of sin, and the need for, and way, of salvation. But the matter of living a holy life takes a whole lifetime. This is the reason for the history of the children of Israel, the illustrations of life as related

7

in the Bible, and the modeling of Jesus Christ through 33 years of life. All these are to help us pattern our lives after God's will for us.

Part of the ministry of the Holy Spirit is to guide the child of God into all the truth, (John 16:13,14) and to transform him into the moral qualities of God. (II Cor. 3:18) The word *glory*, as used in Scripture, always refers to God's moral qualities, and the Holy Spirit's work is to re-characterize Christians so that we reflect those moral and spiritual characteristics of God, as His children. The results are seen in Scripture and quantified as the *fruit of the Spirit*, of which there are nine elements given. To become more Christ-like is not for one to psyche himself up to carry out these elements, but rather to allow the Holy Spirit to re-characterize him, so that one's behaviors reflect the Lord Jesus Christ. In this way we bring glory to Him.

This is the essential purpose of God in the Bible. He has both principles and illustrations to effectively convey His revelation to mankind. The principles are the guidelines for living, and are good constantly, and never change. The illustrations assist us to understand the principles and how to apply them to life's situations. The illustrations were given at a time and location that seem incongruent to modern man, and thereby many not only discount them, but at the same time throw out the principles. This is somewhat like "throwing out the baby with the bathwater." Though the illustrations may be antiquated, and we are able to replace them with modern illustrations, the principles remain constant. It is the responsibility of the Christian to ferret out the principles, and allow the Holy Spirit to apply them in life to the individual, (John 16:13) so that the Christian can, "Grow in the grace and knowledge of the Lord Jesus Christ." (II Peter 3:18)

It is these relative things found in the Bible that are the illustrations, and are also the fragmentary elements that are usually open-ended in our understanding. Since the Bible is not a book primarily of science, sociology, psychology, history, economics, etc., there are many things that we do not understand of these areas from the bible. When these fragmentary items are included, they are given to underscore the understanding of the essentials. That this is important to accept is revealed with final truth.

Unfortunately, many have criticized the Bible as being antiquated and not up to date, as far as science is concerned, as the Bible does not give a full dimension in the scientific realm. That is not the intended purpose of the Bible. Scientific knowledge is included only in an oblique manner, to help understand the principles, but not as an end of knowledge in itself. However, because the God who wrote the Bible, was also the Creator of the universe, and is omniscient, it is reasonable to assume that when He speaks in His word, He speaks with final truth. Maybe today's science has not caught up with and may someday understand the truth of what God has spoken. The relative or fragmentary knowledge in the Bible is complementary to the essentials, and can be trusted and accepted, even though we may not understand the full import of them. The Apostle John noted that if all were written of God's truth that, "Even the world could not contain the books that should be written." (John 21:25)

It may be that someday, in eternity, God will see fit to continue to reveal more of Himself and the universe He has created. It seems reasonable that we will not sit in heaven, and become bored with a perfect environment, but that God will continue to teach us. Until then the Bible provides for us, all that we need today, for life and Godliness in this present world. In I Corinthians 13:12 we read, "For now we see through a glass darkly; but then face to face: now I know in part; but then shall I know even as also I am known."

I Corinthians 14:8 reminds us, "For if the trumpet give an uncertain sound, who shall prepare himself to the battle?" The Bible underscores the truth that there is a pattern of authority, that there should be a sense of responsibility, and that there must be a realization of final truth. Therefore, "It is required in stewards that one be found faithful." (I Corinthians 4:2) It was Evan Hopkins that once said, "A Christian is one who is intellectually convinced, morally convicted, and spiritually converted." May this be true of God's children. His word can never fail, and we who are His children and ambassadors for Him, should understand His truth, live by it, and let our light shine before others that they may see the Lord Jesus Christ in us.

O to be like thee, blessed Redeemer,
This is my constant longing and prayer.
Gladly I'll forfeit all of earth's treasures,
Jesus thy perfect likeness to wear.

O to be like thee, O to be like thee,
Blessed Redeemer, pure as thou art.
Come in thy sweetness, come in thy fullness,
Stamp thine own image deep on my heart.

O to be like thee, while I am pleading,
Pour out thy Spirit, fill with thy love,
Make me a temple, meet for thy dwelling,
Fit me for life and heaven above
—Victorious Life, Keswick, NJ

Chapter 3

FOUR BIBLICAL THREADS
WOVEN THROUGH SCRIPTURE

There are four basic concepts in Scripture that thread themselves throughout the Bible. For a student of Scripture to understand the basic thrust of the Bible, and to comprehend how the Bible is a cohesive unit, it is imperative for one to know these four foundational elements. All four of these threads are more fully developed in other chapters in this book. The reason for briefly outlining them here is that they are foundational to, and assumed in understanding, by every writer of the 66 books in the Bible. Therefore, a summary of them is given, so that the reader can understand what the Biblical writers assumed the reader to know.

The first and foremost concept is THE KINGDOM OF GOD. The kingdom concept is not only woven throughout the Bible, it is woven in all of creation. Mankind was created to operate in a hierarchy of order and is unable to live in a state of anarchy. By nature both mankind as well as the animal kingdom operate in a pecking order of responsibility and accountability. Therefore, God's revelation in the Bible is underlaid with a Kingdom concept, as outlined by the *Kingdom of God*, and the *Kingdom of Heaven*.

Briefly, the *Kingdom of God* is His rule throughout the universe at all times. (Psalms 10:16) God always has ruled in the universe, is ruling today, and will rule throughout eternity. There has never been a time when God did not rule. God is both eternal and sovereign over all the universe.

The *Kingdom of Heaven*, as defined in Scripture, is God's rule here on earth, in the historical past as well as the present, through both people (e.g. rulers, see Dan. 4:34-37) as well as situations, (e.g. nature, see Psalms 19:1-6) and in the minds and hearts of people. (Luke 17:21)

The full explanation of these two kingdoms and their relation to each other, is more fully developed in the chapter, The Kingdom of God.

God's manner of conveying Himself and relating to mankind in the Bible, comes through the second thread woven throughout the Bible, namely, THE COVENANTS. A covenant was an agreement between God and mankind, in which certain elements common to both were accepted and agreed upon and provided promises and responsibilities to follow and carry out. In the Bible we see both *Conditional* and *Unconditional Covenants* between God and mankind.

A *Conditional Covenant* was that of God giving to mankind certain conditions of behavior which they were to agree upon and follow, with promises of blessing by God if followed, and consequences of punishment if not followed. An example of a conditional covenant was God giving the Ten Commandments to Israel, by the hand of Moses, and the people of Israel ratifying the covenant, through agreeing to be obedient. See Exodus 19.

An *Unconditional Covenant* was exemplified in God's promise to Abraham in Genesis 12, that God would make of Abraham a great nation, and that through him all the nations of the world would be blessed. This promise came true, in that Jesus Christ was of the seed of Abraham, and through His work on earth, God provided blessing to all who would believe and accept Jesus Christ as Lord and Savior of their lives.

The Bible speaks of eight various covenants, both conditional and unconditional, that God has made with mankind through the ages. These covenants provide a basis of God's dealings with all mankind down through the centuries, from Adam to today, as well as in the future. For a detailed understanding of them, see the chapter on, The Eight Biblical Covenants.

THE THREEFOLD POSITION OF MANKIND. God's creation of mankind, beginning with Adam and Eve in the Garden of Eden, was constituted in mankind having a threefold position before God. This third thread woven throughout Scripture speaks to the fact that God originally created mankind as a Prophet, a Priest, and a King.

As Prophet, Adam knew God by direct revelation, in that God directly revealed Himself to Adam, who was perfect before God, as they walked together in the Garden of Eden. A Prophet is one who tells forth to others what God has revealed to him. Adam was to relate to his family and progeny what God revealed to him.

As Priest, Adam was sinless in that he had a right standing before God so that he did not need anyone to make intercession in his behalf before God. He was sinless and righteous.

As King, God placed him over all the creation. The fear and dread of Adam was instilled in all the animals, and the ground would bring forth fruit abundantly, without any problems. God told Adam he was king over the creation.

When Adam sinned, (Genesis 3:1-7) he turned from being God-centered to being self-centered, and thereby lost his first estate as being Prophet, Priest and King. He no longer was a Prophet of God, for his sin separated him from God, so that God no longer communed with Adam in revelation. He ceased to be a Priest, in that his sin separated him from God, and now he needed someone to mediate or intercede in his behalf before God. Finally, he ceased to be a King over the creation, for God kicked him out of the Garden of Eden. The animals became wild and the earth produced weeds, thistles, etc. to give Adam a hard time. God noted that Adam would eke out a living, by the sweat of his brow, because of his sin. This has been the lot of mankind from that day until today.

Therefore, we need to come to an understanding of the overall whole of the Old Testament. It is the story of 1) how God raised up a group of prophets, who spoke in behalf of God to the people of Israel; 2) a group of priests from the Tribe of Levi, who were God's mediators between the people of Israel and God, and 3) a group of kings out of the Tribe of Judah, who ruled over Israel and God's human leaders. For a fuller development of this theme, see the chapters, "As In Adam All Die" and "God's Times and Methods of Revelation."

13

The New Testament is the story of Jesus Christ, the greater son of Adam, (I Corinthians 15:45-47) who in His coming to earth would re-unite all three functions in Himself. 1) He came as God's final and last Prophet to mankind (II Corinthians 4:6; Hebrews 1:1,2) in order to reveal an understanding of God to all mankind. He came as our great High Priest, who made reconciliation for all mankind's sins. (Romans 5:1,10,11; Ephesians 2:16; Hebrews 7:22-25) And, He came as King over the creation. (Luke 1:31-33; Rev. 19:15,16)

As the first Adam, before he sinned, had all three functions in himself, so Christ, the last Adam (I Corinthians 15:45-47) who was sinless, re-united them in Himself. This is why the Apostle Paul calls Jesus Christ, "The last Adam." Jesus Christ was God's final and last complete revelation to mankind.

Finally, the fourth thread woven throughout the Bible relates to THE THREEFOLD PURPOSE OF THE BIBLE. The Bible is not a book that provides a revelation to us about everything one wishes to know about God and the universe. No, the Bible is a highly selective book, that has a threefold purpose to explain: 1) SIN, 2) SALVATION, and 3) SANCTIFICATION.

When one examines these three elements, qualitatively, it is seen that they are of equal importance, and need to be followed in that order. However, when one looks at them quantitatively, very little space is taken up in the Bible to explain the entrance and consequences of sin, and it doesn't take much of the Bible to explain the way of salvation with its eternal benefits. But, the doctrine of Sanctification, Holy living, that fills most of the Bible by way of illustration and application. Once a person accepts the principle of being a sinner in need of a savior, and makes a commitment to Jesus Christ as Lord and Savior of their life, then the rest of life is to be spent in growing toward spiritual maturity. This takes a whole lifetime of growth, and the Bible is the principled guidebook toward that end. For a further development of this subject, see the chapter, "The Threefold Elements of Sanctification."

What should be our response to these four key threads that weave themselves through Scripture? In Psalms 119:11 it states, "Thy word have I hid in my heart, that I might not sin against thee." Therefore, we should respond in two ways: 1) to grow in the grace and knowledge of the Lord Jesus Christ. (II Peter 3:18; I Peter 2:2) 2) to let our maturing spiritual life shine before others, so they see the Lord Jesus Christ reflected in us. (Matthew 5:16; Ephesians 4:12-15)

Holy Bible, book divine,
Precious treasure, thou art mine;
Mine to tell me whence I came;
Mine to teach me who I am;

Mine to chide when I rove;
Mine to show a Savior's love;
Mine thou art to guide and guard;
Mine to punish or reward;

Mine to comfort in distress,
Suffering in this wilderness;
Mine to show by living faith,
Man can triumph over death.

Mine to tell of joys to come,
And the rebel sinner's doom;
O thou holy book divine,
Precious treasure thou art mime.

—Victorious Life, Keswick, NJ

15

Chapter 4

AS IN ADAM ALL DIE

Most Christians would accept the following article of faith that says, "We believe that mankind was created in innocence, but fell into sin through Adam, and is now totally unable to redeem himself." Three parts to this statement are: 1) that mankind was created in perfect innocence; 2) because of Adam all mankind died spiritually, with the consequences of physical death; and 3) that mankind is unable to spiritually redeem himself from either physical or spiritual death.

1. The Origin of Mankind: In Gen. 1:26,27 it states that the human race was brought into existence by the creative act of God. The first woman was potentially created in the man, and brought into individual existence by a special formative act of God. Thus, the entire human race is descended from this original pair by natural generation. (Acts 17:26)

2. The Nature of Mankind: In the Genesis account it states that mankind was created in the *image* of God and after His likeness. This image was a natural likeness to God, morally, with personality, and intellect, sensibility and will. As to Adam's moral likeness he had the Holiness of God in him, though he was not confirmed in Holiness (Note: the prohibition of eating of the tree put him on *probation* to see if he would follow God implicitly.) Adam also had a mirroring of the metaphysical moral attributes of God. Prior to his eating of the tree he was perfectly holy with God's moral attributes.

17

God in His essence has two attributes: 1) Moral and 2) Non-moral. His moral attributes (His holiness) were perfectly reflected in Adam before he sinned. God's non-moral attributes (His omnipotence, omniscience, omnipresence, and omnirighteousness) were attributed to Adam in a limited degree. Mankind has some power, some understanding, a limited body, etc. Only God has the full non-moral attributes. This is what separates God from mankind and allows Him to be God and man to be man.

I Thess. 5:23 speaks of mankind having a Spirit, Soul, and Body. His Spirit is his closest point of resemblance and contact with God. Being created with a moral side to his nature tells him he ought to do right by God's standards. (Rom. 2:14-16) When he sinned, his moral nature was marred, not obliterated, though it did separate him from God. He was created as the highest in the scale of created life, for only he had the moral nature of God within him. Even though he became a sinner, he is treated with high dignity and worth, because of who he is by creation. (Matt. 12:9-12)

3. The Fall of Mankind Adam was created with a moral value or nature that was good. (Gen. 1:26,31) His testing consisted of two elements; a positive command not to eat of a certain tree, (Gen. 2:17) and exposure to temptation through the serpent. (Gen. 3:1) The subtle steps of temptation by the serpent (who at this point was Satan's emissary) are seen in Gen. 3:6. It was a physical allurement, *the lust of the flesh*, "good for food;" it was aesthetic, *the lust of the eyes*, "pleasant to the eyes;" and it was intellectual, *the pride of life*, "make one wise." Satan's methods were: a subtle doubt as to God's goodness, a boldness in denying God's word, and a promise to personal benefit as a result of disobedience.

The fall consisted of two elements: an inward act of disobedience of the will, in deciding for himself, what was good and evil, and an outward act of carrying out the decision he had made. The results of Adam's action are seen in Gen. 3:14-19. It resulted in the curse upon the serpent; (v.14-15) a curse upon the woman, (v.16) with multiplied conception to make up for the multiplied deaths because of sin, pain in childbirth, and a natural attraction to men, to overcome the thoughts of painful birth; a curse upon the man; (v.19) a curse upon the earth;

(v.17-18) and God beginning the process of bringing mankind back to Himself through redemption. (Rom. 5:12, 18-21)

4. Mankind Totally Unable To Redeem Himself: The teaching that mankind is *totally depraved* needs to be clarified. It <u>does not</u> teach: that the unsaved have no disposition to do right; that the unsaved never do anything good; that some men commit every kind of sin; that men are as bad as they can become; and that all men are all making the same progress in sin.

The Bible <u>does</u> teach: that all have sinned and have a sinful nature, which under favorable conditions is capable of the worst of sins, that sin has adversely affected the whole being of mankind, that even when the unsaved do right, it is often for quite selfish motives, and never for the honor of God, that the unsaved are wholly without the love of God, that the sinner always becomes worse—though they may improve in outward behavior, actually become worse within, and there is no capacity for recovery within man himself.

5. What Is The Nature of Sin? The Bible describes sin in three forms: as an act, as a thought (intent or purpose) and as a state (disposition, or nature). Note Matt. 15:17-20. In Psalms 32 and 51, David used three words that suggest the course of sin. Sin, in the general or universal sense is anything that is contrary to God's moral nature. Then there are three words subsumed under the general term that are used in the Psalms: 1) <u>Sin</u> - meaning to fall short or not measure up, like an arrow falling short of its mark. In this sense David did not measure up to what God anticipated of him as king; he failed his subjects. 2) <u>Transgression</u> - which means to go against, like a hunter trespassing on a field. David went against three of God's commandments in that he coveted another man's wife, he committed adultery with her, and then had her husband killed in order to have her as wife. 3) <u>Iniquity</u> - which is the basic nature of the person, out of which come the acts of sin. David's sinful nature caused him to both fall short as well as transgress.

Sin is thought of in the Bible as an offense against three parties— against the sinner himself, (Prov. 8:36) against society, (Rom. 5:12) and against God. (Ps. 51:4) This is why the Bible states, "All have sinned and fallen short of the glory (moral character) of God." (Rom. 3:23)

6. The Beginning of Sin: The Bible is explicit as to where sin originated. There are three areas of beginning: 1) It began in the universe through Satan, who at one time was Lucifer, the arch angel of God. (Isa. 14:12-14; Ezek. 28:12-19) 2) It began in the human race through Adam. (Rom. 5:12) 3) It begins in the heart of every individual. (Mark 7:21,22) Thus, it extends to all of the human race. (Rom. 3:10,23)

7) The Consequences of Sin: The Bible speaks of sin as the defilement of the body, (Ps. 38:3-5) the speech, (Ps. 58:3) and that it corrupts the whole nature of mankind; flesh, spirit, mind, and conscience. (Rom. 3:10-20) It also brings disorder against nature. (Rom. 1:26,27) II Tim. 3:3 says that mankind is *without natural affection*. Sin produces moral paralysis (See Eph. 4:18) - "past feeling," (I Tim. 4:2) "consciences seared with a hot iron." Then sin brings bondage, (Rom. 7:22-24) produces misery, (Prov. 14:12,13) guilt, (Rom. 3:19) and ultimately everlasting death. (Rom. 6:23) Both spiritual and physical.

God has made provision to eradicate any and all of these sins from mankind, through Christ's work on the cross in our behalf. It is each individual's responsibility to acknowledge they have sinned, and confess that to God; then accept Christ's redemption for them by trusting in Him. There is only one unpardonable sin, of which the Bible speaks, and that is called "blasphemy against the Holy Spirit." (Matt. 12:31,32, Mark 3:28,29, Heb. 10:29) This has no reference to swearing, as some would mean, but refers to a conscious refusal of what Christ has done on the cross for each person, and not allowing the Holy Spirit to bring regeneration of spiritual life and reconciliation to God. To refuse the convicting and pardoning work of the Holy Spirit and regeneration, is the only sin in life that God cannot pardon. It would adversely affect God's holiness, without which no one can measure up to God's requirements. (Heb. 12:14)

8. Release From Sin and Its Effect: Commitment of one's self to Christ's redemptive work on the cross in His death, burial and resurrection, for the forgiveness of sin, brings release from the bondage of sin as well as from the eternal penalty for sin. (Rom. 6:23; I Cor. 15:3,4; Titus 3:3-8; Rom. 10:9,10; John 3:16,36; John 5:24)

There are many effects of this commitment for the Christian. First, and foremost, it makes one a new creation in Christ Jesus. (II Cor. 5:17) Now, the Christian enjoys the indwelling presence of the Holy Spirit, who brings a new nature to life, and a whole new outlook on life. (Rom. 8:14-16; I Cor. 12:13) This new outlook is summarized in II Tim. 1:7, "For God has not given us the spirit of fear, but of power, (to live constructively) and of love, (to live sacrificially) and of a sound mind" (to live reasonably). It also gives one an assured hope for the future, (Phil. 1:6) as well as having peace with God, (Rom. 5:1) and a maturation in life that brings an inner peace from God. (Col. 3:15)

The Christian physician who attended the skeptic Voltaire on his death bed recorded these words: "When I compare the death of a righteous man, which is like the close of a beautiful day, with that of Voltaire, I see the difference between serene weather and a black thunderstorm. It was my lot that this man should die under my hands. Often did I tell him the truth, 'Yes, my friend,' he would often tell me, 'You are the only one who has given me good advice. Had I but followed it, I should not be in the horrible condition in which I am now. I have swallowed nothing but smoke. I have intoxicated myself with the incense that turned my head. You can do nothing for me. Send me a mad doctor. Have compassion on me. I am mad.' I cannot think of it without shuddering. As soon as he saw that all the means he had just employed to increase his strength, had just the opposite effect, death was constantly before his eyes. From this moment on, madness took possession of his soul. He expired under the torment of the furies."

What a contrast in this account, to the hymn written by Bernard of Clairvaux, when he penned the words:

Jesus the very thought of thee,
With sweetness fills my breast
But sweeter far thy face to see,
And in thy presence rest.

O hope of every contrite heart,
    O joy of all the meek
To those who fall, how kind thou art,
    How good to those who seek.

But what to those who find, ah this.
    Nor tongue nor pen can show,
The love of Jesus, what it is,
    None but His loved ones know.
                    —Victorious Life, Keswick, NJ

Chapter 5

THE KINGDOM OF GOD

As one looks at an overview of the Bible, the significant thread that weaves itself throughout is the kingdom concept. It is the tie that binds every aspect of the Bible together. It is the underlying theme of the Bible, and just like the bones in one's body give structure to the frame, so does the kingdom concept give structure to Scripture. The Bible speaks of two kingdoms, the Kingdom of God and the Kingdom of heaven. It is imperative that we understand the meaning of each, how they interweave, and how each applies to both Israel and the Church; past, present, and future.

By definition the Kingdom of God is His universal kingdom in which He has always ruled in the universe, is ruling, and will always rule. It is His overall rule from eternity past to eternity future. There never has been a time that God has not ruled. The Kingdom of Heaven is the rule of God in a mediatorial way. He has and is ruling in the kingdom of mankind through second causes. In other words He mediates His rule over mankind through individuals whom He allows to exercise rulership, and He controls them for His ultimate purposes. The Kingdom of Heaven is subsumed within the overall Kingdom of God. This concept is adequately seen throughout the history of the Bible, as well as in its underlying concepts.

To understand the essence of these two kingdoms, and how they operate in the history of the world, is to be able to understand how the Bible fits together. To not comprehend this concept, is prohibitive of truly being able to understand God's dealings with mankind. The reason for this is that the kingdom concept is ingrained within each one of us, so that whether in the family, in business, in politics, or in any organization, we do not operate in a vacuum, or an anarchy. We function some semblance of order and structure. That is part of the fabric of human nature. And, so it is with God, Who ordained all of this.

To begin our understanding of these kingdoms, let us first and foremost, consider the Kingdom of God. We will call this the Universal Kingdom, since it is all encompassing, universally, as well as from eternity to eternity. The Bible conveys three aspects of this universal kingdom: 1) Psalm 10:16—The Kingdom of God has always existed in the sense that, "The Lord is King for ever and ever." There has never been a time when God has not ruled in the universe, 2) Psalm 103:19 states that, "The Lord has prepared His throne in the heavens, and His kingdom ruleth over all." There is nothing that exists beyond His control. It is a universal kingdom. 3) Isa. 10:5-18—God's universal rule is extended to earth, where He rules through second causes, rulers whom He has set up, and nature which is under His control. Verse five notes, "Woe to the Assyrian, the rod of mine anger, in whose hand is the club of my wrath." God allowed Assyria to punish Israel for their wickedness, but it was still God Who was in control, exercising rulership. These concepts constitute God's universal rule, which permeates all of Scripture. As one tries to comprehend an understanding of the Bible, this basic element must constantly be kept in mind.

A larger more complete understanding of the kingdom concept is seen in the Kingdom of Heaven, which occupies more of the text of the Bible. It relates more directly to mankind, especially the nation of Israel, as well as the church. Therefore, the rest of this chapter will deal with this kingdom. At the conclusion we shall see how the two kingdoms relate to each other.

The Kingdom of Heaven, by definition, is the rule of God, through a divinely chosen representative who speaks and acts for God. This rule is with special reference to the human race, especially seen in Israel, but eventually embraces the whole universe. We shall note the development of this through the Bible under six headings: 1) in Old Testament History, 2) in Old Testament Prophecy, 3) in the teachings of Christ, 4) in the period of the Acts, 5) during the present Christian Church era, and 6) During the Coming Age.

In order to understand the relationship between the Kingdom of God, and the Kingdom of Heaven, it is seen in the Bible that the Kingdom of God is His overall rule from eternity to eternity. The Kingdom of Heaven is not a geographical location, namely *up in the heavens*, but rather heavenly rule here on earth among peoples. The preferred rule of Christ to the Jewish nation, which they rejected, was to have been Christ's rule over the Jewish nation, which would have been the heavenly kingdom of Christ, with Him ruling over Israel.

Someday, in eternity, when everything is under the authority of Jesus Christ, then the Kingdom of Heaven and the Kingdom of God will be one and the same, as the concept of heaven will be everywhere, including this earth. When we look at the kingdom concept in the Old Testament, as well as the New Testament, we see that the concept in God's mind was His rule over Israel as operative through "second causes," namely the priests and kings. Historically, this was the heavenly kingdom operating on earth. Though this was the way God ordained for Israel, the whole concept failed, because Israel refused to follow God. They broke the covenant they had accepted at Mt. Sinai. (Ex. 19-31)

When Christ came, (John 1:11) "He came unto His own, (Israel) but His own received Him not." When Christ began His public ministry He said, "My kingdom is not of this world." (John 18:36) When you put the two concepts together, what Christ was saying was not that He did not come to bring in the kingdom which the prophets had prophesied, but that He did not come to restore the historical kingdom to Israel. Had He done that, the second administration of the first kingdom would fail for the same reason the first kingdom failed. Because of the sins of the people of Israel. What Christ preached was repentance from sin, and that He had to go to the cross to become an acceptable sacrifice for the sins of the people. Once the sin issue was cared for, then He would bring in the kingdom, and the second time around it would not fail. Christ would be on the throne of His father, David, and all would be righteous. That did not materialize because Israel rejected what He offered. That is why Christ turned to the Gentiles, and began the "Church."

25

1. <u>The Kingdom of Heaven in Old Testament History</u>: It started with the call of Abraham in Genesis 12. God told him to leave Ur of the Chaldees and go into a land God had prepared for him, i.e. Palestine. He told Abraham that He would make of him a great nation, that he would have seed as the seashore, that the land would be his forever, and that kings would reign forever over the people. These were unconditional promises God made.

Later on the development of the kingdom came through Moses leading Israel out of Egypt, through the wilderness, and under Joshua into the Promised Land. During this time God mediated Himself to Israel through the priestly system. When Samuel became the priest of God to Israel, the people demanded of him a king, and this bothered Samuel. (I Sam. 8:1-6) God told Samuel to listen to the people, for He said, "They have not rejected you, but they have rejected me, that I should not reign over them." (I Sam. 8:7) Now we perceive that Israel turned from being a Theocracy, the rule of God to a Monarchy, the rule of man.

However, God still blessed Israel, as long as the kings followed God; the nation reached its zenith in the rule of David and Solomon. After Solomon died, his son Rehoboam took the throne and because of his youthful brashness, the kingdom became divided. The northern part with ten tribes became known as the kingdom of Israel, and the southern part with two tribes became known as the kingdom of Judah. The northern kingdom had a series of wicked kings, and in 721 B.C. went into captivity. The southern kingdom had a number of good and wicked kings interspersed, so it lasted longer, but finally in 586 B.C., it too went into captivity to Babylonia.

The close of the kingdoms was symbolized by God removing His "Shekinah" glory; His dwelling glory in Israel. The glory of God had rested upon Israel, but now God removed it—signifying God's blessing and protection of Israel was finished. The nation was susceptible to invasion and captivity. (Ezek. 9-11) The kingdom failed for two reasons: 1) a lack of spiritual preparation as seen in the *Golden calf* experience at Mt. Sinai, (Ex. 32:1-6) where Israel deviated from Jehovah, even while God was giving Moses the law. This set the pattern of sin in Israel, that bore the fruit of captivity 700 years later, and 2) imperfection of God's human leaders, the rule of wicked kings both of Israel and Judah.

As Israel came closer to captivity through continuing sin, the prophets whom God had raised up to speak in His behalf to Israel, were ignored or persecuted, yet spoke of a future coming day when there would be a perfect king over Israel. (Ezek. 11:20; Heb. 8:6-11) A king that His subjects will follow Him. (Ezek. 11:19) The close of the historical kingdom was marked by the destruction of Jerusalem in 586 B.C. by Nebucadnezzar of Babylon.

2. The Kingdom of Heaven in Old Testament Prophecy: Arises out of a prophetical/historical setting. The prophet's predictions had a *double reference*, meaning that what they said was both historical for that day, as well as futuristic. The prophets spoke of impending judgment if Israel did not repent, as well as a future day when Israel would follow a righteous king. Early prophets spoke mainly to Israel of their day, but as Israel became more wicked, the message of the prophets spoke to a greater degree in the future.

The futuristic aspect began with a reference in Gen. 3:15, where God promised that the *seed of the woman* would crush the serpent's head. This reference was to the ultimate coming of Jesus the seed of the woman—Gal. 4:4, who in His death and resurrection would crush the power of Satan. The prophetical message became a single gleam in II Sam. 7:16, where the prophet promised to David, "Thy throne shall be established forever." This ultimately would be fulfilled in Jesus, the greater son of David, of whom the angel said at His birth, "He shall reign over the house of Jacob (Israel) forever; and of His kingdom there shall be no end." The future aspect of the kingdom grew as the historical aspect declined.

3. The Kingdom of Heaven in the Teachings of Christ: In Matt. 3:1,2 the Gospels open with the announcement of a kingdom. This kingdom and that prophetical kingdom of the prophets is the same. In Daniel 7:13,14 the future kingdom message is tied in with the *Son of man*, (Jesus' favorite title which He applied to Himself). Further, in Christ's teachings may be found every aspect of the prophetic kingdom. The reason that no formal announcement of Christ's kingdom was made when He began His public ministry, was that the prophets had taught of His coming. Over 330 prophecies in the Old Testament gave

27

evidence to His coming and all were fulfilled during His lifetime here on earth.

Christ taught that the kingdom was at hand, because He, the king was present. It was announced to Israel alone, when He sent His disciples out to proclaim, "Go not into the way of the Gentiles, ...but go rather to the lost sheep of the house of Israel. And as you go, preach, saying, the Kingdom of heaven is at hand." (Matt. 10:5-7) The establishment of the kingdom He came to bring, depended upon Israel's acceptance of His message of repentance. (Matt. 11:13-15)

He was not caught by surprise at Israel's rejection. He sent His disciples out to take their *Gallup Poll*, asking the Jews who they thought was this "Son of man?" When they returned Jesus asked them, and they gave various answers, after which He asked them who they thought He was. Peter replied, "Thou art the Christ, the Son of the living God." Christ answered, "Peter, you have well said." (Matt. 16:13-21) At this point Christ introduced two new concepts to His disciples, when it was established that Israel had rejected Jesus as their king: 1) He spoke for the first time of the *Church,* a called out people for His name, and told the disciples they would be the spreaders of this gospel, 2) He instructed them concerning His death, burial, and resurrection. There had been a veiled reference to this by the prophets, but only now was His impending death understood by the disciples. The aspect of the church was unforeseen by the prophets, since their prophecies spoke to Israel accepting the future king. (Eph. 3:3-6; Col. 1:24-29; Matt. 13:11)

The Kingdom was not abandoned by Christ, only postponed. The reason: God had made unconditional promises to Abraham, Isaac, Jacob, David, etc. concerning a king and kingdom forever, but He also had chosen Israel to be His channel through whom the revelation of God would go out to all the world. Instead of Israel disseminating God's revelation to them, they cloistered it to themselves, and became proud of their heritage *in* with God, and called the other nations, *Heathen.* When Christ came they were so self-righteous that their sin kept them from acknowledging Jesus as their Messiah. If God's revelation to all mankind was to be disseminated, He had to obtain a new conduit or channel. This was the reason for the church and the commission it has had for the past two thousand years as seen in Matt. 28:19,20. Christ

Himself said of the church that His message this time around, "The gates of Hell shall not prevail against it." Satan had worked in the national life of Israel to stifle God's revelation through them by their sin of pride, etc. The church would prevail through the indwelling Holy Spirit. (I John 4:4) During Christ's trial before the high priest of Israel, He reaffirmed His kingship. (Matt. 26:63-65) He was rejected because Israel would not accept that He had brought—first a spiritual kingdom, *within you* followed by the restoration of the historical kingdom, promised in the Old Testament. Israel wanted the political restoration without the repentance of their sins and acceptance of the spiritual kingdom Christ came to bring in His death and resurrection. Their own sins and hardened hearts caused their rejection of Him.

4. The Kingdom of Heaven in the Period of the Acts: The Disciples failed to harmonize Christ's death with their hopes of the restoration of the kingdom. (Luke 24:21) The kingdom was not abandoned, only postponed, so that through the church, God's revelation would go out to the world. (Acts 1:6-11) After His resurrection the disciples wondered if *now* He would restore the kingdom, since His mission to bring reconciliation to mankind was accomplished. Christ told them it was not up to them to "know the times or the seasons," but that they were to go into all the world and proclaim the Gospel.

As the book of Acts records the spreading of the Gospel through the Apostles, *sent ones* the *signs* that God gave them to affirm their message failed to convince the Jews, for the problem was not intellectual, but spiritual. (II Cor. 3:13-15) The veil of sin was upon their heart.

The final rejection of Christ, both as Messiah and king is witnessed in Acts 28:17-31, where the Apostle Paul, a believing Jew, under house arrest in Rome, called the Jewish authorities to him, "to whom he expounded and testified the kingdom of God...and some believed, and some believed not." After they had departed, Paul said, "Be it known therefore unto you, that salvation of God is sent unto the Gentiles, nations, and they will hear it." The account tells us that Paul proclaimed the Gospel to any and all who would hear it. He recognized that His own Jewish people had spiritual blindness to the Messiahship and kingship of Jesus Christ. The mantle of revelation had passed to the church, and it was their responsibility to disseminate God's revelation to the world.

5. The Kingdom of Heaven During the Present Christian Era: The kingdom exists today, in the sense that Christ is preparing the people who will spiritually inherit the kingdom that will come. In Col. 1:13 and Gal. 3:26-29 we see that regeneration of heart in the life of the believer translates one into the kingdom of His dear Son. Today, that kingdom exists spiritually in the life of the Christian. Someday, the reality will appear, when Christ returns to set up the kingdom.

Christ set forth the aspects of the kingdom in parables, or analogies, which refer to the *Mysteries* of the Kingdom. In Col. 1:24-28 and Eph. 3:1-7, it is seen that the mysteries were not something mysterious, as we may think, but mean that these elements were divinely hidden from past ages and peoples, but now are revealed to the Christian, through the discernment of the indwelling Holy Spirit. The parables and analogies are to help the Christian, who lives in the time and space world, understand the *other worldliness* of what heaven will be like. An analogy makes a parallel of a *known* with the *unknown*, so the meaning of the unknown can be grasped.

Today, we see a parallel growth of righteousness and evil in the world. And though it may seem that "righteousness is on the scaffold, and wrong is on the throne," that is not the way it will always be. God is sovereign, and His program is on track, for He is Sovereign, "His kingdom rules over all." (Ps. 103:19) Someday the separation will come. (Matt. 25:31-46) The righteous will prevail, and the unrighteous judged, when Christ returns.

6. The Kingdom of Heaven During the Coming Age: The age to come will be ushered in by the authority and power of Christ. God's silence will be broken by the *Trump of God*, the Rapture, the Tribulation, and the personal presence of the King, Jesus Christ. (Rev. 11:15-17; Rev. 19:11-16)

The kingdom the Jews will be ushered in. This will be God's fulfillment of His unconditional promises to Abraham, and reiterated to David, Solomon, etc. The Old Testament Prophets spoke extensively of it. (Rev. 20:1-6) After the thousand years of the Millennium and the judgment of Satan, the Kingdom of Heaven will merge with the Kingdom of God, and God will be all in all. Heaven is not a geographical location, but an existence with God, regardless of location. So, heaven will be *up there*, earth will be heaven, the universe will be heaven. In I Cor. 15:24-28 we see that Christ will deliver up the Kingdom of Heaven, over which He rules, to God the Father, that "God may be all in all." Then the Kingdom of Heaven will be subsumed within the Kingdom of God, Who has ruled from all eternity past, to all eternity future. What God envisioned for mankind when He created him and placed him in the garden of Eden, will become a reality forever. God and mankind will have eternal fellowship, and mankind will be enjoying the threefold fulfillment God intended him to have: 1) fellowship with God eternally, 2) a perfect reflection of God's moral attributes, and 3) king over God's creation. (Ps. 8:4-6)

Revelation 22:3-5 gives us a beautiful picture of eternity that we shall enjoy with Christ. There will be no more curse, and there will no night there, "And they need no candle, neither light of the SUN, for the SON giveth them light; and they shall reign for ever and ever." The eternal Son of God will be our light, and we shall reign with Him eternally.

The Market place is empty, no more traffic in the streets,
All the builders tools are silent, No more time to harvest wheat;
Busy housewives cease their labors, in the courtroom no debate,
Work on earth is all suspended as the King comes through the gate

Happy faces line the hallway those whose lives have been redeemed
Broken homes that He has mended, those from prison He has freed;
Little children and the aged, hand in hand stand all aglow,
Who were crippled, broken, ruined, clad in garments white as snow

I can hear the chariots rumble, I can see the marching throng,
The flurry of God's trumpets, spells an end of sin and wrong;
Regal robes are now unfolding, Heaven's grandstands all in place,
Heaven's choir is now assembled, start to sing Amazing Grace!

31

O, the King is coming, the King in coming,
I just heard the trumpets sounding, and now His face I see;
O, the King is coming, the King is coming!
Praise God He's coming for me!

—Hymns for the Family,
Paragon Assoc., Inc.,
Nashville, TN

Chapter 6

GOD'S TIMES AND METHODS OF REVELATION

In order for one to understand God's overall relationship to mankind, it is imperative to take a telescopic overview of His revelation to the human race. God's understanding of mankind deals with three classes of individuals: the peoples of the world, Israel as God's chosen people, and the Church, those who have acknowledged Him as Lord and Savior of their lives. The Old Testament deals primarily with God's relationship to His people, Israel. The New Testament deals basically with the Church, which is His body of believers through Jesus Christ. The world is under the ultimate judgment of God, though He is, "Not willing that any should perish, but that all should come to repentance." (II Peter 3:9)

There is a well defined pathway to understand what the Prophets told to Israel and the Church. God has a purpose in history, as well as a purpose for mankind on the earth. In His sovereignty He is seeing to it that His purpose is being carried out. (Isa. 46:9-13; Ps. 33:11) This purpose is seen in Psalm 8:4-6, and relates to the creation of mankind in three ways: 1) God created the human race for fellowship with Himself; (v.4) 2) as a reflection of God's moral qualities or attributes (v.5) - this is the *image* of God reflected; and 3) to place mankind, as king, over all the creation. (v.6)

The entrance of sin through Adam and Eve temporarily thwarted the fulfillment of these three purposes. But, since God's purposes are eternal, He outlined the coming of the "Seed of the woman," Who would undo what Satan had done when he seduced mankind into sin. See Gen. 3:15; Gal. 4:4,5. Hebrews 2:5-9 states that someday God will restore mankind to that position which Adam had before sin entered, and this will be the eternal and ultimate fulfillment of these three original purposes. God guarantees this through the resurrection of Jesus Christ. (I Cor. 15:1-58)

There are three distinct periods of revelation from God to mankind, as seen in the Bible: 1) from Adam to Moses, 2) from Moses to Christ, and 3) from Christ to the end. We shall consider the importance of these epochs and the impact on mankind.

1) God's Revelation From Adam to Moses: Until Adam and Eve sinned, God and Adam had total communication between them, and God continuously revealed Himself to Adam, who comprehended all that God taught him. It was all perfect and eternal. After Adam and Eve sinned, they hid themselves from God, (Gen. 3:8) and realized they were morally naked, because a barrier came between them and God. Now the stakes had changed, and no longer did Adam know God by direct revelation. Consequently, God instituted a new order of communication with mankind because of his sin.

The first revelation in the new order came in Gen. 3:15-19 where God confronted Adam and Eve with a pronouncement that would affect all mankind until He concluded all things in judgment—sometime in the distant future. It was a reference to the immediate judgment for sin, that is, they would experience physical and spiritual death as a consequence, but also that God would provide eternal restoration through one Whom He called, *the seed of the woman*, Whom we understand because of further revelation to be the Lord Jesus Christ. (Gal. 4:4) This promise was fulfilled in Christ's first advent. (John 3:16; Heb. 2:5-9) He came to undo what Satan had accomplished through deception. This is the basis upon which God will ultimately fulfill in regenerated mankind throughout eternity, the threefold purpose He had in creation.

The next revelation from God came through Enoch. (Jude 14,15) He prophesied before the flood that God would destroy mankind because of his sin. This came at the time of the flood. Jude carries this over into the end of all things, when God will ultimately destroy all sin. Noah survived the destruction of the flood because of his righteousness before God. Through him the earth was repopulated. These revelations in history are to show by analogy, that situations in the world today are quite similar to those in Enoch and Noah's day, to the effect that God will someday destroy the world, not by a flood of water, but by the fire of His judgment.

Just as in the days of Noah, there were eight righteous people who escaped, so God has His remnant today who will escape the coming judgment. Furthermore, as God raised up a righteous standard prior to the flood, so today God has His people who are standing for Him. Many even stand today in the declension that is engulfing mankind; which will bring God's final judgment. (II Peter 2:5; 3:1-14)

God revealed Himself to Abraham many years after the flood. God promised him that He would raise up a nation through him. God would call His people Israel. This revelation that God would make of Abraham a mighty nation, consisted of a number of things. He made unconditional promises of earthly seed without number. (Gen. 13:16) God would give a land to His people forever. Palestine would become a lasting possession, (Gen. 13:14,15) with kings over the people and land. (Gen. 35:11,12) The history of the Old Testament is a record of how all this came to pass. It had its greatest fulfillment through Moses and Joshua with an entrance into the land of promise (Palestine).

2) God's Revelation From Moses To Christ: Moses enjoyed a personal relationship with God as God's first and greatest prophet. Moses was God's instrument to reveal Himself to Israel. In this capacity, Moses spoke in behalf of God to meet the needs of His people, as well as to reveal future elements that would ultimately affect Israel forever. The revelation to Moses consisted of three things.

First, God used Moses as a type or figure of the future coming of the Son of God as a greater prophet. In Deut. 18:15-18, Moses speaks to this future coming of a Prophet—like unto me; unto Him you shall listen," which was a veiled reference to the ultimate coming of Jesus Christ. The New Testament confirmation of this is seen in Acts 3:22; 7:37 where both Peter and Stephen quote from Deuteronomy and ascribe the prophecy to Jesus Christ. It is also significant to note the reference to Jesus Christ as Prophet in Heb. 1:1,2 and II Cor. 4:6. So, just as Moses was a Prophet of God to Israel, and a type of Christ, so Jesus Christ as God's last and final Prophet is to mankind today. Jesus

Christ heralds a message of repentance from sin, and acceptance of Him as an escape from the wrath to come. (I Thess. 5:9)

Second, Moses predicted the history of Israel, both the blessings and the cursings (Deut. 28-30) which has been largely fulfilled. The historical record of the nation of Israel, both through Biblical sources, as well as through secular history, is an accurate account of that which Moses predicted.

Third, Moses predicted the return of the Lord to and for His people Israel, their restoration to the promised land, and the eternal blessings they would enjoy. (Deut. 30: 1-10) These were literal promises, but always predicated upon God's redemptive work of Jesus Christ. There were other Prophets that God raised up throughout the history of Israel, who spoke in behalf of God to the nation. The earlier Prophets spoke to the Israelites of repentance from their sins, and the consequences of judgment. The later Prophets, those who came at the time of exile and afterwards, spoke more of a coming king. This king would care for the sins of Israel, and set up a kingdom that would not be destroyed. For further understanding see Chapter 4 - The Kingdom of God & The Kingdom of Heaven.

The problem of the people of Israel was not unlike mankind today, they wanted peace, but were not willing to live righteously according to God's standard to obtain it. (Hosea 5:15; 6:1,2 with Matt. 23:37-39) Zechariah put his finger on the problem (6:12,12; 8:8) when he pointed out that there would never be real peace on the earth, until the righteous one, Jesus Christ as the Prince of Peace, would come to reign. When there is righteousness then there will be peace. Thus we come to the end of Old Testament prophecy and turn to the New Testament, as God's revelation concerning His Son, Jesus Christ.

3) God's Revelation From Christ to the End: In Galatians 4:4 we read that Jesus Christ came when it was the *fullness* of God's timing. Since God does not operate out of a time and space world as mankind does, the writers of the Bible utilize time and space world language, so that we are able to understand God's revelation within the framework of our comprehension. God sent Jesus Christ into the world according to His plan for mankind. Christ came, *made of a woman* to fulfill God's promise in Gen. 3:15 that the *seed of the woman* would crush Satan's head, and He came to "redeem them that were under the law." (v.5)

36

This is a fulfillment of God's promise of the Messiah, as revealed by the Prophets.

Thus, the New Testament speaks of three classes of people: the Jews, the Gentiles, and the Church of God. (I Cor. 10:32) God's chosen people in the Old Testament were the Jews (Israel); then when Christ came He instituted a new concept, the *Church*, as seen in Matt. 16:18. For more detailed understanding of the church see the chapter on the Kingdom of God. The *Gentiles* refers to the unregenerate peoples of the world.

In the Old Testament God spoke to Israel through the Prophets, (Heb. 1:1) but when Christ came, God spoke through His Son, (Heb. 1:2) and has continued that message in the Bible, as applied to the Christian through the Holy Spirit. (John 16:7-15)

When Christ came, as God's final and last Prophet to mankind, He came first unto His own people, the Jews. (John 1:11) He came with a proclamation of the Kingdom, (Matt. 10:5-7) but they rejected Him as their Messiah and King. Therefore, He turned aside to proclaim a new concept for people, called the Church. (Matt. 16:17-21) Because Israel was no longer God's channel through whom His revelation would go out to the world, the new channel was the Church. God would know use the church to evangelize the world. The commission to the church is given in Matt. 28:19,20. For the past two thousand years God has seen fit to use the Church as His instrument, along with the Bible and the Holy Spirit, to proclaim His message of love, grace, and redemption to all the world.

After Christ's ascension, with His charge to the Disciples, His followers, whom He recommissioned as Apostles (sent ones) as seen in Acts 1:8, God revealed His will through the Apostles to the Church, who were empowered by the Holy Spirit. When they carried the Gospel message of salvation from sin, the Holy Spirit regenerated all who believed, and indwelt all believers through Spirit Baptism. (I Cor. 12:13) This was in fulfillment of the teaching of Christ to the Disciples in His public ministry. (John 14:26; 16:13-15)

Today, God is in the process of gathering out of the peoples of the world, a people for His name, Christians—followers of Christ. (Acts 15:14) When this task is completed, Christ will return to gather His

Church, all true, believing Christians to Himself in Heaven. (I Thess. 4:13-18)

After Christ's return the Anti-christ will be revealed, and the Tribulation will begin, which will last for seven years, followed by Christ's return to earth to put down Satan and the Anti-christ at Armageddon, and set up the Kingdom for Israel. This kingdom, which will last for a thousand years, (Millennium) will be God's fulfillment of His unconditional promises made to Abraham, Isaac, Jacob, David, and all Israel. (Isa. 9:6,7; Luke 1:32,33) This will be the kingdom offered to Israel when Christ came the first time, but postponed by Him, because Israel refused to acknowledge Him as the Messiah, as prophesied by the Old Testament Prophets.

The eternal conclusion of God's original purpose for mankind through the creation, (Ps. 8:4-6) will become a reality for both believing Israel and the Church, and each will take their rightful place in God's eternal kingdom. (Rev. 21:12,14; I Cor. 15:20-28)

It may be at morn, when the day is awaking,
    When sunlight through darkness and shadow is breaking,
That Jesus will come in the fullness of glory,
    To receive from the world His own.
O, Lord Jesus how long, how long, ere we shout the glad song Christ
    returneth, Hallelujah,
Hallelujah, Amen, Hallelujah, Amen.

O joy, O delight, should we go without dying,
    No sickness, no sadness, no dread and no crying,
Caught up through the clouds with our Lord into glory,
    When Jesus receives His own.
O, Lord Jesus how long, how long, ere we shout the glad song Christ
    returneth, Hallelujah,
Hallelujah, Amen, Hallelujah, Amen.

—Victorious Life, Keswick, NJ

Chapter 7

THE EIGHT BIBLICAL COVENANTS

One of the primary elements of God's communication with mankind, as developed in the Bible, is that of His relating to human beings through a covenantal agreement. The Bible speaks of eight covenants that God made with mankind, that have constituted the relationship between God and His people.

The original covenants were an agreement between God and Adam and Eve, then with Noah, later with Israel, and finally with Christians, in which God agreed to certain commitments and mankind would respond accordingly. This became a binding relationship between the two parties.

The Covenants were of two kinds: 1) Conditional, and 2) Unconditional. A Conditional Covenant was one in which God's actions would be in response to some action on the part of mankind to whom the covenant was addressed. This conditional covenant guaranteed that God would do what He promised with absolute certainty, when the human requirements were met. However, if the person or Israel failed, then God was not obligated to fulfill what He had promised.

An Unconditional Covenant was a declaration of God to fulfill promises originally to mankind, later to Israel, and still later to the Christian, that He would do whatever He had promised without any condition on mankind's part. This promise would be fulfilled, unconditionally, in God's time and manner.

Of the eight Biblical covenants, only the Edenic and Mosaic are conditional. However, even under the six unconditional covenants there is a conditional element as it applies to certain people. This will be evident as we explore them.

1) <u>THE EDENIC COVENANT</u>: The first covenant between God and mankind was in the Garden of Eden between Adam and Eve. (Genesis 1:26-31; 2:16,17) It was a conditional one, which depended upon them to fulfill their responsibilities—being the progenitors of the human race, subduing the earth, and not eating of the tree of the Knowledge of Good and Evil.

The failure of Adam and Eve to fulfill that God-directed responsibility is seen in that they disobeyed God's command. They turned from being God-centered to being self centered, which resulted in mankind falling into sin, and the evident spiritual and physical death. Their sin plunged the whole human race into its pattern of sin and death. (Romans 5:12) Thus, the covenant was broken by their behavior.

2) <u>THE ADAMIC COVENANT</u>: This covenant was made with mankind, i.e. Adam and Eve, as the representatives of the whole human race. This unconditional covenant was imposed by God upon all mankind after their fall into sin. (Genesis 3:16-19) Since this was an unconditional covenant, God declared to mankind what their lot in life would be because of Adam and Eve's sin.

This included a curse upon the man by the sweat of his brow he would eke out a living, the animals would become wild, and thorns would give him a hard time. To the woman, God pronounced multiple births due to the death of people because of sin. She would experience pain and sorrow in motherhood, and be subject to her husband.

Along with the curses placed upon all humanity, God also promised a Redeemer. One who would buy them back from their sins by paying a price for them. He who would provide for reconciliation to God. This was a veiled promise in Genesis 3:15, unknown to Adam and Eve at that time, but revealed to us today through the revelation of God in Christ and the New Testament.

3) <u>THE NOAHIC COVENANT</u>: This was made with Noah and his sons concerning God's judgment on the world of that day, due to the exceeding sinfulness of mankind. (Genesis 9:1-18) Only Noah and

his family were righteous before God, and therefore God gave them an unconditional covenant that saved them from destruction, and through Noah's family the whole world would be populated.

This covenant introduced a new principle of human government as a means to curb sin. Man was given the responsibility to punish sin and to understand right and wrong, and the consequences of wrong behavior. He was also given permission to eat the flesh of animals instead of only vegetables.

It included a prophecy concerning the descendants of Noah's three sons and their wives, and designated Shem as the line through whom the Jewish nation would arise, and ultimately the Lord Jesus Christ, the Redeemer, in the veiled promise previously given to Adam and Eve.

4) THE ABRAHAMIC COVENANT: In this unconditional covenant we have one of the greatest promises and revelations of God to all mankind concerning future history. These profound promises were manifested in three lines.

First, promises were given to Abraham that he would have numerous posterity, (Genesis 17:16) that he would have much personal blessing, (Genesis 13:14-17; 15:5,6,18) that his name would be great, (Genesis 12:2) and that he personally would be a blessing. (Genesis 12:2)

Second, that through Abraham the promise was made that a great nation would emerge. (Genesis 12:3) This manifested itself in the twelve tribes of Israel, and eventually the great nation of Israel. The promise was made to this nation to possess the land of Palestine forever. (Genesis 12:7; 17:7,8) It should be noted here that the timing of this promise was not given and history has born out the fact that Israel did not possess the land for years though she has some of it today. The ultimate fulfillment of this promise awaits a future development, when Jesus Christ will rule over the nation of Israel. At that time this promise will have its ultimate and eternal fulfillment.

Third, that through Abraham blessing would come to the entire world. (Genesis 12:3) This fulfillment came in the person of Jesus Christ two thousand years ago, when He came to make reconciliation for all mankind. (Romans 5:8-11; II Peter 3:9)

5) THE MOSAIC COVENANT: this was a conditional covenant, and embodied the principle that if Israel was obedient, God would bless them, but if Israel was disobedient, God would curse them and discipline them. See Exodus 20:1 to 31:18, and especially Deuteronomy 28:1-68.

In this covenant over 600 specific commands are classified into three major areas: 1) the Ten Commandments; (Exodus 20:1-26) 2) judgments relating to the social and civic life of the nation; (Exodus 21:1 to 24:11) and 3) the ordinances. (Exodus 24:12 to 31:18) It was basically a covenant of works: this is why the covenant failed, in that the people couldn't live up to its demands, even though they agreed to do so. (Exodus 19:8 and 24:7) When Israel failed to live up to what they agreed, God was absolved of following through to that which He agreed to do. It was conditional.

6) THE PALESTINIAN COVENANT: This unconditional covenant refers to Israel's final possession of the land. (Deuteronomy 30:1-10)

Though it was an unconditional covenant, it had conditional elements for any particular generation. God's blessing upon any generation of Israel was conditioned upon their following God. When they turned aside unto idols and forsook God, He allowed them to go into captivity due to their sins, but He also promised eventual restoration of the nation, never again to be uprooted, and ultimately for their Messiah (Jesus Christ) to reign forever over the nation.

This Palestinian covenant accordingly included Israel's dispersion for unbelief and disobedience, but eventually ultimate and eternal restoration. (Deuteronomy 30:1-3)

7) THE DAVIDIC COVENANT: This was an unconditional covenant in which God promised David an unending royal lineage, a throne, and a kingdom, all of them forever. (II Samuel 7:4-16) The New Testament affirmation is seen in Luke 1:31-33, as promised by the angel of God, a thousand years after David.

The Davidic covenant was most important in assuring Israel of the ultimate Millennial Kingdom, in which their Messiah, Jesus Christ, the greater son of David, would reign over the nation of Israel, as well as over the whole world. This kingdom awaits future realization, and is known as the thousand year reign of Jesus Christ. (Revelation 20:1-3)

8) <u>THE NEW COVENANT</u>: The Prophets in the Old Testament prophesied of this covenant, which would eventually have its fulfillment in the body of Christian believers in the New Testament, as well as in the futuristic Millennial, thousand year Kingdom. (Jeremiah 31:31-33; Luke 22:20; I Corinthians 11:25; Galatians 3:26-29; Hebrews 10:10-17; 13:5,6)

The new covenant is between God and any individual, and consists of a relationship between the two, based upon the work that Jesus Christ did on the cross in caring for the sins of every person. On God's part, His holiness is guaranteed in having a relationship with the individual. On the person's part, his reconciliation to God comes in a personal commitment to God, through accepting the work of propitiation that Christ did on the cross in that person's behalf. (Romans 3:23-26) The result is that God is holy, and at the same time is able to justify, declare righteous, and reconcile the believing person to himself through the blood that Jesus Christ shed to cover that person's sins. (John 6:27-29)

This covenant is noted in two aspects: 1) In every case God has declared unconditionally that the believing person will have his sins taken away, never to be judged for them. (Hebrews 10:17) God promises what He will do for those who place their trust in Him, (John 5:24; 6:37) and that is, they become the recipients of eternal life. 2) The future salvation of Israel is also promised under the new covenant. (Romans 11:26,27) This new covenant is unconditional and eternal, and can never be rescinded. It is guaranteed by Jesus Christ Himself, the author of the new covenant, in His resurrection from the dead. (John 14:19; 11:25)

As to these eight covenants; emphasis should be placed on the sovereignty of God, the almighty and eternal power of God over the universe, in contrast to the failure of mankind. What God undertakes and promises, will come to pass.

Thy word is a lamp to my feet,
A light to my path alway,
To guide and to save me from sin,
And show me the heavenly way.

Forever, O Lord is thy word
Established and fixed on high;
Thy faithfulness unto all men
Abideth forever nigh.

At morning, at noon, and at night
I ever will give thee praise;
For thou art my portion, O Lord,
And shall be thru all my days!

Thru Him whom Thy Word hath foretold,
The Savior and Morning Star,
Salvation and peace have been brought
To those who have strayed afar.

Thy word have I hid in my heart,
That I might not sin against thee;
That I might not sin,
That I might not sin,
Thy word have I hid in my heart.

—Victorious Life, Keswick, NJ

Chapter 8

THE SOVEREIGNTY OF GOD

Though Christians place their trust in a sovereign God, there is a tendency at times to wonder if God is really in control. This happens when things in the world look confused. Granted, we believe that He created and sustains the world, but is He really in control over every little thing, as well as the nations of the world? Does He really number the hairs of our head, and furthermore does He care, even when we dismiss our fallen hairs so casually?

If we are to trust Him, not only for our Christian life, but for caring for us on a daily basis, and certainly for our eternal future, it is imperative that we understand what is meant by the sovereignty of God and how it is applied to our questions. Therefore, we need to start with a definition of the sovereignty of God: God is the creator of all things visible and invisible; He is everlasting sustainer of all things created; that He is the owner of all, and therefore has an absolute right to rule over all, which He does in exercising this authority in the universe. (Matt. 20:15; Rom. 9:20,21; Eph. 1:11) This sovereignty is not based on any capriciousness or whimsicalness of God, but is the sovereignty of wisdom, holiness, and love. Scripture abundantly teaches that God is sovereign in all the universe. (I Chron. 29:11; Ps. 115:3; Isa. 45:9; Ezek. 18:4; Dan. 4:35; I Tim. 6:15; Rev. 4:11) Our study of God's sovereignty will be exercised under two aspects: Preservation and Providence.

When one thinks of the word preservation, we believe that it has to do with permanently upholding, and controlling something to keep it for the future. The Biblical understanding of God's preservation is that God, by a continuous agency, maintains in existence, all the things which He has made, together with all their properties and powers. Preservation is distinguished from creation, in that creation had a beginning, and in itself is not self-existent nor self-sustaining. God has established an order of natural forces, which we may call the laws of nature, and by which He preserves, sustains, and continuously motivates things through these laws, in the universe. (Neh. 9:6; Col. 1:17; Heb. 1:3; Acts 17:28; Ps. 37:28; John 10:28)

When we study Scripture we see that God's will is not the only force in the universe, but that God concurs in all the operations, both of matter and mind. (I Cor. 12:6; Acts 17:28) He has given mankind a will of his own, which he has used in rebellion against God, and God has allowed him to act in accordance with his own selfishness. (Jer. 44:4; James 1:13,14) This rebellion of man against God resulted in separation from God, and this is the reason why God programmed Jesus Christ to come into the world of mankind. He entered the time and space world to reveal God and His purpose of reconciliation to God. The basis of the reconciliation came through the death, burial, and resurrection of Jesus Christ. The application of that event to the separated person comes through the individual making a willful acceptance of Jesus Christ. Though God is sovereign over all, He has given to mankind a will of his own, which God cannot override, but has made provision for all to return to the creator, and this comes out of a person's willingness to submit to God's program through Jesus Christ. Thus we see a balance, in human life, between the sovereignty of God and the free will of mankind.

The second aspect of God's sovereignty refers to His divine providence. God has not only created the universe, and has preserved it, but He also exercises sovereign control. This is called providence; it is the continuous activity of God whereby he makes all the events of the physical, mental, and moral phenomena to work out His purposes, and that is nothing short of His original design in creation. It is true that God has allowed evil to enter the universe, but by the same token, God does not allow it to thwart His overall purpose.

46

There are four main areas of existence in the universe over which God maintains sovereign control. The first is over the physical universe. (Ps. 103:19; Ps. 104:14; Matt. 5:46; Acts 14:17) The second is over the animal kingdom. (Job 12:10; Ps. 147:9; Matt. 6:26; Matt. 10:29) Thirdly, God is sovereign over the nations of the world. (Job 12:23; Ps. 22:28; Ps. 75:6,7; Acts 17:26; Rom. 13:1) Finally, He exercises control over all individuals in the following ways: a) over mankind's birth and lot in life, (Jer. 1:5; Gal. 1:15,16) b) over successes and failures of individuals, (Ps. 75:6,7; Prov. 21:1) c) over even the insignificant things in life, hairs of our head, and sparrows that fall, (Prov. 16:33; Matt. 10:30) d) over the needs of God's children, the Christians, (Rom. 8:28; Phil. 4:19) and finally, e) over the destinies of both Christians and non-Christians. (Ps. 73:24; Ps. 37:23,24; Ps. 11:6)

God has four distinct ends toward which His providence is motivated. These are primarily directed toward the eternal welfare of mankind, which He created for fellowship with him throughout eternity. For this was why all creation was made. First, God has an eternal view toward the happiness of mankind. (Acts 14:17; Rom. 2:4; Ps. 84:11; John 10:10; Rom. 8:28) Then, God's providence has in view the mental and moral development of the human race. In the Old Testament, the Levitical priestly system was ordained preparatory to the coming of Christ. All the types and figures were symbolized toward that end. Along with that came the moral and ethical concepts of Christianity, as illustrated and exemplified in the moral law of Moses. (Acts 17:24-28)

When Christ came into the world, He provided for spiritual re-birth and subsequent spiritual maturity of life in the individual, which has resulted in the re-characterization of life and the fruit of the spirit.

The third end toward which God's providence is directed is with a view to the salvation of all mankind. In II Peter 3:9 it says, "The Lord is...not willing that any should perish, but that all should come to repentance." I Timothy 2:4 points out that God, "will have all mankind to be saved." God never created any person to go to hell, but that everyone would be reconciled to Him, so that together they may have fellowship throughout eternity. It is totally inconsistent with God's attributes to ever create anyone and destine that person to eternal damnation. However, because God has given to each a free will, mankind has separated himself from God, and thereby incurred the wrath of God, because God's holiness cannot countenance sin. This is why God had to send Jesus Christ to die in man's stead, so that by one trusting Christ's work on the cross, God's holiness could remain unsullied. He extends His love and grace in redemption to any who would believe. (Romans 3:21-26; Ex. 19:5,6; Titus 2:14; I Peter 2:9; Eph. 3:9,10;5:25-27)

But, some may ask, what about the person who has never had the opportunity to hear and accept the redemption in Christ, that God has provided for the whole world. Will that person go to hell? If God's redemption has paid for the sins of the whole world, and this person has never heard, why should he be eternally judged? To answer these questions from a Biblical perspective, one must always begin with Who God is. The Bible tells us that the primary attribute of God is His holiness, in which He is totally set apart from anything that is contrary to His attributes—thus His holiness.

One of God's attributes is His omniscience, that is, there is nothing that God doesn't know. He knows the innermost thoughts of every individual. Christ died for the sins of the world, and God is not willing that any should perish. (II Peter 3:9) God knows the heart of every person. I am convinced that God in His omnipotence and omniscience would not let anyone perish whom He knows in their heart is seeking their creator, and will provide the opportunity to be saved.

An excellent illustration of this is seen in the life of David Livingston. As a young lad living in England, he desired to become a sailor. He hired himself out to a sea captain going to India. The ship on which he was sailing was caught in a storm around the horn of Africa, and Livingston was cast ashore. Some years later Stanley came from England hunting Livingston, and found him in the heart of Africa, evangelizing many natives of that continent. It is easy to realize that God knew there were people at that time, and in that location, who given the message of salvation, would accept it. He put it in the heart of Livingston to adventure out to sea. God caused the storm that wrecked the ship, and saved Livingston, so that His word might get to those people at that time.

If we accept God's omniscience and His omnipotence, then we must also realize that when mankind stands before God in judgment,

48

there will never be anyone standing there sentenced to eternal judgment, who will be able to say he never heard the message of salvation, and had he done so, would have accepted it. No, God is seeing to it that anyone will have the opportunity whom He knows will accept if they hear, and will open the door to their understanding. Many more hear than accept, because God has given us a will of our own to accept or reject, but no one will be judged who has never heard, but would have accepted had they heard. God is sovereign, and He rules over all, to the intent that He never created anyone to be sent to eternal judgment, but that all should come to repentance. (I Tim. 2:4; 4:10)

Finally, the primary end of God's government over His creation, is for His own glory, His moral attributes. (Psalms 86:12; John 17:1; Romans 15:6) He uses a variety of means, to achieve that end: 1) *His Word*; (Josh. 1:8; Isa. 8:20; Col. 3:16) 2) *His appeal to mankind's reason*; (Isa. 1:18: Acts 6:2) 3) *He also uses persuasion*; (II. Cor. 5:20; Jer. 44:4) 4) *His use of checks and restraints*; (Acts 16:6-8) 5) *His use of outward circumstances*; (I Cor. 16:9; Gal. 4:20) 6) *God inclines mankind's heart in one direction or another*; (Ps. 119:36; Prov. 21:1; II Cor. 8:16) 7) *Sometimes He guides by dreams and visions.* (Matt. 2:13,19,20; Acts. 16:9,10) In God's overseeing of the world and mankind, He utilizes many and varied elements to ultimately direct everything after the counsel of His own will, for His honor and the ultimate good of all mankind. It is difficult for us, at times, to understand God's program, but as the Apostle Paul states in I Cor. 13:12, "Now we see through a glass darkly;" it is for us just to trust God's overall good. We only see today; He sees the whole of eternity.

It is important for us to realize and understand the necessary balance between the sovereignty of God, and the free will of mankind. In God's creation part of the *image* of God which He infused into us was *will*. Originally, Adam exercised his will perfectly in following God. But, Satan deceived Adam and Eve into turning from being God-centered to being self-centered, which was the original sin. The sin of Adam has translated itself to every individual, (Rom. 5:12) so that we have all sinned and come short of the glory of God. (Rom. 3:23) God's sovereignty is still intact. But now He has to work His sovereign will, with mankind's self-will that is opposed to God's will. This constant conflict throughout the ages has caused the problems seen in the world, and also has kept mankind from seeing clearly, and from submitting his will to that of God's sovereignty.

Some may reflect upon this understanding wonder why the Christian needs to pray—if God is sovereign, and in spite of mankind's self-will, God's overall will is being worked out in life? Prayer is not for God's benefit, since He is sovereign, and He knows what we will pray for even before we pray. It is for our benefit, as prayer keeps us sensitive to God, it helps us to unload on Him, and it is our way of communicating with God as His children. God's Word is His communication with us, and prayer is our response to Him. This completes the circuit between a loving heavenly Father and us His children, whom He loves. Note: James 4:2,13-15,16

A sovereign God who designed and created the universe and all that is in it, did so for the good and blessing of each individual, created in His likeness and for fellowship with Him. Because of this, God gave to each of us our will, so that we would respond to Him out of our own volition, not because we had to out of a lack of another option. God did not want a robot or a puppet who would follow Him, but one who would do so out of love. The deception of Satan through mankind, with the consequent separation from God, only incited God to pronounce the decree that He would send His Son, Jesus Christ, He would provide reconciliation to God, through His death and resurrection, and by our receiving what He provided for us in love. Our will, which we act upon freely, projects itself in accepting the provision that was made. God's sovereignty has made this all possible. (Heb. 2:9-18; Titus 3:3-7)

In loving kindness Jesus came,
My soul in mercy to reclaim,
And from the depths of sin and shame,
Through grace He lifted me.

From sinking sand He lifted me,
With tender hands He lifted me;
From shades of night, to plains of light,
O, Praise His name, He lifted me.

50

He called long before I heard,
    Before my sinful heart was stirred,
But when I took Him at His word,
    Forgiven He lifted me.

Now on a higher plane I dwell,
    And with my soul I know 'tis well;
Yet how or why I cannot tell,
    He should have lifted me.

From sinking sand, He lifted me,
    With tender hands He lifted me;
From shades of night, to plains of light,
    O, Praise His name, He lifted me.

—Victorious Life, Keswick, NJ

Chapter 9

THE CONFLICT THROUGH THE AGES

In Genesis 3:15 there is the first prophetic notice in Scripture of a divine major announcement. It signaled the commencement of an age long unceasing conflict between God and Satan, with mankind in between. This is a declaration of war between God and that old serpent, Satan, as Rev. 12:9 states, the Bible provides us with a picture of both sides in this ongoing conflict. It is important to understand each side, so that we, as Christians, might comprehend the *wrestling* that goes on. It is not in the world of time and space, but in the spiritual, metaphysical world, between God and Satan. This spiritual battle impacts mankind. (Eph. 6:12)

God's side of the conflict has four basic truths. The foundation of these elements is found in Gen. 3:15. First, in the context of Gen. 3:14-19, we note the word spoken by God resulted in a curse upon the man, the woman, the ground, and Satan. The serpent was the embodiment and representative of Satan at this point. This was a pronouncement by God, not a question. It must be remembered that though Satan has supernatural power, God is omnipotent. This curse has remained through the history of mankind until today.

Second, all God's goodness to Adam and Eve did not prevent them from being beguiled by, and yielding to, the serpent. What he presented was very attractive, and he won a victory over God at this point. He spoiled God's creation, he alienated the affection of mankind toward God, and he brought mankind under his spell. Though Satan won a victory here, there is no note of despair in God's speech.

Third, from this time on there would be two groups of people: 1) Satan and his seed, and 2) the woman and her seed. The word **enemy** in v.15 means a mutual state of hostility, a continual struggle between an evil supernatural power and struggling mankind. This is seen in John 10:10 and I Peter 5:8.

Fourth, in this conflict both sides would suffer. Satan would ultimately bruise the heel of the seed of the woman at Christ's death for the sins of the world. (Heb. 2:9) The seed of the woman, Christ Jesus, (Gal. 4:4) would crush Satan's head; in that Christ's resurrection would forever destroy Satan's power. (Heb. 2:14; I John 3:8) The seed of the woman expressed by the pronoun, "He," (Gen. 3:15) would terminate in a single individual, the Lord Jesus Christ.

From God's point of view, we turn now to Satan's side of the picture. In John 8:44,45, the Lord Jesus Christ pointed out Satan's two basic ways of fighting. In the context of John 8 we have the so called Pharisaical truth squad that hounded Jesus wherever He went to set the record straight from their perspective. In v.19 they wondered aloud if He knew who His father was. Some versions use a capital "F," meaning God the Father, but it should be a lower case letter, because the Pharisees weren't referring to God. They were questioning Jesus' legitimacy. Then in v.41 they accused Him of being born of fornication; and finally in v.48 they accused Him of being a half-breed. Even still in Jesus' day Samaritans were the intermingling of Assyrian colonists and the poor Jews left in Palestine, when they depopulated Israel in the conquest of 721 B.C.

In v.44, Jesus turned on the Pharisees and said, "You are of your father the devil, and the lusts of your father you will do. He was a murderer from the beginning, and abode not in the truth, because there is no truth in him." In this judgment, Christ put his finger on Satan's two basic ways of fighting: 1) Destruction—from the beginning of Old Testament history to the cross, Satan trafficked primarily in destruction and murder. 2) Deception—from the resurrection to the end of the age, he has used primarily deception. This is not to say that he never used deception before the resurrection, nor that he never uses destruction in this present age. But, if one examines the Old Testament and the New, it is easily seen just how Satan has operated, as Jesus pointed out.

After the primary deception of Adam and Eve, Satan caused the first murder; Cain killed his brother Abel. Later Satan threatened to kill Joseph, through his brothers, and ultimately annihilate the people of Israel in Egypt, by the edict of the Pharaoh, who wanted to kill all male Hebrew babies. When Israel became a nation he used Saul to try to kill David, and later two wicked queens, Athaliah and Jezebel, to destroy the royal line from David to Jesus Christ. When the Jews were in exile, he tried to use the edict of Haman in Esther's day to kill all the Jews.

Having failed to destroy God's chosen people, Satan used all his evil schemes to try to kill Jesus. At His birth, Satan prompted Herod to make a decree that all Hebrew children under two years of age should be destroyed. Herod even used the wise men to try to discover where the Christ child was. But God intervened and told them to go home another way, and then told Joseph to take Mary and the baby into Egypt until Herod was dead. One can easily see the conflict between God and Satan, over the person of Jesus. You can see how the world of the spirit impacted the world of time and space. This is the import of Eph. 6:12.

During the public ministry of Jesus, Satan tempted Him three times. (Luke 4:1-13) He tried to get many groups to kill Jesus. (John 5:18) But the record notes that He "passed through their midst, because His time was not yet." Satan never killed Jesus; Christ laid down His own life at the judicious time according to God's plan. (John 10:18)

Finally, when Jesus was crucified, Satan used all his evil schemes and power to try and keep Christ in the grave. He placed a huge stone to seal it; he ordered a legion of soldiers around the grave; and he put the seal of the Roman government on the grave. (Matt. 27:65,66) But, all his wicked designs failed to keep Jesus in the grave. When Christ arose, He forever sealed the doom of Satan (his head was crushed). In I Cor. 15:1-58 there is a powerful testimony, by way of summary, as to the conflict, and God's omnipotence over Satan. It is also a note of victory to those of us who are God's children.

What then is left for Satan? Deception. From the resurrection to the end of the age, that is what Satan is using to destroy mankind. I

55

John 3:8 states that Christ came to destroy the works of Satan. This He did in His death, burial, and resurrection. In the book of Acts there are seven verbs used in reference to Christ's death, but not one states that anyone destroyed Him. But Scripture plainly states Christ destroyed the power of Satan. What then is left for Satan but deception. And, this is what he has so effectively played upon mankind since Christ's resurrection.

Christ realized Satan's designs of deception, when He gave the parable of the wheat and the tares. (Matt. 13:24-30) As He stated to His disciples, that the sower sowed the grain; then another sowed tares (weeds). The Disciples said they should take out the weeds, but Jesus said to let the two grow together until the harvest, and the farmer would separate the grain from the weeds. In this analogy, or parable, He stated that the seed was the good Word of God, and the weeds the deception of Satan. Thus we see in today's world that both righteousness and wickedness are prospering, and just as weeds outstrip the grain with little or no food, so wickedness seems to prosper and righteousness has a difficult time. But, this is not the way it will always be. God will some day come in judgment and destroy wickedness forever. (John 5:22-27)

Satan has used three great deceptions today, in seducing mankind away from the truth of God's revelation in Jesus Christ. It is important for the Christian to understand these, because we are not immune to Satan's deception, even though we are God's children. Granted, the Christian has the indwelling Holy Spirit to give discernment, (I Cor. 2:14; I John 4:4) so that we can be aware of the deception, whereas the unbeliever has no help from falling into Satan's trap.

The first great deception is that of Doctrine—Matt. 24:4,5. After coming out of the temple in Jerusalem, Christ spoke of its destruction, which elicited three questions from His Disciples. (v.3) He answered only the second, "What shall be the sign of your coming?" He then stated, "Take heed that no one deceive you. For many shall come in my name, saying, I am Christ and shall deceive many." (v.4,5) The first and foremost deception of Satan is in reference to Biblical truth. He has tried, through the centuries, to produce many false christs, so called Prophets, and he has tried to undermine the truth of Scripture by addition or subtraction. He has used religious people to convolute

56

Scripture, to try and get it to say something that it doesn't. All these things are intended to deceive unsuspecting people. Whereas, Christ said, "I am the way, the truth, and the life, no one comes unto the Father but through me." (John 14:6) By that He meant the only way of reconciliation of mankind to God is through acknowledging Christ as the only way to have eternal life.

If Satan is unable to deceive one through a false Christ or false teaching, he then turns to the second great deception, that in regards to Sin. (Heb. 3:13) "But encourage one another daily, while it is called today; lest any of you be hardened through the deceitfulness of sin." In today's world there are two popular words, *rationalize* and *justify*, used by people to do what they wish to selfishly do, in order to avoid guilt and the consequences of their behavior. "Everyone is doing it, isn't it alright?" Many under this rubric, the dirt of sin is swept, and people go on about their business, feeling they are getting away with it. God calls this being deceived in sin. In II Cor. 5:10 it says that we must all stand before God in judgment to, "Receive the things done in his body, according to that he has done, whether it be good or bad." Then in Heb. 4:13 it notes that, "All things are naked and opened unto the eyes of Him with whom we have to do." Just because the person of the world feels it is all right for him, does not necessarily mean that behavior is right for the Christian. The child of God marches to the beat of a different drummer.

The third and most subtle deception of Satan is in regard to Humanistic Philosophy, (Col. 2:8) "See to it that no one takes you captive through hollow and deceptive philosophy, which depends upon human tradition and the basic principles of this world rather than on Christ." (NIV) The basic humanistic philosophy is that mankind's nature is good, even though he has fallen upon hard times, and needs help. Whereas, the Bible states that, "All have sinned and come short of the glory of God." (Rom. 3:23) Mankind has separated himself from God through sin. Satan tries to gloss this over through educated philosophical manipulation, intended to overwhelm people into believing they are okay, and thus be deceived into believing to be somebody they are not. In Col. 2:9,10 God tells us, His children, that only in Christ dwells all the fullness of Deity, and that through regeneration in Him we are complete.

57

I Tim. 4:1 points out that "In the latter times some shall depart from the faith, giving heed to deceiving spirits and doctrines that demons teach." Demons deceive first in doctrine. Most cults and isms deny the Deity of Jesus Christ, the inspiration of Scripture, the work of Christ on the cross, and His resurrection. II Tim. 3:1,2 states that in the "Last days perilous times shall come. For mankind shall be lovers of SELF." We see a proliferation of self-centeredness in our world today; the "Me" generation is prospering as never before, and mankind desires to get *all the gusto* out of life he can. Verse 13 says, "Evil men and deceivers shall wax worse and worse, deceiving and being deceived." The Christian should not be surprised at what is transpiring in the world today, because God foretold this in His Word.

As Christians we are not left without admonition, as to how we should respond to all these things. In II Tim. 3:14-17 there is God's commendation to us, as to how we should live in a wicked world. The Apostle Paul used a personal illustration in the life of Timothy to apply to us all. He told him to continue to do the things he had been taught in a godly way, by his Mother Lois, and his Grandmother, Eunice. (II Tim. 1:5) A godly heritage is one of the finest things parents can pass on to their children. Paul noted that Timothy had, "From a child known the Holy Scriptures, which are able to make you wise unto Salvation through faith which is in Jesus Christ." (v.15)

Finally, in II Tim. 3:16 we have God's antidote to Satan's three deceptions of False doctrine, Sin, and Humanistic Philosophy. "All Scripture is given by inspiration of God and is profitable for doctrine, as the antidote to false doctrine, for reproof, for correction, as the antidote to sin, for instruction in righteousness, as the antidote to humanistic philosophy." God's conclusion is found in v.17 which tells us, "That the child of God may be brought to maturity, thoroughly equipped unto all good works." God's Word is, "A lamp unto my feet, and a light unto my pathway." (Ps. 119:105)

Satan does not deny the historical Jesus, even the cults don't do this. He denies that Jesus was the Christ, the Son of God, the only Redeemer that can save mankind from his own self destruction.

In 1952 in the New York Times Sunday supplement magazine it stated there were 113 notable books published, according to their reckoning, that had impacted our nation, between 1850 and 1950. It is interesting to see that not one of those books was written to honor the Lord Jesus Christ. So, how easily it is seen that Satan has riveted the chains of deception upon our country today. We are reaping what we have sown. "The one who sows to please his sinful nature, (SELF) from that nature will reap destruction; the one who sows to please the Spirit, from the Spirit will reap eternal life." (Gal. 6:8) (NIV)

In the dark of the midnight, Have I oft hid my face,
While the storms howl above me, and there's no hiding place.
'Mid the crash of the thunder, precious Lord hear my cry,
Keep me safe 'til the storm passes by.

Many times Satan whispered, there is no use to try,
For there's no end of sorrow, there's no hope by and by,
But I know thou art with me, and tomorrow I'll rise
Where the storms never darken the skies.

When the long night has ended, and the storms come no more,
Let me stand in thy presence, on that bright, peaceful shore.
In that land where the tempest never comes, Lord may I,
Dwell with thee, when the storm passes by.

'Til the storm passes over, 'til the thunder sounds no more,
'Til the clouds roll forever from the sky.
Hold me fast, let me stand in thy hollow of thy hand,
Keep me safe 'til the storm passes by.

—Hymns for the Family,
Paragon Assoc., Inc.,
Nashville, TN

Chapter 10

BY GOD'S WILL

In the providence of God, there are four aspects of His complete plan for us His children, that are all encompassing from eternity past to eternity future. Though they are found in various aspects of Scripture, there is a summation of them in Hebrews 10:10-18. In Chapter 2 we saw the three aspects of life for ourselves that we need to be aware of: 1) The entrance and problem of sin; 2) The need for and way of salvation; and 3) The way of sanctification, Holy living of life. In this chapter our lives are seen from God's perspective, and what He has done to bring reconciliation of mankind to Himself.

I. By God's Will We Have Been Sanctified. (Heb. 10:10) This acts delivers the believer's Position from sin. God set apart all those who would accept His son as their Savior, before the foundation of the world was even laid. This was a positional setting apart. In Romans 8:29 it says, "For whom He did foreknow with God's omniscience He also did predetermine to be conformed to the image of His son." I Peter 1:2 tells us that we have been, "Elected according to the foreknowledge of God the Father."

God brought His plan to fruition in Christ's redemptive work on the cross, as seen in this verse, "By the will of God we have been sanctified through the offering of the body of Jesus Christ, once for all." The Greek present tense denotes a present condition, based on a past action.

Christ's offering dealt with the believer's position in sin. Since sanctification by Christ's sacrifice is judicial, God set the believers apart unto Himself, positionally putting us into a holy class before He could do anything for us personally. To illustrate, an adopted child must be legally adopted, he must have a position as a child of the new parents before they are able to do anything about raising him as their own. So, God had to set us apart unto Himself, through Jesus Christ, before He could begin the life transforming power in us. Therefore, Christ's offering was once for all sanctifying and setting us apart as God's own possession. Once for all; the believer, past, present, and future.

II. <u>By God's Will We Have Been Justified</u>. (Heb. 10:11-13) This act of God removes the believer's <u>Penalty</u> for sin. This, too, is a judicial act of God, because mankind is incapable of paying the penalty for his sins. Because God is infinite, our sins against Him are infinite in cost. But, God now is able to declare the believer righteous and justified through the work Christ did on the cross.

Romans 3:24-26 explains that God justifies us through the redemptive work of Christ, (v.24) and then enlightens us by noting that Christ was a propitiation to actually pay for our sins, which we accept by faith. It is important to note in verses 25 and 26 that Christ did not make atonement paid a covering over for our sins, but propitiated, actually cared for, our sins. The word *atonement* is strictly an Old Testament concept, since the sacrifice of animals didn't care for the sins of the people. (Heb. 10:4,11) It only covered them over until Christ came and actually cared for, and propitiated the sins of both Old and New Testament believers which is strictly a New Testament concept. Under the Old Covenant God *forebore* (v.25) the sins of the Old Testament saints until Christ came. In v.26 it tells us that God is now able to be just as His holiness is exercised and the justifier, declares him righteous who believes in Jesus. Again it is worthy to note that the word *atonement* is never used in the New Testament for it is strictly an Old Testament Covenant concept. Conversely, the word *propitiation* is never used in the Old Testament, for it is strictly a New Testament Covenant concept.

In Hebrews 2:14,15 we see that Christ became flesh and blood. In other words He came into the realm of life in which we participate, in order to meet sin head on and conquer it, since sin was committed in the realm of flesh and blood. Christ's resurrection conquered death and Satan, so that all believers, past, present, and future could be delivered from the bondage of sin. On the basis of Christ's propitiatory work on the cross as well as His resurrection, God is able to justify the believer in Jesus Christ. Hebrews 10:13 looks forward to the culmination of this victory.

III. By God's Will We Have Been Regenerated. (Heb.10:15,16) This provides for the believer's Power over sin.

In verse 15 we see the Holy Spirit doing the work of regeneration and also indwelling the believer, to give him power to overcome sin. In verse 16 we see the two aspects of sin: 1) volitional and 2) intellectual.

The volitional is understood by, "I will put my law into their hearts," which provides for the believer a new nature that overcomes the old disposition or set of the human will in selfishness. Philippians 2:12,13 explains we are to, "work out your own salvation with fear and trembling." The salvation we have through regeneration is a gift of God, for which we can do no work. What is meant here is that we are to work out in a maturing of our spiritual life, what God has given to us through the gift of eternal life. We don't fear God in the sense of being afraid, but in the sense of awe or respect of God for Who He is. Verse 13 explains that it is the indwelling Holy Spirit within us Who provides a willingness as well as an enablement to carry out our spiritual maturation.

The intellectual aspect of our new nature is seen in, "I will write my laws into their minds." This provides moral and spiritual discernment for the Christian. (Heb. 8:10) In John 14:16-26 Christ taught His disciples of His return to Heaven, and He promised them **another Comforter** whom He said would be the Holy Spirit, to continually indwell them and abide in them. Then in John 16:7-14 Christ instructed the disciples concerning the Holy Spirit by saying that "He will guide you into all the truth." The work of the Holy Spirit in the life of every Christian is to give us moral and spiritual discernment. In I Cor. 2:9-14 we see that only the Christian has what the Bible states is *spiritual discernment*. This enables us to comprehend the truth of the Bible in our understanding, and then as we allow the Holy Spirit to apply these truths to our development we become more spiritually mature. This is primarily what God wishes for His children. (I Peter 2:2; II Peter 3:18)

Regeneration brings a new life, a new heart, and a new will. Only the Christian has all these by the power of the Holy Spirit. The person of the world has intellectual understanding, but the Christian has the discernment of God's principles for wholeness of life.

IV. By God's Will We Have Been Glorified. (Heb. 10:14,17,18) This deals with the very Presence of sin.

Today, in the life of every Christian, there is a progressive transformation into God's likeness, that is taking place. But in these verses that God-likeness in us is seen as already completed, in God's mind. Because God does not operate in a time and space world as we do, everything in His plan is in the present. All that God has, is, and will do for us is already completed by Him, ages ago.

This is why Romans 8:28-33, which follows through from eternity past to eternity future, states, "All things work together for good, to them that love God." It has not only been planned in eternity past, it is and will be carried out by God's sovereignty and omnipotence. On this we can rely.

Heb. 10:14 says that we are *perfected forever*, which means "bearing through to the end." In Phil. 1:6, the Apostle Paul said, "I am confident of this very thing, that the Holy Spirit who has begun a good work in you through regeneration, will bring it to completion at the day of Jesus Christ." I John 3:2 tells us that, "We shall be like Him, for we shall see Him as He is." I Thess. 5:24 notes that, "Faithful is He that calleth you, who also will do it."

This is why Heb. 10:17 states, "Their sins and iniquities will I remember no more." For every child of God there is only looking forward to that great day of eternity with our heavenly Father. Therefore, by God's will, from eternity to eternity, we have been, sanctified, justified, regenerated, and glorified. Praise God!

"I stand amazed in the presence of Jesus the Nazarene,
And wonder how He could love me, a sinner, condemned, unclean.
How marvelous, how wonderful, and my song shall ever be;
How marvelous, how wonderful, is my Savior's love for me.

When with the ransomed in glory, His face I at last shall see,
'Twill be my joy through the ages, to sing of His love for me.
How marvelous, how wonderful, and my song shall ever be;
How marvelous, how wonderful, is my Savior's love for me."

—Victorious Life, Keswick, NJ

Chapter 11

THE THREEFOLD MINISTRY OF CHRIST

In Revelation 19:10 we read, "For the testimony borne to Jesus is the spirit of prophecy." This thought is probably the most all encompassing verse of the Bible. It underlies all of the revelation of God to mankind, as seen in His Word.

The word *Prophecy* has as its primary meaning, *To tell forth* and a secondary meaning of *Foretelling*. The Prophets of old told forth the revelation of God to Israel, and a portion of their prophecies were futuristic. But, primarily, they were the mouthpieces of God to Israel, to reveal Himself and His commandments.

Prophecy, as a predictive element has but one objective, that is to give testimony concerning the Lord Jesus Christ. Therefore, if we look at Prophecy in this manner throughout the Bible, we are able to say that in the Old Testament He is coming, in the Gospels He is here, and in the Epistles He is coming again.

Genesis 3:15 is the seed of all Messianic prophecy. The seed of the woman culminated in Jesus Christ, Who in His death and resurrection, forever crushed the power of Satan. (Gal. 4:4) All history is the story of two men: (I Cor. 15:47) 1) Adam—from him issued forth ruined mankind, the rejection of Jesus Christ, and the eventual acceptance of the anti-Christ, 2) Jesus Christ—from Him issued forth salvation to Adam's race, and ultimate dominion over all the world. Adam's fall centered the hope of restoration upon Jesus Christ, the second man. It is important to study these two men by way of contrast.

I. Concerning the Creation and Position of Adam. The Bible tells us four things about him. He was the first man; and there was no one before him. (I Cor. 15:45) Second, he was the father of all mankind. (Acts 17:26) Third, he was the federal man in that he held the governmental headship for all the peoples of the world. (Rom. 5:12) When he sinned he placed all of mankind in the realm of sin. Finally, he was a type of the second man, Jesus Christ, (Rom. 5:14) in that Christ became the man Jesus, and took on human flesh in a world of time and space. He came into the world of sin to undo what Adam had done in placing all of us in sin. (I John 3:8; I Cor. 15:22)

II. Concerning the Privileges and Failures of Adam. He enjoyed a standing before God in his sinless estate, as a Prophet, a Priest, and a King. As a Prophet, he knew the will of God by direct revelation. Adam and God walked together and enjoyed sweet fellowship, and God continued to reveal Himself to Adam, who in turn was to convey his understanding to his family. As Priest, Adam had a right standing before God, since he was sinless. As King God placed him over all the creation. He told Adam that the animals were subservient to him, that the ground was his to work, and it would produce abundantly. All of this Adam and his family were to enjoy. Furthermore, he was to fill the earth with his progeny, and all this would continue eternally, with no death.

But, when Adam sinned he ceased to be a Prophet, because now there came a separation between God and him due to his sin. He needed to be taught the mind and will of God, since he no longer had it by direct revelation. He couldn't tell forth the revelation of God, because of the separation. He also ceased to be a Priest, for now he needed a mediator in his behalf before God. Thirdly, he ceased to be a King over the creation. Now the animals became wild, the ground brought forth weeds, and by the sweat of his brow he would eke out a living. Adam was cast out of the garden of Eden. These were the consequences of his sin. His turning from being God-centered to becoming self-centered. All this was due to the deception of Satan, as embodied in the serpent, who deceived both Adam and Eve. All of the world's problems from that time to the present are seen in the self-centeredness of mankind. Thus the need for a successor to Adam.

68

III. <u>Concerning Adam's Successor</u>. This brings us to the point of Genesis 3:15.

In this verse the seed of the woman was now promised. The first man, Adam, left to posterity alienation from God. But, in the promised Messiah, the Christ, the *Last Adam*, (I Cor. 15:45) complete triumph over Satan is promised. Satan, through the serpent, bruised the *heel* of the woman. The deception of Adam and Eve has carried down through the ages to every person, evidenced in our sin nature. But, the promised seed of the woman, Christ Jesus, would crush the power of Satan forever. (I John 3:8) This was guaranteed to all mankind in the resurrection of Christ from the dead. (I Cor. 15:20-26)

At this point of the story, God used three methods to prepare for the advent of the seed of the woman. He raised up a succession of <u>Prophets,</u> who were God's mouthpiece to Israel. Then, He raised up a family of <u>Priests,</u> from the tribe of Levi, who were men of special sanctification to mediate between Israel and God. Finally, He raised up a race of <u>Kings,</u> from the tribe of Judah, who were a special choice of God to rule over Israel. The Old Testament is a record of how these three classes fulfilled their function.

Yet, in all the Old Testament, not one Prophet, Priest, or King, was found upon whom the Spirit of God could rest and remain as Savior for Israel. The reason? The "Seed of the woman" had not yet appeared. (Gal. 4:4) The Old Testament concludes with all these longings as yet unfulfilled.

The point of the text in Revelation 19:10 shows that in the Old Testament the Spirit of prophecy was bearing witness to the fact that one would come, who would: 1) As <u>Prophet</u> fulfill in His life and work all the prophecies of the Old Testament; and 2) As <u>Priest</u> explain in His death and propitiation, all the ceremonies of the Levitical priesthood; and 3) As <u>King</u> satisfy, in His resurrection and coming again, all human longings.

We now turn to the New Testament to see the record or testimony borne to Jesus Christ, as Prophet, Priest, and King.

1) <u>As Prophet</u>: Moses, who was the great Prophet of the Old Testament, and a type of Christ, gave reference to the promise of the coming Christ in Deuteronomy 18:15 when he spoke of another Prophet, like unto him, and said, "Unto Him you shall listen." In Acts

3:22, the Apostle Peter was preaching, when he quoted from Deut. 18:15, and likened what Moses prophesied to the Lord Jesus Christ. Stephen, in Acts 7:37, did likewise in his defense of Jesus Christ.

Moses was the lesser Prophet, and gave only fragmentary prophecies, whereas Christ the greater Prophet, fulfilled them all. In Hebrews 1:1,2 we note the contrast between the Old Testament Prophets, (v.1) and Jesus Christ, God's Son, who brought God's final and last prophecies. (v.2) Christ is God's completed revelation to mankind. (II Cor. 4:6)

2) <u>As Priest</u>: Under the old covenant, Aaron was the High Priest, who was a type of Christ. This is seen from Heb. 5:1-10, where it states that Aaron was chosen from among men, and appointed of God. So was Christ. The difference between them was that Aaron could not put away sin, (Heb. 7:26-28) whereas Christ could and did. (Heb. 10:14) Furthermore, Aaron's priesthood was carried on upon earth, but Christ's is carried on in heaven. (Heb. 8:1-5)

Aaron entered into the holiest place in the Tabernacle, and no one dared follow. Christ entered into heaven itself, not only to carry on intercession for us, but has left the way open for all to follow, and bids us enter. (Heb. 6:20; 4:14-16) Therefore, Christ was, and is, the perfect priest of God for us.

3) <u>As King</u>: When God spoke in times past, there were many implications that He was preparing for the great and coming king. The many kings of the Old Testament foreshadowed the King of kings. In Hebrews 7:1 the king who is mentioned as a type of Christ is not David, Solomon, or Hezekiah, but Melchizedec, King of Salem. He is described as the "Priest of the most high God." (Heb. 7:1)

Melchizedec is a type of Christ, and in Hebrews 7 there is a play upon words, both in his name and his title. In Hebrews 7:1,2 it points out that Melchisedec is compound from two Hebrew words. The first part *Mel* means *king* in Hebrew language; the last part *Chizedec* is a transliteration of a word that means *Righteousness*. The word *Salem* means *Peace*. In verse two the interpretation is explained. The reason for all this is that Christ is both *King of righteousness* as well as *King of peace*.

In Zechariah 6:12,13 it prophetically states that the "BRANCH," who is Christ, will be both a king and priest on His throne. When Christ comes to rule the world, He will institute everlasting righteousness. Then, and only then, will the world enjoy the peace it so sorely desires. (Jeremiah 23:4-6)

Hebrews 7:11-17 it points out a fact that all Jewish people understood; that a king dared not enter the Priesthood or vice versa. The two offices were separate, as commanded by God. But the Hebrew passage points out that the Levitical Priesthood could not bring in perfection, so the law was changed by God. Therefore, Christ came both as King and Priest since He came to rule, as well as to care for sins and effect perfection.

For Christ is the true King of Righteousness and after that, King of Peace. Throughout His Millennial reign He will fulfill God's divine order, first righteousness, then peace.

Return to the text of Revelation 19:10. The testimony to Jesus in this passage is of a prophetic character and a threefold nature: Prophet, Priest, and King. In the book of Revelation there are no less than three indicators of this: Revelation 1:4 states, "From Him which is Christ as Priest, and which was Christ as Prophet, and which is to come Christ as King." See also Revelation 1:5: "From Jesus Christ, who is the faithful witness as true Prophet, and the firstborn of the dead, as the true Priest, and the Prince of the kings of the earth as Lord omnipotent, King of kings."

Finally, in Revelation 19:1-16 the four "Alleluias" (v.1,3,4,6) denote Christ as: Prophet, (v.11)—"Faithful and true:" Priest, (v.13) "Garment sprinkled with blood" and coming King (v.16)—"King of kings and Lord of lords." Revelation 19 depicts the battle of Armageddon, where Christ will return to the earth to rule and reign over the nations. In the context of this chapter, the Apostle John is so overcome with emotion in the vision he is witnessing, that he falls at the feet of the escorting Angel, who says, "John don't worship me, I'm just a fellow servant; worship God: for the testimony borne to Jesus is the essence of all Biblical prophecy." This speaks of the Lord Jesus Christ, who is God's final and last Prophet to mankind, the only Priest who could put away the sins of world, and the coming King over all the earth; worship Him!

I hear the Savior say,
    Thy strength indeed is small,
Child of weakness watch and pray,
    Find in Me thine all in all.

Jesus paid it all,
    All to Him I owe;
Sin had left a crimson stain,
    He washed it white as snow.

Lord, now indeed I find,
    Thy power and thine alone,
Can change the leper's spots,
    And melt the heart of stone.

For nothing good have I,
    Whereby thy grace to claim,
I'll wash my garments white,
    In the blood of Calvary's lamb.

And, when before the throne,
    I stand in Him complete,
"Jesus died my soul to save,"
    My lips shall still repeat.

Jesus paid it all,
    All to Him I owe;
Sin had left a crimson stain,
    He washed it white as snow.
                    —Victorious Life, Keswick, NJ

Chapter 12

THE COURSE OF THIS WORLD

In the world of conflict and turmoil which we constantly see, the primary battle is not in the material world which we understand, but in the spirit world which we do not sense with our sensory perceptions.

Ephesians 6:12 states, "For we wrestle not against flesh and blood, but against principalities, against powers, against the rulers of the darkness of this world, against spiritual wickedness in high places above the time, space, and material world, the world of the spiritual." Again, in I John 5:19 it says, "And we know we are of God, and the whole world lies in the lap of the wicked one." This conveys the idea that the world is under the control of Satan. God has allowed mankind, of his own free will, to exercise his self-centeredness to the extent that Satan has brought the world under his control, by catering to mankind's selfishness.

In Luke 4:1-13 it is seen that Satan even tried to bring Christ under his control, by playing upon Jesus' human vulnerability, when He was tired and hungry. Satan tempted Jesus in three ways, each designed to allow Satan to gain control over Him. Jesus rebuked Satan at every turn, yet Satan continued to tempt Jesus through using the Pharisees, the Roman government, etc. throughout Christ's public ministry.

Over the period of time in the history of mankind, we see the course of the world as antagonistic to the purpose for which Jesus Christ came into the world.

I. The Purpose For Which Christ Came: In Hebrews 2:14,15 we understand that since sin was committed in the realm of *Flesh and blood*, that Christ came into this realm to meet sin head on and conquer it. Satan introduced sin into the realm of mankind, through the deception of Adam and Eve in the Garden of Eden. Therefore, God sent Jesus Christ into the human realm to deal with sin where mankind lives.

Negatively, I John 3:8 tells us that Christ, "Was manifested that He might destroy the works of the Devil." This He did when God resurrected Jesus from the grave. Mankind's sins caused Christ to die; Satan tried to keep Him in the grave, hoping to overcome Jesus and what He had done to take away mankind's sins. The moment He arose from the grave, it forever sealed the doom of Satan! Today, Satan is living on *borrowed time*, awaiting judgment.

Positively, in II Corinthians 4:4-6 it tells us that God sent Jesus Christ, "To give the light of the knowledge of the glory of God in the face of Jesus Christ." He came into our world of time, space, and matter to be a reflection of the Godhead, so that we who live in the confines of this world could comprehend the Godhead, who did not exist within our framework of knowing.

II. The Philosophy of Mankind: Since all humans operate on a personal philosophy or worldview, it is important to understand the Biblical view of mankind's philosophy of life.

Basically, all mankind begins with a self-centered nature, which is separate from God, and diametrically opposed to God's control. This is seen in God's dealings with Israel as stated by the Prophet Jeremiah, (22:21) when God spoke to Israel saying, "I spoke unto you in your prosperity; but you said, I will not hear. This has been your manner from your youth, that you have not obeyed my voice."

Again, this refers back to the Garden of Eden, when Satan deceived Adam and Eve to turn from listening to God, and instead exercise their own selfish desires. In Genesis 3:6 this selfishness is well evidenced. When they saw the tree of the knowledge of good and evil, prohibited by God from eating, to be *good for food*, the lust of the flesh, *pleasant to the eyes*, the lust of the eyes, and *desired to make one wise*, the pride of life, they ate and thereby incurred sin—not only for themselves, but for all humanity. (Romans 5:12) Note the contrast of a God-centered life as seen in I John 2:15-17.

Isaiah 29:13 is an excellent illustration of mankind's religious external ritual of the worship of God, with an inward hypocrisy of the heart: "The Lord said, Forasmuch as this people draw near me with their mouth, and with their lips do honor me, but have removed their heart far from me, and their fear toward me is learned by rote." Much of religious worship is simply going through ritualistic and liturgical motions, as seen in the constant recital of the Lord's prayer, without a heart of love for the Lord Jesus Christ. This is Satan's philosophy riveted upon mankind for deception. This is the course of this world.

III. <u>The Present Condition of the World</u>: The New Testament, though written two thousand years ago, is an excellent commentary on the present condition of the world today. In II Timothy 3:1-7 we have a litany of things that engulf the self-centeredness of mankind, in an ever increasing fashion. It is basically that of self love. In II Peter 2:10-14 there is presented an outline of the anarchy that is rapidly overtaking mankind today. II Peter 3:3-9 points out the retribution of God's coming judgment because of mankind's sins.

II Peter 2:4-9 speaks to three historical first occurrence events of God's judgment on the world, saying to us that the *Fire* of God's coming judgment on the earth is a sure thing. Ezekiel 16:49,50 tells of God's judgment on Sodom and Gomorrah, whose sins are seen in the world in which we live, and just as God took them away, He will judge the world of iniquity today.

Conclusion: The Christian's response to the self-centered philosophy of the world is found in I Peter 2:11-15. He tells us that our manner of life should be honest, exercise good works, be submissive to the laws of the land for the Lord's sake, give honor to others, love fellow Christians, honor the Lord Jesus Christ, and honor our leaders in government. We are not to use the liberty we have in Christ as a cover up for evil.

Finally, in II Timothy 3:12-17, we note that as evil progresses Christians will suffer persecution more and more. Our response is stated clearly: we are to continue to abide by the Word of God, not be deceived by evil people, and allow the Scriptures to be our guide and strength. Trust our Heavenly Father who is sovereign and in control.

How firm a foundation, ye saints of the Lord,
    Is laid for your faith in His excellent word.
What more can he say than to you He has said,
    To you, who for refuge to Jesus have fled?

Fear not I am with thee, O be not dismayed,
    For I am thy God, I will still give thee aid;
I'll strengthen thee, help thee, and cause thee to stand,
    Upheld by my gracious omnipotent hand.

When through the fiery trials thy pathway shall lie,
    My grace, all sufficient, shall be thy supply;
The flames shall not hurt thee, I only design
    Thy dross to consume, and thy gold to refine.

The soul that on Jesus has leaned for repose,
    I will not, I will not, desert to his foes;
That soul, though all hell should endeavor to shake,
    I'll never, no never, no never forsake.

—Victorious Life, Keswick, NJ

Chapter 13

A NEW CREATION IN CHRIST

In II Corinthians 5:17 we read, "Therefore, if anyone be in Christ, he is a new creation: old things are passed away: behold, all things are become new." What does that verse mean, how does it apply to the individual, and what are the various elements that go into an understanding of this verse?

Once a person has made a personal commitment to Jesus Christ as Lord and Savior of their life, the Holy Spirit enters into the heart and regenerates it. That individual person is *born again* and becomes a Christian. Now, as a Christian, God desires every child of His to, "Grow in grace, and in the knowledge of our Lord and Savior Jesus Christ." (II Peter 3:18) In I Peter 2:2 it tells us, "As new born babes in a spiritual birth crave the unadulterated milk of the word, that you may grow spiritually." The primary desire of God for each of His children is spiritual maturity. Therefore, being *In Christ* is a life-long altering transformation.

There are seven important elements that go into the total spiritual transformation, from being a self-centered person to a God-centered individual. These elements are God given, beginning at salvation and extending throughout life. We shall evaluate each with its definition, understanding and application to the life of the Christian.

1) JUSTIFICATION: to justify is for God to declare the Christian righteous in His sight. This is a change of STANDING before God. Now, the believing person has a right standing with God. (Romans

77

3:24-26; 5:1) The believer has been declared righteous by God, and now has peace with God, through the work that Jesus Christ accomplished in his behalf.

2) REGENERATION: This is a change of NATURE from God. When we were naturally born we were generated, or made alive by our parents. Regeneration by the Holy Spirit of God, means one has a spiritual new birth, that comes into him from the entrance of the Holy Spirit. (Titus 3:5; John 1:13; 3:3; Ephesians 5:26) It produces a *new life*—a spiritual life given to us by God Himself. The result is that the Christian has a spiritual life that is God-given, and God-directed.

3) REPENTANCE: This is a change of MIND about God. The word itself means to change one's mind. Before one was a Christian, the basic mindset was to be self-centered. When one becomes a Christian, it not only changes one's standing before God, but changes the mind about desiring to do God-centered things, and accepting Biblical principles and precepts. One may repent of their sins, which means to acknowledge one's sinful ways, and change their mind as to behaviors conforming to God's way rather than the self centered manner. Acts 17:30.

4) CONVERSION: This is a change of LIFE for God. The Christian converts, changes, from being a self-centered person to becoming a God-centered person. Instead of constantly being absorbed with self, one now concentrates on, and desires to do God-centered things in life. It is no longer a concentrated selfishness, but a willingness to allow the Holy Spirit to change one's thoughts, desires, lifestyle, and relationship with others, and conform to God's way for his life. (Acts 15:3; 26:18)

5) ADOPTION: This results in a change of FAMILY in God. Before becoming a Christian, one's life is bound up with Satan's allurement and worldly things, that cater to the self life and all that it implies. When regenerated, with the corresponding new life in Christ, that person joins the family of God by adoption. However, the Bible speaks of this adoption as being infinitely more than a legal concept; it is a re-birth, a regeneration into the family of God, which is spiritual not natural. The result is that the Christian is now a member of the family of God. (Galatians 4:5-7)

6) SANCTIFICATION: This produces a change of SERVICE unto God. For a fuller development of this subject, see the chapter on "The Threefold Elements of Sanctification." Upon accepting Jesus Christ into one's life, there is an immediate change of POSITION—as one moves out of Satan's family into God's family. (Hebrews 10:10,14) Next, there is a PROGRESSION of a life-long development and spiritual growth causing one to become more Christ-like in character and behavior. It is the work of the Holy Spirit, re-characterizing the Christian, to conform to the personhood of Jesus Christ, Who is our model. (I Peter 1:15,16) Finally, there will be an ultimate PERFECTION of the character and behavior of the Christian, when we get to Heaven, and all together we will be like the Lord Jesus Christ—spiritually and completely holy. (I John 3:2,3; Philippians 1:6)

7) GLORIFICATION: This results in a change of PLACE with God. It will become a reality when we enter Heaven by the grace of God, and it will become the eternal abode of every believer. Glorification is more of a transformation of life, being transformed into His likeness, as well as a place in Heaven. Both will be a reality. We will be as perfect as God is perfect. The word, "Glory" refers to the moral character of God, which is absolutely "Holy," that which is, totally set apart from sin. We will never become little gods, as He alone is God, but we will be like him morally and spiritually. (Romans 8:11,30; Philippians 1:6; I Corinthians 15:51-58; I John 3:2,3)

The above seven elements that constitute the totality of the Christian life, are all based upon the threefold work of Christ in our behalf: Redemption, Reconciliation, and Propitiation. These three Biblical concepts and principles are foundational to our understanding as to how the seven elements come into reality, and pertain to the Christian life. It is of utmost importance to understand these three basic foundational truths, and what every child of God, has in Him.

1) REDEMPTION: The word redeem, as used in Scripture means *to buy back by paying a price*. In relationship to Jesus Christ it means that He bought our redemption, in that He paid the price for our sins, so that God could justify us. (Romans 3:24) We, thereby, are able to be reconciled to Him, from Whom we have been estranged because of our sins. In I Peter 1:18-20 we see that Jesus Christ redeemed us with

His own precious blood, and that God ordained this from before the creation of the world. See also I Timothy 2:5,6 and Hebrews 7:25.

2) RECONCILIATION: This means to bring us together with God. Isaiah 59:2 tells us that, "Your iniquities, sins, have separated you from God." The problem facing God in reconciling mankind, whom He created for fellowship, (Psalms 8:4) was our sin against Him. A Holy God could not reconcile sinful mankind unto Himself. God's Holiness would be compromised, and He would no longer be God. Therefore, the impasse was cared for, in that Jesus Christ paid the eternal penalty for the sins of the world. (John 1:29; II Peter 3:9; I Timothy 2:4) So God could be just and Holy as well as the Justifier of those who trust in Christ's work for their sins. (Romans 3:25,26; II Corinthians 5:19; Ephesians 2:14-18)

3) PROPITIATION: This word is used exclusively in the New Testament, never in the Old Testament. The Old Testament counterpart to it is the word, *atonement*, which is never used in the New Testament. The two words have distinctly different meanings, yet they do have a relationship.

In the Old Testament animal sacrifices were made to *atone* for one's sins. This means the sins were, *Covered over*—somewhat like *sweeping the dirt under the rug*—hidden, but still there. Though the Old Testament believers made animal sacrifices, which could never care for their sins, (Hebrews 10:4) they were justified by faith on God's promise of a future Messiah who would actually be the payment for their sins. (Romans 4:4,21-25)

When Christ came and offered Himself as the sacrifice for the sins of the world, He *propitiated* the sins of the world, in that he paid for the sins, not just covered them over. In actuality He appeased God's wrath against sin. (Romans 3:25; I John 2:2) Therefore, every believer who trusts in Christ's sacrificial work, knows his sins are not covered over, but actually paid for by Christ. That is why it says in Hebrews 10:17, "Their sins and iniquities will I remember no more." The result is the reconciliation of the believing person with God, based on Christ's propitiation of that person's sins. (II Corinthians 5:17,18) This is why Romans 3:25,26 tells us that now God can be "just," and Holy, the "Justifier of him who believes in Jesus." Romans 4:28

further enlightens us by saying, "We conclude that a person is justified by faith, apart from the deeds of the law."

These three key concepts in the mind of God, REDEMPTION, RECONCILIATION, and PROPITIATION were all ordained by Him, so that His Holiness could remain unsullied, and at the same time extend Himself to sinful, yet believing mankind, created in the image of God and for fellowship with Him. Mankind chose, out of his own volition or will, to turn from being God-centered to being self-centered, and thereby separated himself from God. These three acts of God through Jesus Christ, became the basis upon which God's threefold purpose in creating mankind could be ultimately and eternally fulfilled. The image of God in mankind was His moral likeness exemplified in Psalms 8:4-6. With which, God created mankind for fellowship, (v.4) to be a reflection of God's moral character, (v.5) and to be king over God's creation. (v.6)

Someday, in eternity, these three purposes of God in the creation will be fulfilled in all of God's redeemed, propitiated, reconciled, and glorified children. This is why the hymn writer wrote, "And when before the throne, I stand in Him complete, Jesus died my soul to save, my lips shall still repeat, 'Jesus paid it all, all to Him I owe, sin had left a crimson stain, He washed it white as snow.'"

Redeemed, how I love to proclaim it!
Redeemed by the blood of the Lamb;
Redeemed through His infinite mercy,
His child, and forever, I am.

Redeemed and so happy in Jesus,
No language my rapture can tell;
I know that the light of His presence,
With me doth continually dwell.

I think of my blessed Redeemer,
I think of Him all the day long;
I sing, for I cannot be silent;
His love is the theme of my song.

I know I shall see in His beauty
The King in whose law I delight;
Who lovingly guardeth my footsteps,
And giveth me songs in the night.

Redeemed, Redeemed,
Redeemed by the blood of the Lamb;
Redeemed, Redeemed,
His child and forever, I am.

—Victorious Life, Keswick, NJ

Chapter 14

A NEW NATURE, A NEW HELP, A NEW ASSURANCE, A NEW HOPE

Biblical principles are God's way of conveying to mankind how to live, and to Christians the path of progressive maturity in the faith. These principles are interwoven into the fabric of human beings and nature, so that as we relate to them we are able to understand God's way of life for us. Primarily the New Testament was written in a format first of Principle or Doctrine, then a Practice and Duty concept.

In this chapter we shall see examples of faith and promises in the Bible, followed with admonitions for Christian living. The admonition to Christian living is usually denoted by the words, *therefore* or *wherefore*, which then provides the practical application of the principle.

An example of this is seen in Hebrews 11:40 followed by Hebrews 12:1. (Note: Sometimes the chapter divisions get in the way, as seen in this illustration.) The thought in Chapter 11 is followed by the application in Chapter 12. In Chapter 11 we see examples of faith in the lives of the Old Testament saints. Verse 40 tells us that God has better things for all His children, but that the Old Testament saints will not be perfected without the New Testament saints. Then Chapter 12 is the admonition to us, based upon the thought of the previous chapter, introduced by the word, *wherefore*. Then the practical application of the principle is outlined for us, with behaviors to follow. The principle of God's dealings with the Old Testament saints is a model for us to follow in the development of our lives today.

I. A New Nature: (I Peter 1:23 with 2:1-8) In v.23 the promise of God to us is that the child of God has been regenerated with a new nature that cannot die or be taken away. This is assured to us by the Word of God. Then in 2:1-8 is the admonition to Christian living, based upon the promise of God and introduced by the word, *wherefore*.

The context of this passage is an imperative that we are to grow spiritually (v.2)—"Crave the unadulterated milk of the Word, that you may grow thereby." Part of the process of growth through the divine nature is for one to be rid of (v.1) malice; an evil intention to injure others, guile; using deceit, cunning and fraud, hypocrisy; pretending to be what one is not, envy; a desire to possess what belongs to others, and slander of every kind. These are not conducive to spiritual growth, and putting them aside is indicative of growth.

II. A New Help: (Col. 3:1-4 with 3:5-10) The exercise of faith is seen in v.1,2, where it states that the Christian has a heavenly position with Christ, and when He returns we shall appear with Him in glory, (v.4) meaning that we shall enjoy the fullness of God's moral attributes eternally. God tells us in verse 2 that we are dead to sin, in that it doesn't have us in its grasp because we are *In Christ*, and our life is in Him. This help we have is through the power of the indwelling Holy Spirit, given to us by the promise and authority of Christ Himself. (John 14:16-26; 16:7-14)

Verses 5-10 begin the practical application of this new help by the word, *therefore*. Because of our new life in Christ, and the help that we have in the Spirit, we are to *mortify*; put to death in our lives those elements of our selfish desires: immorality, impurity, lust, evil desires, and greed—which is idolatry. (Rom. 8:13) These are inward sins which can be exercised without external communication.

Then, in verse 8 we note the outward sins, which are usually reflected from one person to the another: anger, rage, malice, slander, ill will, and filthy language.

Remember, God's principles are always perfect, as coming from a Holy God, and though we cannot live up to them perfectly, they are goals toward which we should strive in this life, by the submission of the Self to the Holy Spirit. As we willingly allow Him to control us,

He transforms, re-characterizes us to conform our lives to God's will for us. All this leads to the "Fruit of the Spirit" as seen in Galatians 5:22-24. This is the help that we have from Him.

III. A New Assurance: (Ephesians 3:13-20 with 4:1-3) In v.17-19 the exercise of faith is seen in the Apostle's prayer for the Christian,— that we may be grounded in the faith, to understand the mind of God, and to be filled with the love of God and His fullness. The promise of God is stated in v.20—God is able to do an exceedingly good work in us according to His power that indwells us. With all that He has promised, how can we fail?

"Therefore" (4:1-3) the Apostle commends to us that we, "Live a life worthy of the calling we have received." We are to exercise ourselves unto being, "Humble and gentle, patient, bearing with one another in love, making every effort to keep the unity of the Spirit through the bond of peace." The way by which that can be attained is through the assurance from God, of all that we have in Him, and through all that He is willing to do for us. We do have all the resources we need to live a Godly life, if we allow the Spirit to control us.

IV. A New Hope: (I Corinthians 15:1-57 with 15:58) In v. 3,4 we have a statement that gives us the essence of the Gospel of Christ's death, burial, and resurrection. Verse 17 points out our exercise of faith based on the statement. If Christ is not raised then our faith is in vain. But, in v.20 it says that Christ is risen, and not only is our faith valid, but because He lives we too shall live. (John 14:19) The resurrection of Christ guarantees our resurrection someday.

God's promise to the Christian as a result of all this is seen in v.51-57. The "sting of death" has been removed from the child of God; the grave no longer will be victorious over us; and someday, "at the last trump" our corruptible body will be transformed into an incorruptible body. This is God's eternal promise to us. What a future the Christian has!

The admonition to the Christian—verse 58—"Therefore, my beloved people, be steadfast, unmoveable, always overflowing in the work of the Lord, forasmuch as you know that your labor is not in vain in the Lord."

Dying with Jesus, by death reckoned mine,
   Living with Jesus, a new life divine.
Looking to Jesus till glory doth shine,
   Moment by moment, O Lord I am thine.

Never a trial that He is not there,
   Never a burden that He does not bear,
Never a sorrow that He does not share,
   Moment by moment, I'm under His care.

Never a heartache and never a groan,
   Never a teardrop and never a moan;
Never a danger, but there on the throne,
   Moment by moment He thinks of His own.

Moment by moment I'm kept in His love,
   Moment by moment I've life from above;
Looking to Jesus till glory doth shine,
   Moment by moment, O Lord I am thine.
                    —Victorious Life, Keswick, NJ

Chapter 15

GOD'S WILL AND MAN'S CHARACTER

After one has made a personal commitment to Jesus Christ, as Lord and Savior of his life, the primary desire on God's part is for that person to come to Spiritual maturity. It becomes a life-long endeavor to grow spiritually. There are several verses that emphasize this aspect of the Christian life. (I Peter 2:2; I Peter 4:1,2; II Peter 3:18; Col. 1:27,28)

In John 14:16-26, Christ spoke to the disciples concerning His return to Heaven, and told them He would send another Comforter, who would be the Holy Spirit, to indwell the believers. Then in John 16:13, He said of the Holy Spirit that, "He will guide you into all the truth." It is the work of the Holy Spirit to guide each one toward this goal of maturity, that is to re-characterize the believer from being self-centered to being Christ-centered and more like Him.

The problem that every Christian has in this work is the basic sin nature that is common to all. The character that we possess is from two elements: 1) genetically inherited tendencies, and 2) learned behaviors which we acquired from our family of origin, as we watched our parents model before us. Both of these sources, plus our basic sin nature, tend to cause us to be the self-centered person we are, which is opposite from being God-centered, which is what He desires for us.

It is the work of the Holy Spirit in the life of the newborn Christian, to begin the life-long process of producing a change of character in the child of God. The promise and hope for us is God's promise that this continuing transformation will be perfect and complete at the coming of Jesus Christ for His children. This is seen in Phil. 1:6 and I John 3:2,3, and is guaranteed to us by the resurrection of Christ. (I Cor. 15:20-23; See also John 14:19.)

I. How This Is Accomplished: It starts with the WILL. Since mankind's will is opposed to God's will for him, the Christian must begin here. In Matt. 6:33, Christ said, "Seek ye first the kingdom of God, and His righteousness, and all these things shall be added unto you." The last part of the verse is God's promise to us based upon our acceptance of the first part. God knows our needs better than we know them, and He said, "My God shall supply all your needs according to His riches in glory by Christ Jesus." (Phil. 4:19)

Then, in Rom. 12:1,2 we have the *what* in verse one—we are to present our bodies as a living sacrifice. (Christ gave up His body unto death for us; isn't it reasonable for Him to ask that we be a living example for Him?) Verse two provides the *how* to do it. We are not to conform ourselves to be like the world, but to allow the Holy Spirit to transform our lives into Christ's likeness, that we may prove what is that good, and acceptable and perfect will of God for us. His will for us is always good, acceptable and perfect—customized for each person by the Holy Spirit.

In I John 2:15-17 we have the admonition not to love the things of this world, "The lust of the flesh, the lust of the eyes, and the pride of life." John tells us these things will pass away, but the Christian who does the will of God will abide forever. Remember that Satan used these three elements, in the Garden of Eden, to deceive Adam and Eve. In Gen. 3:6 as the serpent presented the tree to them they saw that it was, "Good for food" (the lust of the flesh), and that is was "Pleasant to the eyes" (the lust of the eyes), and a tree to be, "Desired to make one wise" (the pride of life)," and they succumbed to Satanic deception.

Once the Christian has made up his mind to follow and serve the Lord, by listening to the Holy Spirit, then Psalm 37:3-7 provides the framework of how to go about making the choices and decisions of life. First, one is to TRUST in the Lord, and do good according to Biblical principles. Then follows a delight in wanting to carry out the principles in behavior. Next comes a daily committal of one's life to the Holy Spirit's control, allowing Him to bring to pass His best for the development of the individual's day. The admonition is to wait patiently for the Lord, as He is in control. This does not mean that one cannot plan ahead. We must always commit those plans to the Lord, and be willing to change as the Lord directs us otherwise. We must develop a sensitive ear to the Holy Spirit and God's principles. It is the best way to go.

II. <u>Guaranteed Results</u>: Every person desires joy, happiness, fulfillment, peace, prosperity, success, etc., and God wishes these for His children. But, we must accomplish them in God's way, and by His means, if we are to be truly fulfilled in life.

There are two ways by which we achieve our goals in life: God's way through following Biblical principles which guarantees success, or the Christian may follow his own selfish ways, which will guarantee failure and sadness. There are three Scriptures that have bearing on this: Joshua 1:8; Psalm 1:2,3; Rom. 8:6. Let's examine these important ideas.

In Joshua 1:8 Israel's new leader, Joshua, is about to lead Israel into the land of Canaan. God instructs him as to prosperity and success in their new venture: meditate upon the law of God, day and night; then both prosperity and success would be guaranteed. It is interesting to note that the word, *success* is used only once in the Bible. It is in this verse. The admonition to us today is clear: as we move forward in the unchartered waters of life, as we allow the Word of God to permeate and control our lives, God is the guarantor that we will be both prosperous—as God evaluates prosperity, and successful in His eyes. By following His Word, we become re-characterized through the work of the Holy Spirit. The result is a change of character to become more Christ-like and the evidence is the "Fruit of the Spirit." (Gal. 5:22-24)

Psalm 1:2,3 gives to us, by analogy, an affirmation of what was seen in Joshua 1:8. God tells us that when we delight in the law of God day and night, to allow the Holy Spirit, through the Word to permeate our life, then we will be like a tree that is well planted, well watered, produces good leaves, and is prosperous. When one sees that kind of a tree, we realize that it is a good tree. God tells us we can be like that as we allow His Word to control our life.

Finally, in Romans 8:6, we have a basic principle of life that is plainly understood: "For to be fleshly minded and self-centered is death, but to be spiritually minded is life and peace." As the Holy Spirit controls and guides the Christian, the fullness of life, with inward peace, becomes the controlling factor in that person. This is God's supreme will for every child of His.

Every individual desires to get ahead in life, and God has a formula for that, as found in Deuteronomy 28:13, "The Lord will make you the head, not the tail, if you pay attention to the commands of the Lord your God that I give you this day and carefully follow them, you will always be at the top, never at the bottom." God wants us to be on the cutting edge of life, not on the trailing element. This is the God ordained way to be there.

III. How One Can Know God's Will: There are two ways by which the Christian is able to generally discern the will of God for his life.

The first is the Internal principle. Submission of one's will to the control of the Holy Spirit, allows Him to change the thoughts and intents of the mind and heart, to bring one's internal ideas into conformity to the principles of God's Word. One's desires are now in the process of change, as guided and controlled by the Holy Spirit.

Then comes the External principle. Conditions outside of one's life, over which there may he little or no control, are controlled by the Holy Spirit, to bring both the internal desires, and the external conditions into conformity to God's will for His child. All this is for our good and maturation.

God never allows anything to come into the lives of His children, but that which is for their good and His honor. God is not a capricious Father, zapping His children for His pleasure, laying trials and tribulations upon us indiscriminately. Even the adversities of life are for our ultimate benefit, and become experiences through which our character is developed according to His will for us. This is why one can say, "All things work together for good," (Rom. 8:28) not necessarily as we evaluate them, but as God does for our character development.

Therefore, we can give thanks to God in our prosperity (Eph. 5:20) as well as in our adversity. (I Thess 5:18) This is why the Apostle Paul said, "God said unto me, My grace is sufficient for you: for my strength is made perfect in your weakness." Paul was then able to reply that in Christ, "When I am weak, then am I strong." (II Corinthians 12: 9,10) Trusting God for everything strengthens us and provides a continuing maturity in life.

IV. <u>Conclusion</u>: There are parting promises given to the Christian as one is guided and controlled by the Holy Spirit and the Word of God.

Of all people in the world, the Christian should be the most optimistic in life. In Philippians 4:6-8 we are told not to be disturbed about anything that is highly idealistic, because we are influenced by circumstances but, "In everything by prayer and supplication let your requests be made known unto God." That means to lay it on the Lord. The response of God is His promise in verse 7, "And the peace of God, which is beyond our comprehension, will surround our hearts and minds in Christ Jesus."

In John 14:27 Christ tells us, "Peace I leave with you, my peace I give unto you: not as the world giveth, give I unto you. Let not your heart be troubled, neither let it be afraid." Again, in John 16:33 He said, "In the world you will have tribulation: but be of good cheer, I have overcome the world." In Hebrews 13:5,6 God's Word comforts us with, "For He has said, I will never leave you nor forsake you, so that we may boldly say, the Lord is my helper, why should I fear."

Lastly, Christ said in John 10:10, "I am come that you might have life, and that you might have it more abundantly." He said in John 15:11, "These things have I spoken unto you, that my joy might remain in you, and that your joy might be full." God's will for His children is continuing growth to become more like the Lord Jesus Christ, and along the pathway to enjoy life to the fullest. This is God's way for every child of His.

Were the whole realm of nature mine,
    That were a present far too small;
Love so amazing, so divine,
    Demands my soul, my life, my all.

To Him I owe my life and breath,
    And all the joys I have,

He makes me triumph over death,
And saves me from the grave.

Since from His bounty I receive,
Such proofs of love divine;
Had I a thousand hearts to give,
Lord, they should all be thine.

—Victorious Life, Keswick, NJ

Chapter 16

A GUIDE FOR LIFE - THE HOLY SPIRIT

At some point in the ministry of Christ, He began to instruct His disciples concerning His death, burial, resurrection, and ascension into heaven. He was their comforter, but now He would eventually leave them, and send "Another Comforter," whom He stated would be the Holy Spirit. (John 14:16-26; 16:7-14)

The Holy Spirit came upon the Apostles on the Day of Pentecost (Acts 2:1-17) to empower them to carry out Christ's commission that He had instructed them to do. (Matt. 28:19,20; Mark 16:15) The work of the Holy Spirit would be to regenerate, baptize, fill, energize, empower, and give gifts and wisdom to all Christians. Thus, His ministry in the life of Christians today is to provide all these elements in order to bring eternal life to every Christian and assist him to spiritual maturation. Then He helps every child of God to carry out the commission originally given to the disciples to go into the world and let our light shine for Him.

I. The Personality and Work of the Holy Spirit: He is the third person of the Trinity, with all the distinctive marks of personality, and is called God. (Acts 5:3,4) He is the author and interpreter of Scripture. (II Peter 1:21; I Cor. 2:10-12)

In the Old Testament His ministry was not given generally to all Israelites, but to select people only. (I Sam. 16:14) However in the New Testament, the Holy Spirit indwells, baptizes all believers at the moment of regeneration. (Rom. 8:9; Eph. 1:13,4:30; I Cor. 6:19, 12:13)

His work is threefold in the life of the believer: 1) In the Past tense He has regenerated, baptized, indwelt, and sealed every Christian, when one has accepted Jesus Christ as Lord and Savior. (Eph. 1:13) 2) Presently, He is infilling, imparting spiritual gifts, anointing, teaching, satisfying, witnessing, interceding, protecting, and producing fruit in the believer. (I Cor. 6:19,20) 3) In the future He will raise and glorify the resurrected body of the saints. (Rom. 8:11)

II. <u>The Baptism of the Holy Spirit</u>: The baptism of the Holy Spirit is God's divinely ordained way whereby the believer enters into that sphere of relationship with God, by the work of Christ through the Holy Spirit placing the believer into the family of God. The Christian is then said to be "in Christ" through the operation and entrance of the Holy Spirit into the believer's life. (I Cor. 12:13) All believers who have exercised faith in the propitiatory work of Christ are baptized and placed into the body of Christ by the Spirit at the moment of salvation. (Rom. 3:24,25) The Greek word "Baptidzo" means to place into, so it is the operation of the Spirit placing the believer into the family of God. This is a once-for-all-act, at the time of salvation, and is common to every believer. One cannot become a Christian apart from the baptism of the Holy Spirit.

The results are that: 1) It brings us into the family of God; (II Cor. 5:17,21; Gal. 3:27) 2) It gives us access unto God; (Eph. 2:18) and 3) It identifies us with Christ in His death and resurrection. (Rom. 6:2-5)

III. <u>The Infilling of the Holy Spirit</u>: There is a Biblical command in Eph. 5:18 to be filled with the Spirit. The present tense, in the Greek, shows that God wants us to be continually filled with the Spirit. This marks the difference between baptism, which is a once-for-all and complete act (Eph. 2:22; 4:4-6,30; I Cor. 12:13; Rom. 8:9) and infilling, which is *many* acts (Eph. 5:18)

Definition: to be filled with the Holy Spirit is to have Him fulfilling in us all that God intended Him to continually do in us, when God placed Him in us at salvation. It is not the Christian getting more of the Spirit, but the Spirit getting more of the Christian, by submission to His will. In order for this to be accomplished, it is the Word-filled life that contributes to the Spirit-filled life. As the Christian meditates upon the truth of God's Word, and allows the Spirit to permeate their life, the person becomes more like Christ, which is what God desires. Compare Eph. 5:18 with Col. 3:16. In the Ephesian passage it commends to us to be filled with the Spirit. In the Colossian passage it substitutes, "Let the Word of Christ dwell in you richly." The Spirit-filled Christian is the Word-filled Christian.

There are three scriptural conditions for the filling by the Holy Spirit.

1) I Thessalonians 5:19—"Quench not the Spirit." That is, do not stifle or suppress the Spirit's will for us. We are constantly commended to yield to the Spirit's control. (Rom. 6:13)

2) Ephesians 4:30—"Grieve not the Spirit." That is accomplished by sinning. Quenching the Spirit will, in turn, lead to grieving the Spirit by sin, which, in turn, leads to loss of fellowship and the fruit of the Spirit. (Gal. 5:22-24) The remedy for sin is confession. (I John 1:9)

3) Galatians 5:16—"Walk by the power of the Spirit." This means to continually walk by the power of the indwelling Holy Spirit, which is a daily continuing act of the believer delivering one's self to the Holy Spirit's control. Failure to do so will result in the loss of spiritual power and failure in life.

The results of being filled with the Spirit are found in many passages of Scripture. Galatians 5:22-24 shows the fruit of the Spirit-controlled life, This fruit is the evidence of a Holy Spirit re-characterized life. One does not have the fruit of the Spirit by wanting it, but by submission to the Spirit who changes the character, and the fruit is the result.

In John 16:12-15 and I Corinthians 2:9-14 we see that the Holy Spirit teaches the Spirit-filled believer, guides one into knowing the truth of God, and gives *spiritual discernment*, which the non-believer does not have. The Christian has God given insight to understand the Word of God. Though the non-believer is able to read the Bible, he is unable to comprehend it, due to the fact that it is spiritually discerned. (I Cor. 2:14)

Romans 8:14 shows that the Holy Spirit gives guidance to the Christian. While the Bible provides the principles of the Christian life, it is the Holy Spirit Who applies them specifically in the life of the Christian. Roman 8:16 shows the assurance one has of his salvation, through the Holy Spirit. Ephesians 5:18-20 and Colossians 3:16 tells how the Christian is guided in true worship. Romans 8:26 directs one's prayer to God, in the proper way, by the Holy Spirit. Ephesians 2:10 tells how the Spirit directs the believer's service to God. In I Corinthians 2:14-16 we note that only the Holy Spirit can give the Christian discernment between good and evil. All these elements work together to provide spiritual growth and fullness of life.

IV. <u>The Gifts of the Holy Spirit</u>: I Corinthians 12:4-18 speaks of the *gifts* of the Holy Spirit to the Christian.

Though every believer possesses some divinely bestowed gift, (Eph. 4:7) there is a diversity of gifts. (Rom. 12:6) Christians are not all appointed to do the same thing. It is the Holy Spirit who distributes the talents and gifts to the Christian as He pleases, and this distribution is that which is best suited for every personality and character.

Each person has three basic gifts. (Rom. 12;7,8) These are: *helps* which includes whatever can be done to serve others; *giving*, which may be services, not necessarily money; and thirdly, *showing mercy* to withhold judgment with cheerfulness. Every child of God can commonly do these.

I Corinthians 12 outlines the gifts and how they are dispensed and utilized. The Apostle Paul uses the analogy of the physical body. Just as the body is composed of many coordinated parts, each functioning as part of a unit, so the body of Christians, having diversity of talents, should function as one body of believers, coordinated together under the control of the Holy Spirit. In I Corinthians 12:31 we are exhorted to earnestly seek the best gifts that God has for us, and to exercise them well for His service. (Note: I Tim. 4:14)

Christian are not Spirit-filled because they are active in service; they are active in service because they are Spirit-filled. (I Cor. 4:2)

In Ephesians 4:12-14 we note the purpose of the gifts. There are three: 1) for the maturing of the saints, 2) for the work of ministrations, helps, and 3) for the building up, edifying of the body of Christ. In verses 13,14 we see the results: 1) to establish unity in the faith, 2) that Christians might become mature in Christ, 3) to be more Christ like, and 4) to become strong in the faith, not like naive children, so that the Christian is not carried away by false cults and isms.

The ministry of the Holy Spirit is absolutely essential to every Christian. For without Him, one could not become a believer, and only with His indwelling can one come to a full understanding and development as a Christian. This is God's ordained plan for each one of us.

How I praise thee precious Savior,
That thy love laid hold of me.
Thou hast saved and cleansed and filled me,
That I might thy channel be.

Jesus, fill now with thy Spirit,
Hearts that full surrender know;
That the streams of living water,
From our inner man may flow.

Channels only, blessed Master,
But with all thy wondrous power,
Flowing through us, though canst use us,
Every day and every hour.

— Victorious Life, Keswick, NJ

Chapter 17

THE SPIRITUAL LIFE AND THE WORLDLY LIFE

Once a person has made a personal commitment to the Lord Jesus Christ, and has become a regenerated believer, that individual has a new nature that cannot sin. It is diametrically opposed to his original self-centered nature, which desires to continue to do self centered things. There is, therefore, a continuing conflict between the two natures which produces constant conflict throughout life.

The Holy Spirit within the believer is given to help the Christian to grow spiritually to maturity, and thereby provide spiritual strength to overcome the pull of the self-centered nature. It is up to the Christian to make up his *WILL* as to which of the two natures he allows to control him. (Rom. 12:1,2)

Originally, in the Garden of Eden, God gave to Adam and Eve a will which they could exercise: follow God's way and refuse to eat of the forbidden fruit of the tree, or exercise their own will and eat, going against God's prohibition. They listened to the serpent's deception and ate, and thereby incurred a self-centered, sinful nature, as well as separation from God. This nature has been passed down to each of us. (Rom. 5:12) Christ came to save us from this nature, as well as destroy the work of Satan against us. (I John 3:8)

When we accept what Christ did for us, we are regenerated and receive, through the Holy Spirit, the nature of God which cannot sin. God does not eliminate our old nature when we become a Christian, but allows it to work against our new nature. As we submit to the Holy

Spirit transforming our character, and the interaction between the two natures, our new nature is strengthened. This helps us to "Grow in the grace and knowledge of our Lord and Savior Jesus Christ." (II Peter 3:18) The key to overcoming of the old nature, and growing in the new nature depends on our WILL. This is why there is so much emphasis upon our will in the Bible.

In order for us to have a clear understanding of the two natures, it is important to know the contrast between the two, as well as the results. Then we are able to better understand what we should do.

The Spiritual Life	The Worldly Life

1. Love - God gives to us
    John 3:16
	1. Hate - At odds with others
	    Matt. 24:10; Luke 6:22

2. Christ-Centered life
    John 3:30
	2. Self-Centered life
	    II Tim. 3:2

3. Fruits of the Spirit
    Gal. 5:22-24
	3. Works of the flesh
	    Gal. 5:17-21

Results	

1. True Character of life
    Rom. 12:2
	1. Two facedness (Masking)
	    Ps. 12:2; James 4:8

2. Serving Others
    John 13:35
	2. Serving Self (Ego minded)
	    Rom. 12:3,16

3. Seeks first God's Way
    Matt. 6:33
	3. Seeks Materialism/Power
	    Rom. 8:6

4. Genuine love for others
    John 15:12
	4. Beware of cares, lust,
	    deceit Mark 4:19

5. Hope of Eternal Life
    Phil. 1:6
	5. Transient Life
	    I John 2:15-17

In conclusion it is well to note what the Word tells us concerning our new nature, and the exercising of it in love: I Corinthians 13:1-13; I John 4:7-21; and II Timothy 1:7.

"For God has not given us the spirit of fear, but of POWER, and of LOVE, and of a SOUND MIND."

POWER—To live constructively

LOVE—To live sacrificially

SOUND MIND—To live reasonably

Therefore, in Christ we have all things we need to live a Godly life, to develop our Christian nature, to let our light shine to the world. We have the resources for all of this through our submission to the Holy Spirit's control. What more can we ask, or do we need?

O Master let me walk with thee,
In lowly paths of service free;
Tell me thy secret, help me bear,
The strain of toil, the fret of care.

Help me the slow of heart to move,
By some clear winning word of love;
Teach me the wayward feet to stay,
And guide them in the homeward way.

Teach me thy patience, still with thee,
In closer dearer company,
In work that keeps faith sweet and strong,
In trust that triumphs over wrong.

In hope that sends a shining ray,
Far down the future's broadening way;
In peace that only thou canst give,
With thee, O Master, let me live.

—Victorious Life, Keswick, NJ

Chapter 18

PERSONHOOD AND BIBLICAL PRINCIPLES

In a recent research project on children who were personally secure, it was found that there were four significant factors that contributed to their security:

1) A great amount of ACCEPTANCE by their parents.

2) Clearly defined and consistently ENFORCED LIMITS

3) The parents related to the child with RESPECT.

4) The parents needed to have personal self esteem, in order to provide a good ROLE MODEL for the child.

Christians, who are the children of God, need to search for this pattern in the Bible, in order to reinforce one's personhood and spiritual security in the maturation process of life. There are a number of references to guide one in this way.

In Luke 2:52 it says, "And Jesus (emphasis on the human person) increased in wisdom (that's mental maturity), and stature (that's physical maturity), and in favor with God (that's spiritual maturity), and man (that's social maturity)." Here is the Christ-like model for you and me; a well-rounded and balanced life.

In Philippians 1:6 the Apostle Paul said, "I am confident of this very thing, that the Holy Spirit who has begun a good work in you, through regeneration, will bring it to completion at the day of Jesus Christ." I John 3:2,3 tells us that when Christ comes for us that, "We shall be like Him, for we shall see Him as He is." This does not mean we will become little gods, but that we will be like Him in all His moral glory; all God's moral attributes will be fully developed in us, perfectly. Then, in I Thessalonians 5:24 it says, "Faithful is He that calls you, who also will perform it." Finally, in Hebrews 13:5,6 the Lord tells us, "I will never leave you nor forsake you, so that we may boldly say, the Lord is my helper, why should I fear, what can mankind do unto me?" All these promises are based on John 3:16, "That God so loved each one of us, that He sent His only begotten Son, that whosoever believes in Him, might not perish but have eternal life." What a model for self-esteem, worth, and dignity in life.

Our response to the foundation of eternal life in Christ which every Christian enjoys, is found in the following verses.

In I Peter 2:2 and II Peter 3:18, there is the admonition for every child of God to grow to spiritual maturity. Once a person enters the family of God, the primary motivating factor through life is spiritual growth. This is a constant admonition.

Unlike the world, which is interested in producing, climbing the ladder of success, and obtaining material wealth through greed and power, God is primarily interested in the development of our personhood. Our being. In II Corinthians 8:12 it says, "For if the willingness is there, the gift of giving of one's self to God's control is acceptable according to what one has, not according to what he does not have."

Furthermore, since each person is a unique creation of God, God does not wish us to compare ourselves to each other, as the world does. He tells us in II Corinthians 10:12, "We do not dare to classify or compare ourselves with some who commend themselves. When they measure themselves by themselves and compare themselves with themselves, they are not wise." God so loves each one of us as individuals, uniquely fashioned according to His will, and endowed with His Holy Spirit, that we have all we need in Him to develop as human beings, with love, security, and a sense of well-being, because of all He has done and is doing for us.

In Romans 8:28-30 we have God's model of provision for His children, which He has programmed in our behalf, even before He created us. Therefore, in His eternal plan, all these areas that we need for our personal development and security are set.

Notice how all these things work out in Scripture:

1) Justification by faith is the model of God's ACCEPTANCE of us. (Rom. 5:1,8) Jesus provided the perfect MODEL. (Luke 2:52)

2) Sanctification (See Chap. 23 for explanation) of life is the LIMITS of God's WILL for us in the Bible. (Rom. 12:1,2; I Thess. 4:7; II Tim. 2:19)

3) Glorification is the ultimate and complete FREEDOM that will be ours, when we arrive in Heaven. We are in process now, through our sanctification and maturation. (Phil. 1:6; I John 3:2)

The theology of salvation fits the development of a positive sense of personhood.

Conclusion: In life, success—divided by expectation—equals one's perceived value of life. If one's success exceeds one's expectation, then one's perceived value of self is great. If one's success in life is less than the expectation, then the value of life is diminished. If we use this formula in the Biblical sense we see a positive perception not only in this life, but in the one to come.

The ultimate success of the Christian is Heaven. (I Peter 1:3; I Thess. 4:13-18) Our expectation or hope in this life is a struggle to maturity. (Rom. 5:2-4) Therefore, since the struggle in this life will be rewarded with eternal life, and a perfect environment throughout eternity with the Lord, our perceived value to us, here and now should be "fullness of life." (John 10:10)

That is why the Apostle Paul said in Romans 8:18, "For I reckon that the sufferings of this present time are not worthy to be compared with the glory which shall be revealed in us." The Apostle noted in Romans 8:38, 39 that nothing could separate us from the love of God in Christ Jesus. God's principles applied to each Christian, by the power of the Holy Spirit, not only provide peace and security in this life, but an assured hope beyond the grave, with an eternity spent with our blessed Lord and Savior, Jesus Christ. What a life, and what a hope!

Fade, fade, each earthly joy, Jesus is mine;
Break every tender tie, Jesus is mine.
Dark is the wilderness, earth has no resting place;
Jesus alone can bless, Jesus is mine.

Tempt not my soul away, Jesus is mine,
 Here would I ever stay, Jesus is mine;
Perishing things of clay, born but for one brief day,
 Pass from my heart away, Jesus is mine.

Farewell ye dreams of night, Jesus is mine,
 Lost in the dawning bright, Jesus is mine.
All that my soul has tried, left but a dismal void;
 Jesus has satisfied, Jesus is mine.
—Tabernacle Hymns #3

Chapter 19

TO BE OR NOT TO BE
(Performance vs. Character)

Everyone desires to come to wholeness and enjoy the fullness of life. How that is achieved throughout one's time in this world is quite another matter and depends upon a number of variables in each person's life.

Principally there are two general ways by which this is attained: 1) the self-centered way, by design of the individual, and 2) God's way and His will for His child. It is up to each Christian to determine which way to follow. There are consequences, both good and bad, depending upon one's choice.

Life today—with its accomplishments—is based primarily on one's performance, with the results being reward or lack thereof. The emphasis is to do better than the other person. This gives a false sense of security, since the standards are constantly shifting. In school there is achievement through grades and advancement. In work advancement comes by doing a better job and then promotion with salary increase, the rise up the corporate ladder, and ultimate success. Society values achievement, acceptability, respect, and honors those who attain them.

All of this is contrary to God's plan for His children. (Prov. 14:12; Isa. 55:8) He is not as concerned with what one does, so much as He is with who one is; that is, with a person's being, not his accomplishments. (Rom. 8:29; Col. 3:10; II Cor. 3:18) In God's eyes, each individual is a unique person. God's principles are applicable for everyone, yet individually applied by the Holy Spirit to each person. The Bible never compares a person with a person, but each one is compared with God's standards. (II Cor. 10:12)

In the world of today, with its constant stress, and the emphasis upon achievement, there are valuable results in following God's plan for us, rather than the model that the world imposes. Primarily, God's way produces much less stress, for there is not the strain to measure up; we are accepted by Him, unconditionally. The significant elements in Scripture are to: "Rest in the Lord;" (Ps. 37:7; 62:1) "Abide in Him;" (John 15:7) "Trust Him;" (Ps. 37:4,5; Prov. 3:5; I Tim. 4:10) "Grow in Him." (I Peter 2:2; II Peter 3:18) The results are found in Matt. 11:28-30, "Come unto me all you that labor, and are heavy laden, and I will give you rest. Take my yoke upon you...for my yoke is easy, and my burden is light."

We hear of people having a feeling of low self-esteem, lack of confidence, and many insecurities. The world's model for life has produced this, with all the problems that follow. God's model provides fullness of life, and inner peace, even in a world of tribulation. The result is a sense of security, not in one's self, but in God's indwelling and fulfilling His word in us. The Christian can enjoy a sense of well-being and wholeness.

Parents can instill these truths in their children, to provide a growing sense of security, that will enable them to become useful adults, and to counteract the influence of the world and peer pressure. There is nothing better for a child than unconditional love from parents, and a Christian heritage. The resulting security comes from love, encouragement, acceptance, affirmation, discipline, and spiritual modeling by Christian parents.

There are three basic passages of Scripture to guide us in following God's pattern of fullness and wholeness: Joshua 1:8, which shows us how we can become prosperous—in God's measurement not mankind's—and how we can attain unto good success; Psalm. 1:2,3, meditating on the truths of the Bible will produce life fulfilling *fruit*; and Romans 8:6, which shows the contrast, "to be self-centered is death, but to be God-centered is life and peace."

In Scripture there are three "bones" that we would do well to follow: the "Wishbone" - "Delight yourself in the Lord, and He will give you the desires of your heart" (Ps. 37:4); the "Jawbone" - "Speak Lord, for your servant hears" (I Sam. 3:9); and the "Backbone" - "Watch, stand fast in the faith." (I Cor. 16:13) When one follows God's plan for life, there is fullness and abundance.

May the mind of Christ my Savior, live in me from day to day,
    By His love and power controlling, all I do and say.

May the word of God dwell richly, in my heart from hour to hour,
    So that all may see I triumph, only through His power.

May I run the race before me, strong and brave to face the foe,
    Looking only unto Jesus, as I onward go.
—Victorious Life, Keswick, NJ

Chapter 20

TOWARD A CHRISTIAN PHILOSOPHY OF LIFE

II Timothy 1:7 says, "For God has not given us the spirit of fear, but of power, and of love, and of a sound mind."

Power—to live constructively

Love—to live sacrificially

A Sound Mind—to live reasonably

The question is, how do we live reasonably in life? This then relates to one's philosophy of life. From the ancient Greek philosophers came the questions: Where did I come from? Why am I here? Where am I going? Today, the same questions confront each individual, who then has a personal responsibility to consider. Why? Because one's philosophy of life will determine what track it will run on. A life of reproach or a life with God's favor. That is why it is important for each one to have a well thought out biblical worldview of life.

I. The Reasoning: Every person starts with basic assumptions in life. Assuming that one accepts the Bible as a revelation from God to mankind, and as an objective guide for understanding life, let us consider some basic assumptions.

A) All truth is God's truth. The truth of the Bible tells us that God created mankind: spirit, soul, and body. (I Thess. 5:23) The spirit is the life that we have from God, the soul is our psyche, our emotions, mind, and will and the body is our flesh. Therefore, the basic assumption must be, that God who created us, should know best how we operate in life, to give us the fullness we desire. He has given us this information in His revealed Word, the Bible.

The Bible is to the person somewhat like the automobile handbook is to the car. It is the manual of operations to help us run the car efficiently. So, God has given us a spiritual manual of operations, so that we enjoy the fullness of life. (John 10:10) The Bible is the genesis and sourcebook of understanding mankind, his life, his emotions, will, and his body.

B) The best understanding of a God-directed philosophy of life and the psychology of well-being for wholeness of life, comes from the Scriptures—illustrated in the Biblical characters—with God's principles woven into the fabric of human nature. God's principles are always perfect, coming from a holy God. But, He takes us where He finds us, less than perfect, and elevates us to a positional perfection in Christ Jesus. (Eph. 2:6) He gives to us the Holy Spirit to re-characterize our lives, that our behaviors may be brought into line with our position in Christ. This takes a life time of work in the Christian to be achieved.

This is accomplished by our allowing the Holy Spirit to take what we read in the Bible, as we see the struggle of God's people illustrated, and accepting the principles that arise out of human interaction with God. Though the people of the Bible lived in a different environmental context than we do, they live in an agrarian society and we in an esoteric, complex one. Human nature has remained quite constant, so the principles are constant. If we replace the human illustrations of the past, with those of modern day, the principles remain. It is these principles that we should know, understand, and apply to our lives, if we desire to know God's best for us, and lead a full life.

II. The Problem: The basic problem that exists between modern humanistic philosophy and psychology, with the Biblical and Christian points of view is that the humanist evaluates mankind through a different *grid* or *filter* than does God. This skews mankind's perception of himself. Note some differences between the two:

A) Philosophy—Mankind is basically good
    Bible—Mankind is basically sinful and self-centered
        (Jeremiah 17:9)

B) Philosophy—No objective criteria as to what is good or normal

Bible—Biblical objective for normalcy

C) Philosophy—Subjective, Self-Ego-I

Bible—Objective, God-centered

The conclusion to this is that modern day philosophy is basically a distortion of the understanding of personality, and a trial and error method of correcting mankind's problems.

The Christian should not shy away from understanding philosophy or psychology just because it does not square with the Bible. But, the Christian needs to gain a proper perspective of both philosophy and psychology from the Biblical point of view. The basic need is first to know the principles of the Word of God, then the study of philosophy and psychology, sifting them through the grid of God's Word, the Bible. This will give one an objective God-centered view of the personality of mankind.

III. The Biblical Resolution: The New Testament book of Colossians is God's revelation of the philosophy for mankind. The primary passage is Colossians 1:24 - 2:10.

In this section, the Apostle Paul is speaking of three mysteries, relating to mankind. Note: The word *mystery* does not mean something mysterious, but rather something that previously has been divinely hidden and now divinely revealed. The first mystery is in Col. 1:24-26; the mystery of the CHURCH. God, in the Old Testament, dealt with Israel; now He is dealing with the body of Christ—known as the *Church*—spiritually speaking, is His body of believers on earth.

The second mystery is that of the CHRISTIAN in Colossians 1:27, in which the revelation of God has gone out to all mankind telling us that the salvation we have in Christ, is that which transforms us into the glory, the moral qualities of God. (Romans 10:13,14)

Finally, in Colossians 2:2 we have the mystery of CHRIST, "in Whom are hid all the treasures of wisdom and knowledge." See also II Peter 1:3. This refers to the fact that all the Christian needs for life and Godliness is found in the Lord Jesus Christ, as seen in His Word, the Bible.

In Colossians 2:8 there is a warning concerning humanistic philosophy, which the Apostle notes is, "after the elements of the world, and not after Christ." Conversely, we see in I Corinthians 2:9-14 that for the Christian, God, through the Holy Spirit, reveals that which He wants us to know, "that we might know the things that are freely given to us of God." Furthermore, he points out in verse 14 that the Christian has God-given discernment to know right from wrong through His Word.

The conclusion to one's searching for reality in life, through a Biblically thought out philosophy, is found in Colossians 2:9,10, "For in Him, Christ, dwells all the fullness of God in bodily form. And, you are complete in Him, Who is the head of all principalities and power." God is over all, in all, and by Him all things are held together. (Col. 1:16-19) Wholeness in life comes through one accepting regeneration from God, willingly being submissive to the Holy Spirit's re-characterizing of his life, and formulating one's worldview based on the principles of the Bible.

As mentioned previously, an excellent model is seen in Jesus Christ, as stated in Luke 2:52, "And Jesus increased in WISDOM, and STATURE, and in favor with GOD, and in favor with MAN." Wisdom is mental maturity, stature is physical maturity, favor with God is spiritual maturity, and favor with mankind is social maturity. Here was a perfectly balanced model of life, after which we would do well to pattern our lives.

In II Corinthians 4:6 we read, "For God Who commanded the light to shine out of darkness, has shined in our hearts, to give the light of the knowledge of the glory (His moral qualities) of God in the face of Jesus Christ," that we might pattern our lives after Him, and come to wholeness of life, according to God's pattern for us. God guarantees the fullness of life to us. (John 10:10)

O soul, are you wearied and troubled?
No light in the darkness you see?
There's light for a look at the Savior,
And life more abundant and free.

Through death into life everlasting,
He passed and we follow Him there;

114

Over sin no more death hath dominion,
    For more than conquerors we are.

His word will not fail you, He promised;
    Believe Him, and all will be well;
Then go to a world that is dying,
    His perfect Salvation to tell.

Turn your eyes upon Jesus,
    Look full in His wonderful face,
And the things of earth will grow strangely dim,
    In the light of His glory and grace.

—Victorious Life, Keswick, NJ

Chapter 21

THE NORMAL CHRISTIAN LIFE - PHILIPPIANS

God's Word, the Bible, has three foundational essentials, that He desires everyone to know and understand: 1) the entrance and problem of SIN, 2) the need for and the way of SALVATION, and 3) the understanding of SANCTIFICATION of life (See Chap. 2 for discussion of these three essentials). Sanctification refers to holy living, the primary and foremost element of the Christian life.

The world is concerned with physical, mental, and social maturity, whereas God is primarily interested in our spiritual maturity. (Luke 2:52) Philippians is the objective, authoritative book on spiritual and emotional maturity for the Christian. It was written by our creator, Who better understands us, and how we develop in life? There are four basic elements, one in each chapter of the book.

I. Chapter 1 - The Principle of the Normal Christian Life: The key to the basic principle of the Christian life is in Phil. 1:21, "For to me to live is Christ, and to die is gain." This displays the TRUST that the child of God has in Him. This does not mean that we live for Christ, but that we are better off dead, because we are then with Him. No, God did not create us to die, but to live, and in our living to be totally dedicated to His will for us. (Gal. 2:20) Our commitment for living for Him should be all-consuming.

For the Christian this answers the problem of PERSONAL IDENTIFICATION in life. Every person desires to be identified with someone or something. Many are constantly searching for meaning in life, and often shifting their focus, which does not produce stability. God wants us to be totally identified with Him, which provides security and fullness of life.

Psychologically, this commitment and concentration of life provides avoidance of FEAR of the future. One's life is totally given over to God's control; He is guiding and caring for His children. (Ps. 37:3-7,23,34; Heb. 13:5,6; I Peter 5:7) It also gives HOPE to the Christian, which is both satisfying and fulfilling.

II. Chapter 2 - The Pattern of the Normal Christian Life: A pattern is a guide, and God desires that we pattern our lives after the Lord Jesus Christ. The key verse in this chapter is 2:5, "Let this mind be in you, which was also in Christ Jesus." If He is our pattern, and we allow the Holy Spirit to re-characterize our lives after Him, this shows the ONENESS we have with Jesus Christ. He stated that He came not to do His will, but the will of the Father who sent Him. (John 5:30) Therefore, as Christ patterned His life after that of His Father, we are to pattern our lives after Him.

This helps answer one's problem of PERSONAL DISPOSITION of life. Since we all have time and energy in life, how do we dispose of it, so that we gain the fullness that we desire. Here is the pattern. God is the guarantor to us, that if we use our personal resources of talents, time, and energy to serve Him, when we arrive at the end of life we will be able to say, we've had a full and productive life.

Psychologically, this gives one ABSOLUTE GUIDANCE for life. (Rom. 12:1,2) Furthermore, it gives us a PERFECT MODEL after whom we can pattern our lives. When we look to others as models, we find some detrimental aspect about them that eventually brings disappointment. But, when we look to Jesus Christ, there is no disappointment in Him. On Him we can depend totally, for ACCEPTANCE and AFFIRMATION of life.

III. Chapter 3 - The Passion of the Normal Christian Life: In life we all experience emotions, which are normal. In this chapter we understand how to exercise our emotions in the manner that God desires, so that we are able to experience the full range of them, in a balanced way. For a Christian to enjoy emotions is to respond with APPRECIATION to God for His fulfilling in us His will, which gives EXPECTATION (hope) to the child of God.

The keys in this chapter are verses 3:13,14,20. The Apostle Paul, recounted his own experiences in the past. As an employee of Rome, he placed Christians into prison, and now he preached to them as an Apostle of the Lord. He realized that though he had not *arrived* in life he could say, "This one thing I do, forgetting those things which are behind, and reaching forth unto those things which are before, I press toward the mark for the prize of the high calling of God in Christ Jesus." One can easily understand that he could have had negative emotions of past behaviors. Instead, he was able to say, by the grace of God, that he looked ahead, rather than allowing the past to overwhelm him.

The lesson is clear: We need to forget those wrong behaviors of the past. We have confessed them to God, who has forgiven and forgotten; (I John 1:9) keep our eyes on Him, and press on in life. I believe that one of the greatest designs of Satan against the Christian—knowing that he can't take our salvation away—is to burden us with false guilt because of past failures. (Eph. 2:8,9) There are times when every Christian needs to tell Satan to, "bug off, I don't owe you anything; I owe God everything." We realize that all we are, all we have, and every breath we take is by the grace of God. Even the Apostle Paul noted that, "In Him we live, and move, and have our being." (Acts 17:28)

Let our lives be guided by the Holy Spirit, through the principle in God's Word. He will help us define God's goals for us to enjoy fullness of life, balanced emotions, and hope for the future with goals we can expect to complete in Him. In I John 3:2 it says, "We know that when He shall appear, the coming of Jesus Christ for the Christians, we shall be like Him, for we shall see Him as He is." What a HOPE and what ASSURANCE!

IV. Chapter 4 - The Power of the Normal Christian Life: In Phil. 4:13 it says, "I can do all things through Christ, who strengthens me." This shows the HELP we have in Him, the ACHIEVEMENT in life, through the power of the indwelling Holy Spirit. It answers the problem of PERSONAL SECURITY in life.

One of the greatest resources a person can have is personal security in life. Much of this comes through learned behaviors from proper parental modeling and affirmation. In addition to these factors, security can be enhanced through spiritual maturity of life. This chapter provides that understanding. Even an insecure person can possess security of life, if willing to accept the principles in this chapter at face value, and live them out on a daily basis. Heb. 13:5,6 says, "For He, the Lord, has said, I will never leave you nor forsake you, so that we may boldly say, the Lord is my helper and I will not fear, what can man do unto me."

Psychologically, this gives one a sense of ASSURANCE in life, as well as a sense of POWER. Phil. 4:19 tells us, "My God shall supply all your needs according to His riches in glory by Christ Jesus." All of God's resources for our personal spiritual development and fullness of life are ours for the taking. What more can be said; what more can we ask; what more do we need?

The Apostle Paul leaves us with the formula for the secret of PEACE in life: Phil. 4:6,7, "Do not be disturbed about anything, but in everything by prayer and supplication; lay it on the Lord with thanksgiving, let your requests be known unto God. And, the peace of God, which is beyond all understanding, shall surround your hearts and minds in Christ Jesus."

Evan Hopkins once said, "A Christian is one who is intellectually convinced, that is mental maturity; who is morally convicted, that is emotional maturity; and who is spiritually converted, that is scriptural maturity." This is God's design for each of His children.

Fight the good fight with all thy might,
    Christ is thy strength, and Christ thy right;
Lay hold on life, and it shall be,
    Thy joy and crown, eternally.

Run the straight race, through God's good grace,
    Lift up thine eyes, and seek His face;
Life with its way before us lies,
    Christ is the path, and Christ the prize.

Cast care aside, lean on thy guide,
　　His boundless mercy, will provide;
Trust, and thy trusting soul shall prove,
　　Christ is its life, and Christ its love.

Faint not nor fear, His arms are near,
　　He changeth not, and thou art dear;
Only believe, and thou shalt see,
　　That Christ is all in all, to thee.

—Hymns for the Family,
Paragon Assoc., Inc.,
Nashville, TN

CHAPTER 22

THE NEUTRAL AREA OF LIFE - Romans 14

Though the Bible has specific principles for the Christian—guidelines for proper living—there is a vast area of behaviors commonly known as the *gray* areas of life. It is these areas that have provoked great misunderstanding and controversy within the church.

Romans 14 is chapter written to provide basic principles that act as a guideline to help us make the proper decisions. Rather than call this a *gray* area, we will refer to it as a *neutral* area, until a decision is made as to whether it is proper or not for the Christian.

God could easily have listed in His Word every controversial element, and prescribed for us godly behaviors. But as a loving and wise Heavenly Father He wants us to be mature spiritually—able to make the proper decisions of life accordingly. Therefore, God has provided principles upon which we are able to make decisions that are not only right according to His standards, but personally beneficial. It is somewhat analogous to the parent/child relationship. Good parenting does not prescribe every decision for children as they develop. But it gives the responsibility to the child, in an incremental manner as the child grows, so that personal responsibility for decisions becomes a part of the maturing process. Just as every parent has ultimate veto power over bad choices of the child, in order for protection, so God can veto our decisions for our good. Also, when we willfully go against God's principles, He does punish us to bring us back into the way of Holiness. (Heb. 12:10,11)

In this chapter there are three guiding principles to help us come to right decisions. As we evaluate these principles it is important to ask ourselves concerning the decision made on any or all of them: will it enhance or detract from our spiritual maturity? The reason for this is that God wants to allow us to come to Spiritual maturity through making right decisions according to His Word and will for us. The process itself is part of the maturing. The guideline for us is the enhancing or detracting of that maturation process.

I. The Vertical Principle - Romans 14:8 This principle has to do with one's relationship to God. It requires one to consider that which is entered into or indulged in—how it will affect his relationship with the Lord. Will it help or hinder that relationship? As Christians, we belong to God by the right of divine redemption. (I Cor. 6:19,20) It is important that we make no decision that would adversely affect our relationship with Him.

II. The Inward Principle - Rom. 14:12 This principle has to do with one's self and the effect the decision has on his life. The question here is: does it build the Christian up spiritually, or does it tear one down? Since maturity in Christ is the primary and foremost desire of God in the lives of His children, (I Peter 2:2 and II Peter 3:18) it is important to evaluate indulgences in the context of how it affects the individual.

III. The Horizontal/Outward Principle - Rom. 14:13 This principle relates to the responsibility each Christian has to others. The Christian has two types of people with whom to relate: 1) the fellow believer, and 2) the unregenerate person to whom one is to be a testimony.

In relation to a fellow Christian, one is not to be a stumbling block to another's spiritual development, but be a positive example so that others may see the character of the Lord Jesus Christ.

As to the unregenerate person, the Christian is to be a testimony of righteousness, so that the individual may be desirous of becoming a Christian. Therefore, the Christian must consider as to that which he indulges in, does it help or hinder the testimony of the Lord to that person?

IV. Postscripts to Amplify the Principles - Rom. 14:14-23 In the remainder of the chapter, there are a number of elements to help one

124

understand how to apply the principles, as well as answering questions that may arise from the application of the principles.

As human beings we realize it is impossible to please everyone at all times; we inherently look at things differently. Therefore, if we are to be careful how we judge things in the neutral area, how can we be assured that which ever way we decide, we won't offend someone? God has given us the Holy Spirit, to give us wisdom to know how to apply these principles, so that we will have the mind of Christ in our decisions. (James 1:5) When we earnestly desire to follow the Biblical principles, and allow the Holy Spirit to apply them to the decision-making process, we can be assured that whatever the outcome, it will be according to His will for us. In this we can rest, even with the knowledge that we can't make perfect judgments.

Verse 14 points out that in the *neutral* area there is nothing unclean or wrong, per se. That which the Christian considers to be wrong, to *him* it is wrong, but not necessarily in itself, nor to another Christian. In the neutral areas it could mean that at certain times or places the decision could go either way, and this is precisely why God did not specify absolutely certain decisions.

An excellent illustration of this is seen regarding a missionary family who went to another country. They included the game of checkers for their children to play. But, when they arrived in that country they found the Christians were aghast that they would allow the children to play checkers, as the game was used there for gambling purposes. So, the missionaries put the game away while they were there, but did allow the children to play the game when they were on furlough. To apply the principle is to understand that the game of checkers in itself is neutral, not inherently wrong. But the association of its use for gambling would cause some to stumble when they saw missionaries children playing. In order to have a beneficial testimony to the natives of that country the missionaries put the game away. In this way they were able to make a proper decision based on Biblical principles.

Verse 15 explains that just because one evaluates something to be alright according to Biblical principles, it does not give one the right to use their liberty to adversely affect another person. (I Cor. 8:1-13) As Christians we are to exercise our liberty in love for one another and be

125

mindful of their weaknesses or immaturity. As verse 16 notes, "Do not allow what you consider good to be spoken of as evil."

Verse 17 points out that the neutral area which may be evaluated differently by Christians are not the essential elements in God's kingdom. The kingdom of God is not essentially determined by these things. Rather, His kingdom is evaluated in our lives by RIGHTEOUSNESS, and PEACE, and JOY in the Holy Spirit. "Make every effort to do what leads to peace and mutual edification," (v.19) rather than selfishly doing as we please. Our responsibility to fellow Christians is to build one another up in the faith.

Verse 20,21 explains the fact that God's work is not destroyed by our wrongful behaviors, when we judge wrongly, but we should be careful that we do not become a stumbling block to someone else. Though we may judge a thing to be alright, it may not be so in other's point of view. Thus, we must decide which is more important, do as we please and maybe hurt a fellow Christian, or be sensitive to their needs and minister to their development as a Christian. In Romans 8:18, the Apostle Paul exhorts us to realize that the sufferings of this life are not worthy to be compared to the glory that will be ours when we arrive in heaven.

Verse 22,23 concludes the Biblical admonition on our judgment of the neutral areas by saying that if we judge a thing to be alright, then we are to enjoy it. But if we have any doubts as to any one or all three principles, then it is not of faith and we should refrain from indulging. "Whatsoever is not of faith is sin."

In Romans 15:1,2 there is a concluding admonition based on the principles of chapter 14, and that is, "We who are strong, mature in faith, ought to bear with the failings of the weak and not to please ourselves. Each of us should please his neighbor for his good, to build him up."

The Bible stands like a rock undaunted,
Mid the raging storms of time;
Its pages burn with the truth eternal,
And they glow with a light sublime.

The Bible stands like a mountain towering,
    Far above the wrecks of men;
Its truth by none ever was refuted,
    And destroy it they never can.

The Bible stands, and it will forever,
    When the world has passed away;
By inspiration it has been given,
    All its promises I will obey.

The Bible stands every test we give it,
    For its author is divine;
By grace alone I expect to live it,
    And to prove it and make it mine.

—Choice Hymns of the Faith

Chapter 23

THE THREEFOLD ELEMENTS OF SANCTIFICATION

Two words in the Bible, sanctify and holy, basically have the same definition: being set apart from sin, and set apart unto God. The fundamental idea is separation from sin. Sanctification or holiness of life has a threefold aspect: 1) Positional, which is the past work of Christ in our redemption, and confers upon the Christian a perfect position, as a child of God; (Heb. 10:10) 2) Progressive, which is the present work of the Holy Spirit in the life of the believer, bringing one's character development into conformity with his position in Christ. This is experiential throughout one's lifetime; (II Tim. 3:16,17; Col. 1:28; II Peter 3:18) 3) Perfection, which is future and will be completed when the Christian arrives in heaven. His character will be as perfect as his position is in Christ. (I Thess. 3:12,13; Phil. 1:6; I John 3:2,3)

I. Positional Sanctification: When Christ provided salvation by redemption for us through His work on the cross, it set every believer apart unto God as His own possession. (Heb. 13:12) This was accomplished in the past, and confers upon every believer a positional standing before God as His child. Christ's work propitiated paid in full the debt due for our sins, and for the sins of every believer. (Rom. 3:25; I John 2:2)

The nature of this work is that it was a finished work of Christ; completed when He died on the cross. Hebrews 10:10 states, "By the will of God we <u>have been sanctified</u> through the offering of the body of Jesus Christ <u>once for all</u>." Hebrews 10:11,12 notes that under the old covenant the priests stood daily offering repeated sacrifices which could never take away sins. But, Christ made "one sacrifice for sins forever, sat down on the right hand of God," thereby signifying His completed work of our Redemption. His sacrifice needs never to be repeated, because it took care of the sin problem, once for all.

This sanctification is not dependent on any perfection of our own character or conduct. It is positional, and as such sets the believer apart from a sinful world, in that one moves out of Satan's family into God's family. It sets one apart forever unto God as His own possession, (I Peter 2:9) and confers on us a perfect positional holiness. Every Christian is considered as, perfect in the sight of God through the blood of the Lord Jesus Christ. (Heb. 10:14)

This sanctification gives defiled saints an entrance into the very presence of God. (John 9:31; Heb. 4:14-16) Furthermore, it is the present possession of all believers. (Acts 26:18) What should be the Christian's response to this? Simply believe. The work that Christ did for the believer is appropriated to us when we accept Him. (John 6:27-29) It is a finished work, we need only to accept it.

II. <u>Progressive Sanctification</u>: The nature of progressive sanctification is the present work of the Holy Spirit. The believer is progressively being set apart from sin and brought toward personal perfection. In contrast to positional sanctification, a once-for-all setting apart as a child of God, progressive sanctification is an experiential progress. One is being set apart from sinful ways, re-characterized by the Holy Spirit through the Word, to make the child "fit" to be God's own possession.

The method by which this is accomplished is through the instrumentality of the Word of God. (John 17:17; Phil. 2:12,13) The Bible serves as an instrument of sanctification in three ways: 1) the Holy Spirit uses the Word to reveal our sinful condition; (James 1:23-25) 2) the Holy Spirit uses the Word to cleanse us from our sinful habits and practices of sin. (Eph. 5:26) It is the Word that washes away our daily defilement.

Some question the need for the washing away of this daily defilement. Doesn't the blood of Christ cleanse us from all sin? Yes, but day by day we sin, and we need to confess those sins. (I John 1:7,9) Also, all sin has two aspects; 1) guilt and 2) habit. The blood of Christ cleanses us from the guilt of sin, and the Bible cleanses us from the habit of sin that results in our daily pollution.

An excellent illustration of this is seen in the feet washing of John 13. According to the custom of the day, when the disciples came into the upper room at the Passover, they had already washed their feet. During the meal, Jesus began to wash the disciples feet. Peter remonstrated with Him as to why He was doing it as they all had their feet washed. Christ's action had a higher spiritual significance than just the physical act. When Peter questioned his actions, Jesus told Peter that if he would not allow Him to wash his feet, that he would have no part with the Lord. Peter replied that if that be the case he wanted the Lord to give him a whole bath. To this the Lord replied, "He that is bathed needs not a whole bath, except his feet." What Christ was telling Peter was that salvation cleanses one wholly, but that because of the daily defilement through sin, we need the cleansing power of the Word.

I fondly remember a railroad worker who was a member of my father's church, testifying in prayer meeting. He said when he came home at night from working in the dirty railroad yards—before he took a bath—he sat down and read a chapter in the Bible. The dirty language of the day had polluted his mind. It was more important to cleanse his mind from the daily defilement of the world than it was to cleanse his body.

Our salvation in Christ, through His blood, has cared for our reconciliation with God, and now we are His children. But, as we travel through life we acquire the dirt of the world, for which we constantly need the cleansing of our minds by the Word of God through the Holy Spirit. This results in a progressive transformation into the likeness of Christ, by transforming our character.

The third way by which the Bible serves as an instrument of our progressive sanctification is the Holy Spirit uses the Word of God to transform us into the *Image* of Christ. The image of Christ is not a physical likeness, but a transformation into the moral qualities or attributes of God. This is the re-characterization by the Holy Spirit, which is progressively making us fit for Heaven.

In II Corinthians 3:18 it says, "But we all, with unveiled face beholding in a mirror the moral qualities of God, are transformed into those same qualities—as from the Holy Spirit of God." In other words, the Holy Spirit not only shows us our sinful condition, but He uses the Word to cleanse us from our daily sinful ways, and re-characterizes us into the moral likeness of God. The result is that because of this character transformation, the Christian lives out in daily life, what the Apostle Paul called, "the fruit of the Spirit." (Gal. 5:22-24) This is progressive sanctification, which is a life-long work. It involves a willingness on our part, and the work of the indwelling Holy Spirit to accomplish it. The Apostle Paul stated in Philippians 1:6, "I am confident of this very thing; that the Holy Spirit who has begun a good work in you, will bring it to completion at the day of Jesus Christ."

This sanctifying work of the Word implies three things: 1) that we will read and heed the Word of God; 2) that we will submit our lives to its cleansing power, and 3) that we will see Christ in the Word.

Sanctification by the Word is based on sanctification by the blood of Christ, and is inseparable from it. One has no sanctification by the Word without sanctification by the blood. (John 17:9) Christ set Himself apart to die for us, that we, through Him, might be sanctified through His Word. (John 17:17)

The Bible gives us motives for our progress in sanctification, they require an active response on our part. God presents these motives to lead us in the way of holiness. They are: 1) God's own Holy nature—what God is; (I Peter 1:15,16; Phil. 2:12,13) 2) God's grace to us—what He has done for us; (Rom. 12:1; II Cor. 8:12) and 3) God's promises to us—what He will do for us. (II Cor. 6:17,18, 7:1)

There are three results that accrue for the children of God as we submit our lives to His cleansing and transforming power: 1) it will help us control our fleshly lusts and appetites; (I Thess. 4:2-7) 2) it will fit us for God's service; (II Tim. 2:21; 3:16,17) and 3) it provides fellowship with Christ. (John 15:3,4) Our attitude toward all that He has done, is doing, and will yet do for us, His children is to OBEY.

III. Perfect Sanctification: This setting apart of the Christian is a work of completion. God will wholly finish the process of our progressive sanctification. (I Thess. 3:12,13 and I Thess. 5:23,24)

It will be accomplished at the coming of the Lord Jesus Christ for His children. At that time He will completely finish the work of regeneration and character transformation in our lives. (Phil. 1:6) Note: Heb. 12:22,23. All God's children are *righteous people* now, and someday we will be *made perfect*.

The results are wonderful! We shall be made like the Lord Jesus Christ, in all His moral attributes, spiritually, and physically perfect. And, we will have an unhindered vision of Christ. (I John 3:2) Today, we behold Him through the *mirror* of the Bible, (II Cor. 3:18) but our *vision* is often blurred by our own sin. Then we shall see Him, "face to face." There is no chance that it might not be done, for it is pledged by the very faithfulness of God. (I Thess. 5:24; Rom. 4:25; John 14:19; I Cor. 15:12-20)

The present effect of our future sanctification should compel us to be better Christians here and now. (I John 3:3) No one can be ready for Christ's coming, unless we are looking for His return. (II Peter 3:10-14) Our personal responsibility is outlined for us in II Corinthians 6:14 - 7:1. Justification, our declared righteousness from God, assures our right standing before God. Sanctification cares for our holy living. In II Corinthians 7:1 it says we are to, "Purify ourselves from everything that contaminates the body and spirit, maturing holiness out of reverence for God." We cannot do it ourselves, through our own strength, but only as we submit to His cleansing power. Note: I John 2:15-17.

Four final admonitions on sanctification:
1. Read the Word of God
2. Obey it
3. See Christ in the Word
4. Look for His coming again

Marvelous grace of our loving Lord,
  Grace that exceeds our sin and our guilt;
Yonder on Calvary's mount outpoured,
  There where the blood of the Lamb was spilt.

133

Sin and despair, like the sea waves cold,
  Threaten the soul with infinite loss;
Grace that is greater, yes grace untold,
  Points to the refuge, the mighty cross.

Grace, grace, God's grace,
  Grace that will pardon and cleanse within;
Grace, grace, God's grace,
  Grace that is greater than all our sin.

—Victorious Life, Keswick, NJ

Chapter 24

TESTING IN THE LIFE OF THE CHRISTIAN
James 1:2-27

In John 16:33, Jesus Christ stated, "In the world you will have tribulation, but be of good cheer, I have overcome the world." Problems are part of everyday life for all. Christ did not tell Christians He would detour them around the problems. He did say, "I will never leave you nor forsake you, so that we may boldly say, the Lord is my helper, why should I fear." (Heb. 13:5,6)

James 1:2 exhorts the Christian to, "Consider it pure joy, my brothers, whenever you face trials of many kinds." The word *trials* (NIV) or *temptation* (KJV) should be rendered as *testing*. The purpose of the book of James is to show how testing demonstrates the faith of the Christian. As we consider this chapter on testing, there are three elements that provide understanding of this difficult aspect of life.

I. There is a service rendered by God, to the believer, in testing. (James 1:2-12) This service has a fourfold teaching element:

A) It is for the maturing of the believer. (vss.2-4) When surrounded by trials and tribulations, count it all joy. From a human perspective this seems contrary to normal reaction. But God notes that it is not the trial per se that is the issue. It is the faith of the believer that is being tested, in order to be strengthened and matured. (v.3)

The testing of one's faith is like metal being fired in the crucible. When heated, the metal becomes molten, the dirt rises to the top and is ladled off. So, God allows the trials in our lives for separation and

135

refinement. This in turn leads to the maturing of the Christian. (v.4) Since He is a God of economy, He never does anything capriciously or willy-nilly, but with specific purposes in mind. He never allows any trial in our lives, but that which is for our good and His glory.

B) It promotes and develops the believer's prayer life. (vss. 5-8) Testing is what the believer lacks, increases wisdom, and knowledge. (v.5) Knowledge without wisdom is dangerous; it puffs one up (I Cor. 8-1) whereas wisdom helps one discern good from evil. (I Cor. 2:13,14; Heb. 4:16) God is the source of all true wisdom. (v.5) (Job 28:28)

However, one must ask in Faith, without doubting, hesitation, or selfishness. (v.6,7) In verse 8 one is admonished not to be double minded, that is, facing in two directions at the same time, seeking to do it God's way, at the same time doing it in a selfish way.

C) It puts praise on the lips of the believer. (vss.9-11) The lowly person is able to praise, in that he is able to ask of God, just as every other believer. (v.9) The rich and mighty, are also able to praise the Lord. The testing reveals their security is in the Him, not in their wealth or power.

D) It promises reward to the believer. (v.12) The promise is the crown of life, as well as blessing, for one who persists in his faith. God is the rewarder of those who love Him. A crown is an evidence of victory over the testing.

II. The source of testing is outlined in James 1:13-18. God is not the source of testing. (v.13) The natural reaction of a person is to cry out against God when things go bad. In adversity one tends to question God as to why He has done it. Conversely, when things go well there is a tendency to take pride in the accomplishment.

In this section it is important to note that the word temptation or trial has a two-fold meaning. As used of Satan or of Self, it means to allure to sin. As used of God, it means to test for maturity. The same word is used in two different contexts. The source or context determines the meaning.

In v.13 we note that God's very nature is Holy and good, and He cannot do evil against anyone, nor does He allure anyone into doing evil. Verse 14 points out that the allurement to do evil comes from either Satan or one's own lustful desires. It is interesting to note that the word *allure* (KJV) or *dragged away*, (NIV) in the Greek, is the

136

same word that refers to a fisherman purchasing lures to ensnare fish. Sin is often camouflaged by that which is attractive to the senses, but has a terrible bite. 1 John 2:15-17 points out the allurement of the world.

From God's perspective, He allows the trials—not to allure us to sin—but to refine and strengthen us. It is our response to the situation that is the key. Do we allow the allurement of the world, flesh, and the Devil to entice us, like the fish is allured to the hook? Or do we trust God to help us through the situation, and thereby become stronger in our faith? God's recommendation in verse 16 is, "Do not be deceived, my dear brothers." The picture here is of two different responses to the temptation: one conquers because of the new nature, the other suffers because of succumbing to the will of the old nature.

The final admonition as to the source of testing is not to fall into sin because of: 1) our justification—"He chose to give us birth," (v.18) and we are His by divine right; (I Cor. 6:19,20) 2) our sanctification—"Don't be deceived," (v.16) we are to "grow in grace and the knowledge of our Lord and Savior Jesus Christ;" (II Peter 3:18) 3) our glorification—*Firstfruits.* (v.18) In Romans 8:29,30 our future glorification is already an accomplished fact in the plan of God. Therefore, because of all these promises, we should press on. We realize that all is from God, who loved us, sent Christ to redeem us, and has given us of the Holy Spirit to mature us. Someday, he will perfect that which He has begun in us.

III. The salvation which enables one to overcome temptation. (vss.19-27) First, we are to know the facts of deliverance from temptation. (v.19-21) In verse 19, we are told to be: "Swift to hear God's Word when tempted," "slow to speak in judgment," and "slow to anger." Unfortunately, many times we do just the opposite. We don't listen to the Holy Spirit speaking to us; we are quick to judge; and quick to anger.

In verse 21 we are admonished to: "Put away on the outside all moral filth, and on the inside any overflow of wickedness." The vacuum should be filled with the Word of God. Then we are to apply the facts of deliverance from temptation. (vss.22-25) We are not to be hearers only of the Word, but doers. If we hear and do not do, then we are like a person looking into a mirror, and doing nothing to correct what he sees.

The doer of the Word examines it, applies it to life's situations, and continues to follow God's Word. God blesses that person. (I Samuel 2:30) One can examine the results of obeying God's Word by comparison, to see how one measures up. Two evaluations as to the worth of a Christian's behaviors are given in verses 26,27: 1) Worthless religion is seen in not being able to control one's tongue, saying one thing and doing another, or being judgmental of others. 2) Valuable Christianity is measured by two criteria: to help others in need, and to keep one's self from worldly contamination.

Therefore, testing in the life of the Christian, is a service from God to promote one's spiritual maturation, and to strengthen one's prayer life. The result is God rewards the Christian who follows His Word. The final admonition is to "Be doers of the Word, and not hearers only."

Be still my soul, the Lord is on thy side,
  Bear patiently the cross of grief and pain;
Leave to thy God to order and provide,
  In every change, He faithful will remain.
Be still my soul, thy best, thy Heavenly friend,
  Through thorny ways leads to a joyful end.

Be still, my soul, thy God doth undertake,
  To guide the future as He has the past;
Thy hope, thy confidence, let nothing shake,
  All now mysterious shall be bright at last.
Be still, my soul, the waves and winds still know,
  His voice who ruled them while He dwelt below.

Be still, my soul, the hour is hastening on,
  When we shall be forever with the Lord,
When disappointment, grief, and fear are gone,
  Sorrow forgot, love's purest joys restored.

Be still, my soul, when change and tears are past,
All safe and blessed we shall meet at last.

—Hymns for the Family,
Paragon Assoc., Inc.,
Nashville, TN

Chapter 25

HOW TO PRAY

Next to spiritual food from the Word of God, the next important aspect of spiritual development is prayer. We must pray because Satan seeks our downfall. (Eph. 6:12,13) Our Lord prayed. (Mark 1;35) It is God's appointed way to receive blessing, (James 4:2) and it leads to fullness of joy. (Jn. 16:24)

In the immaturity of our faith, we do poorly in prayer, but as we become more mature we learn to ask for and obtain those things, which are more consistent with God's will. We learn to ask within His will. (I John 5:14; John 15:7)

To help overcome our problems we need to pray! There has never been a sowing of God in the heart of His child, but what there has been an oversowing of Satan. Less time should be spent in trying to straighten out our problems and relationships, and more time spent in prayer about them.

I. <u>The Basis of Prayer</u>: It is the foundation of approaching to God. (John 16:23) We need to learn to pray effectively. Seek the Holy spirit's guidance. Search God's Word for conditions and promises for fruitful prayer. (John 14:13,14) Believe He hears and answers the prayer of faith. Thank and praise Him for His faithful responses. (I Peter 3:12; John 9:31; I Tim. 2:8) In light of our coming to God in prayer, there should be daily searching. (Ps. 139:23,24; Ps. 51; I Cor. 11:28-31) Prayer is also the exercise of our faith. (Matt. 21:21; Mark 11:24; James 1:6,7; 4:13-15)

It is impossible for one to exercise real faith that God will grant something that is contrary to His expressed will in the Bible. The Holy Spirit gives us the confidence that we need in asking, and we must be sure that we desire His leading in our prayers. (Rom. 8:26; Jude 20; Eph. 6:13; James 4:13-15; See esp. Jer. 9:24)

II. The Elements of Prayer: Two conditions are laid down by Christ for prayer: (John 15:7) a) you must abide in me, and b) my words abide in you. Effective prayer is seen in I John 3:22. We receive what we ask because we keep His commandments and do those things that are pleasing in His sight. We cannot effectively pray when we harbor a bitter spirit. (Mark 11:25,26)

Our approach to God is seen in Heb. 11:6—"Believe that He is," and—John 9:31—"God does not hear or act upon sinners, but only those who truly worship Him." Hebrews 10:22 tells us how we should draw near to God. His attitude toward His children is seen in Psalm 34:18 and 51:17. He hears those that have a broken and contrite heart. We have access to God the Father, through the intercessory work of Christ, and by the power of the indwelling Holy Spirit. (Eph. 2:13,18; Rom. 8:16-26) Some prayers are lost because we do not seek the Lord's will or search Him out. (Jer. 29:13)

A spirit of thanksgiving should accompany all our prayers. (I Thess. 5:17,18) A Christian should engage in secret prayers (Matt. 6:6) as well as public prayers. (Matt. 18:19,20; Heb. 10:25) There are a number of ways by which we are robbed of power in our prayers: James 4:3—because we ask amiss; Ps. 66:18—due to iniquity in our heart. We cannot effectively pray when we harbor a bitter spirit. (Mark 11:25,26) Ezek. 14:3 tells us that idols in our heart make a stumbling block. (Note: an idol is anything that comes between us and God, and takes first place in our life.) Prov. 21:13 says if we have an unwillingness to help others, then God won't help us. Vain repetition in our prayers is especially displeasing to God. (Matt. 6:7,8)

Many passages in Scripture explain to us when and how we should pray: Ps. 5:3—In the morning; Ps. 55:17—Evening, Morning, Noon; Matt. 26:41—We are to watch and pray. In Luke 21:36 and Eph. 6:18—Pray always with all supplications; I Thess. 5:17—Pray without ceasing; this means to be in such an attitude before God, that we can be immediately in contact with Him through prayer. Heb.

4:16—We are to come openly before the throne of Grace; James 5:13—If any are sick, let them pray; and finally, Rom. 12:12—We are to continue in prayer.

The Word gives us guidelines as to what we are to pray for: I Tim. 2:2—For kings and all those in authority; II Thess. 3:1,2—For fellow believers; I Tim. 2:1—For all mankind; Matt. 5:44—For enemies and those who despise us; Phil. 4:6—In everything by prayer and supplication; Ps. 51:1-4—For cleansing from transgressions, iniquity, and sin; (I John 1:9 and Psalms 19:12) James 1:5—For wisdom; Rev. 22:20 For the coming of the Lord.

III. Conclusion: The normal order of prayer for the Christian should be directed to the Father, through the cleansing work of Jesus Christ, and by the communion or help of the Holy Spirit. (II Cor. 13:14) PRAYER IS THE SOUL'S SINCERE DESIRE FOR GOD.

Take time to be holy, speak oft with thy Lord;
    Abide in Him always, and feed on His Word.
Make friends with God's children;
    Help those who are weak,
Forgetting in nothing, His blessing to seek.

Take time to be Holy, the world rushes on;
    Much time spend in secret with Jesus alone;
By looking to Jesus, like Him thou shalt be;
    Thy friends in thy conduct His likeness shall see.
                      —Victorious Life, Keswick, NJ

Chapter 26

WITNESSING FOR CHRIST

Christ's commission to the Christians, of going into the world and making disciples of his (Matthew 28:19,20), has been a great impetus to the Church of Jesus Christ, through the centuries. Most earnest Christians today, desire to let their light shine to the world, in winning people to the Lord as Savior. However, though most have a desire to do so, they are inhibited mainly by one element. Their willingness to witness is offset by a fear of being unable to respond to questions that the person to whom they are witnessing will raise, because they may not be able to give a Biblical answer with proper verses, or dialogue with Biblical understanding and principles. Therefore, the Christian may not project himself in spiritually helping unsaved individuals to accept Jesus Christ as their Savior. The following is provided to assist Christians to have confidence in witnessing for the Lord, with a degree of certainty in being able to answer questions.

First of all, some basic truths that one needs to explain to a seeking person, relative to becoming a Christian. In Romans 4:23 it says, "All hav e sinned and come short of the glory (i.e the holy moral character of God) of God". One has to acknowledge that he has sinned, and needs someone to save him from his sins. Then, one needs to know that Jesus Christ came into the world to give salvation from sin for every person, and through His work on the cross has provided that, as well as reconciling the person to God (John 3:16-18). The next thing is to show the person how this can be accomplished in his personal life,

145

and that is found in Romans 10:9,10. If the person understands this and is willing to take that step, then the Christian should lead him in prayer to that commitment to Jesus Christ, as his Savior.

A follow up to this, is to give to the new Christian some verses of assurance, as to his new found faith and Christian life. A representative group of verses may be: John 5:24; Eph. 2:8,9; and Heb. 10:17. It would be well for the Christian to explain what these verses mean to a new Christian. One thing can be understood in the life of the new believer, is that now he has the Holy Spirit within him, who gives to him spiritual discernment, to enable him to understand Biblical truths. So, the person witnessing, can have assurance, that as he discusses these truths with the new believer, that one now has the ability to know the mind of God. See: 1 Corinthians 2:9-14.

Many times the unbeliever will bring up questions relative to becoming a Christian, that in various ways he has learned about Christianity that are either not true, or have been skewed by misinformed people, or other unbelievers. Here is where the Christian has to know the truth of Biblical principles, to offset the wrong understanding of the one to whom he is witnessing. The following seven questions are the most common ones that are barriers to one accepting Christ, and the Biblical answers are provided to assist the Christian in giving a proper response. Hopefully this will give assurance to the Christian, so that one may have spiritual guidance and confidence in being able to answer these questions.

Question: If one says he believes his good deeds will out way his bad deeds, and hopefully will get him into Heaven. The following verses will guide one in answering this response: John 3:18; 5:24; 6:25-29; 14:6; Eph. 2:8,9. The most common misperception among non Christians has to do with one's works being able to get them into Heaven. This is visualized in what people say is that when they get to the Pearly Gates, St. Peter will weigh their good and bad deeds on a scale, and that will determine whether they are in or not. These verses put it all in Biblical perspective, to show that good deeds, regardless of quality, will not get one into Heaven. This is absolute truth, since God is the one who determines the results, and these verse plainly state the understanding.

146

Question: If one says, aren't there many ways (i.e religions) to God? The Biblical response is found in John 14:6 and Acts 4:12. The passage in John 14:6 is the most divisive absolute in the world, for Jesus claimed absolute authority over all other religions. The truth of this claim lies in the fact that God raised Him from the dead, whereas all other religious leaders have died and not risen. Christianity set itself apart from all other religions because its head, Jesus Christ arose from the grave, and He said in John 14:19, "Because I live, you shall live also". This is the guarantee to the Christian of our eternal life.

Question: If one says, there are many denominations, how do I know which is the right one? Response: one's eternal destiny has nothing to do with one's Church affiliation. It has to do with one's relationship to Jesus Christ, as savior from sin. It has to do with what God's revelation says to mankind in the Bible

The following verses may be helpful in answering this question: Acts 16:31; John 3:7; 3:36; 5:24; 14:6. It makes little difference what the Church's denominational affiliation is, the key element in its proclamations is, does it teach the salvation of eternal life, as obtained through a personal commitment to Jesus Christ, as one's Lord and Savior from sin. All else is secondary.

Question: But, I was baptized as a baby, and have been confirmed in the Church, and become a member of the Church, doesn't that guarantee me a place in Heaven? The answer to that question is an unequivocal, no, it does not. Water baptism does not provide one with eternal life. Only a personal commitment to Jesus Christ does that. Water baptism is an outward symbolic testimony to others, of what one has done through a personal relationship with Jesus Christ. In 1 Corinthians 12:13 it says, "By one Spirit are we all baptized into one body", which means that the Holy Spirit places us into the body of believers in Christ. It is spirit baptism, not water baptism. This is called regeneration or being born again, spiritually. When Jesus said to Nicodemus in John 3:5, "Except a man we born of water and the Spirit, he cannot enter the kingdom of Heaven", he did not mean water in the sense of what we mean by that. Jesus meant water to be a "washing" according to the word of God (Ephesians 5:26). The Bible provides us understanding of what it means to be a Christian. It is the Holy Spirit who places us into (i.e. baptizes) the family of God. It is better to be

147

baptized by the Holy Spirit and never by water, than to be baptized by water, and never by the Holy Spirit.

Question: If one says he knew a person who became a Christian, but has since turned his back on Jesus Christ, and is living a sinful life, has he lost his salvation? In John 10:28, Jesus Christ stated of Christians, "I give unto them eternal life, and they shall never perish, nor shall anyone pluck them out of my Father's hand". In one sentence He says that once a person accepts him as Savior, he is guaranteed eternal life, i.e. non forfeitable life, and he will not destroy himself, nor can anyone pluck the believer out of His hand. If the believer falls into sin, God has unique ways of punishing that one, and restoring the believers fellowship with God (Hebrews 12:6-11). God never punishes vindictively only correctively, for the good of God's child.

However, there are those who have made a "profession of faith" in Christ, but never made a personal commitment to Him. In other words, they are "wolves in sheep's clothing", and the Apostle Peter speaks of them in 2 Peter 2:19-22. At times it is difficult to absolutely know if a person is a Christian or not. We are able to determine only by their change of life, and a willingness to live for the Lord Jesus Christ.

Question : If one says I don't believe in God, or whether there is one or not, how do we answer that? In Hebrews 11:6 we read, "He that comes to God, must believe that He is". One must take that "leap of faith" , which as humans we accept many things by faith. Faith consists in believing, when it is beyond the power of reason to believe. When one does that, then he will realize that faith in God and trust in the Bible, is very reasonable. The truth of the Bible, and its historicity, has been proven by Archaeology, absolutely.

Furthermore, isn't it better to believe in Him and accept Him as Savior of one's life, even if He doesn't exist, than to not believe Him, if God is real? See: Romans 3:19,20 and John 3:18,36.

Question: If one says, but I can't or won't accept what the Bible says, how does one respond? A Christians personal testimony of what Jesus Chri st has done for you, is prima-facie evidence that cannot be disputed. Explain how Jesus Christ has transformed your life, and tell them they can experience the same life transforming power in their life, by committing themselves to Jesus Christ. Only when they make

148

that decision by faith, will they realize that life giving transformation, eternally.

As one projects themselves out to others, for the Lord Jesus Christ, it is imperative that the effort be bathed in prayer, and a willingness to allow the indwelling Holy Spirit take over one's life, and empower one to be His servant, in seeking to make disciples of searching people, who need the Lord.

I'll tell to all that God is love;
    For the world has never known
The great compassion of His heart
    For the wayward and the lone.

I'll tell of mercy's boundless tide,
    Like the waters of the sea,
That covers ev'ry sin of man;
    'Tis salvation full and free.

I'll tell of grace that keeps the soul,
    Of abiding peace within,
Of faith that overcomes the world,
    With its tumult and its din.

—Till The Whole World Knows
Rev. A.H. Ackley, B. D. Ackley

Chapter 27

A PROPHET'S MESSAGE FOR TODAY - Habakkuk

This relatively small and insignificant book, written six centuries before the coming of Christ, is probably as up-to-date as today's newspaper. Yet it has far greater significance; it has come from the hand of God through His Prophet Habakkuk.

Habakkuk prophesied to the country of Judah during the reign of a Godly king, Josiah, but the prophecy would be fulfilled after his departure. The prophecy is *parabolic* in substance, that is, though it had immediate consequences for Judah, the main thrust of the message is for us today. The essence of Habakkuk's message in Chapter 2 reads with the authority of God's Word behind the prophecy. Therefore, it is important for every Christian to see what God has to say to us today.

I. The Prophet's Double Problem. (1:2-17) In chapter one the Prophet cried out to God concerning his double problem: "The law is slack, and justice never prevails." (v.4) As we reflect upon the world today, we are able to concur with Habakkuk and ask God, as did he, "Lord what are you going to do about it?"

Habakkuk saw the violence and the wickedness in his day, and it seemed to him that "Right was on the scaffold, and wrong was on the throne." Just as he was aggravated at conditions in his day, so we are concerned for the spiritual and moral declension we see in today's world. This is why the book of Habakkuk is so pertinent to our understanding of God's dealings with mankind. As God worked a mighty work back then, so God will continue to intervene in our world today, to work His will. Though we do not know God's timing, we can trust and be assured that His program will prevail. It did then, it will now, and in the future. This is the message of the Prophet for us today.

God answered Habakkuk's plea in chapter 1:5-11, "For I will work a work in your days, which you will not believe, though it be told you." (v.5) In his day God allowed the Chaldeans to overrun Judah and punish the nation for their wickedness. In our world today we wonder how long God can allow wickedness to prosper. When will He say, "Enough," and bring catastrophe to mankind because of the spiritual darkness that now encompasses the world. The wheels of God's justice may grind slowly, but they grind surely. God was most gracious and lenient with Israel and Judah over hundreds of years, but He finally brought judgment.

II. <u>God's Divine Principles</u> (2:1-20) The heart of the message of Habakkuk is in chapter 2, which is also the most pertinent for us today, as every aspect of the principles in the chapter pertain to our world today.

As Habakkuk remonstrated with God, he said, "I will watch to see what He will say unto me, and what He shall answer concerning my complaint." (2:1) The Lord answered him with five Woes of Judgment that are very much present in our world today.

1) "Woe to him who piles up stolen goods and makes himself wealthy by extortion." (2:6) This is unholy ambition, yet this is what runs the world today. People take advantage of others, through any means, in order to gain advantage for themselves. As God looks down on the kingdom of mankind, and sees the wickedness, He hates all of it, so that through the prophet He pronounced a woe upon sinful people.

2) "Woe to him who builds his realm by unjust gain to set his nest on high, to escape the clutches of ruin." (2:9) This is simply covetousness, which is one of the ten commandments. Today, the desire to obtain what someone else has, by fair means or foul, is the order of the day. People today also seek to flee from the consequences that come because of the foulness of their deeds.

3) "Woe to him that builds a city with bloodshed and establishes a town by crime." (2:12) We are appalled at the crime and bloodshed

on the streets of our cities and towns. When the "Law is slacked and judgment doth never go forth," the results are oppression and violence. The sin of the human heart knows no boundaries. Unregenerate mankind knows not how to stop the situation because it denies Jesus Christ as Lord and master.

4) "Woe to him who gives drink to his neighbors, pouring it from the wineskin till they are drunk, so he can gaze on their naked bodies." (2:15) Here is immorality that comes from drink and a lack of moral or ethical teaching and behavior. These behaviors are commonplace now, as they were back then, and God will bring people today into judgment as He did then. God's standards for morals are no different today than they were in the Prophet's day.

5) "Woe to him who says to the wood, 'Come to life!' or to lifeless stone, 'Wake up!' (2:19) Here is a judgment pronounced upon idolatry. Though we may not have idols of wood or stone, we have them today in different forms—anything that comes first in a person's life is an idol. If something is greater in priority than God, then that becomes his god. God wants first place in one's life; anything less than that is idolatry.

Interspersed within these five woes upon the world, God provides three eternal truths that His people can rely on and trust, even in the midst of the wickedness seen today.

1) God's way of righteousness, (2:4) "The just shall live by his faith." This phrase is the foundation for three New Testament epistles: Romans 1:17 - which emphasizes Justification by faith; Galatians 3:11 - which emphasizes how we should live; and Hebrews 10:38 - which is the great book of faith. What God gave the Prophet Habakkuk in his day, as to how he should respond to the wickedness he saw, is the same exercise of faith that we can live by in the world of wickedness today. The Christian can truly live through faith and be sustained in the faithfulness of God.

2) God's eternal glory, (2:14) "For the earth will be filled with the knowledge of the glory of the LORD, as the waters cover the sea." Mankind is trying to eliminate God from every aspect of life. But, someday God will bring everything in life, and all mankind, under the judgment seat of Christ. (I Cor. 4:5) Then, as King over all the earth, His glory of His attributes will fill the universe throughout eternity, just as the waters cover the sea. We can count on it. (I Thess. 5:24)

153

3) God's eternal sovereignty, (2:20) "But the LORD is in His holy temple, let all the earth be silent before Him." When Satan is displaced when Christ Jesus returns, the rule of God will be exercised over all the earth. Then and only then, will we have sanctity of life, and serenity in the world. The world is in chaos and turmoil, at present, seeking peace without righteousness. The only way we can have true peace is when we have righteousness. (Isa. 32:17)

III. Habakkuk's Delightful Poem (3:1-19) As a result of God's overwhelming the Prophet with His eternal principle, Habakkuk stood in awe of God's majesty and power. He writes a most delightful poem in this chapter. The heart of the poem reflects upon the majesty of God in judgment.

IV. The Two Eternal Truths of Life In conclusion, consider well the two truths of life as seen in chapter 2:4 and 2:5. In 2:5 we see the *puffed up* man. He is self-centered and conditioned by the circumstances of life. He shall pass. However, in 2:4 we see the *just* man. He is God-centered and conditioned. He shall live. For the Christian the problems of today must be submitted to God in faith.

Over a hundred years ago there was a French scientist who projected that someday mankind would unlock the key to the atom. He noted that when that happened, God would take His great ring of keys off its hook in heaven, come down into the world of mankind and say, "Gentlemen, it is closing time." In the fall of 1942, at the height of World War II, a group of world renowned scientists gathered in Chicago, where they succeeded in unlocking the key to the atom. It became known as the "Manhattan Project," and culminated with the atom bomb being dropped upon Japan. Over a half a century has passed since then. It seems we can hear God rattling His keys in heaven—about to come in judgment on the world—and say, "Gentlemen, its closing time."

My faith has found a resting place, not in device nor creed
I trust the ever living one, His wounds for me shall plead
I need no other argument, I need no other plea,
It is enough that Jesus died, and that He died for me.

—Victorious Life, Keswick, NJ

Chapter 28

"BELOVED — BE" - II Peter 3

Prophecy, or Eschatology is the doctrine of last things. It is God's signature on His sovereignty, and His assurance to mankind of the hope that we have for the future.

The prophetic principles in II Peter 3 cover what we should consider while we live in an increasingly wicked world. God has an answer to the conflicts we experience, and His program for the future is always related to Holy living. The standard for Holy living is God's Word.

The reasons why Christians don't follow the Word are outlined in Mark 4:19: 1) The cares of this world, 2) The deceitfulness of riches, and 3) The lust of other things choke the Word and it becomes unfruitful.

In II Peter 3 there are four principles of admonition to the child of God, as related to prophetic events that will come.

I. "<u>Beloved—Be Mindful</u>" (v.1,2)—Of what are we to be mindful? In vss.1-7 the Apostle answers the question. We are to be mindful of the words which the Prophets of old spoke in God's behalf to Israel, as well as the words of the Apostles. The reason for being aware and understanding what God said through them to us, is that in the last days there would be scoffers who would come questioning the return of the Lord Jesus Christ.

In John 14:3, Jesus told the Apostles He was going back to Heaven, but that He would return to take His children to Heaven with Him.

Scoffers have argued against His coming again claiming that over the centuries the world has experienced continuous cycles of birth and life and death which will continue into the future. The Apostle accused the scoffers of ignorance of God's program.

In II Peter 2:4-6, the Apostle speaks of three instances of what I call, *The law of first occurrences*. He cited three situations recorded in the Old Testament that had never happened before in human history. The argument that because Christ has not returned—therefore, He never will—is contradicted by these three instances.

The first of these is in 2:4, regarding war in heaven between the Angels led by Lucifer and God and His angels. The result was that Lucifer and one third of the Angels were cast out of Heaven. This is cited in Isaiah 14 and Ezekiel 28. This had never happened in all of eternal history past, but it did.

We find in 2:5 the second illustration of *the law of first occurrences*. The wickedness that God saw in Noah's day, caused God to tell him to build an ark. Noah would be saved from the flood that God would bring upon the world. There had never been any rain upon the earth up to that time. God had watered the earth through a mist that went up from the ground. But now God said he was going to let the firmament, the clouds and atmospheric heavens, down upon the earth in the form of rain and flood it. The skeptics of Noah's day jeered him for his faith in God's command. It had never rained before, therefore, it never would. But it did rain and Noah was saved and the rest were drowned. (Gen. 2:6; 6:5-8:22)

The third illustration is in 2:6, where God destroyed the cities of Sodom and Gomorrah. Abraham's nephew, Lot, separated himself from his uncle and lived in these wicked cities. God sent two angels, as men, to Lot's door and told him to get out, because God was going to bring judgment on the cities in the form of fire. The men of the cities asked Lot if he was going to believe two strangers—the judgment they promised had never happened before—therefore, it never would. But it did! (Gen. 19:1-25)

Now, in 3:7, the Apostle warns mankind today, that the "Heavens and the earth which are now, by the same word are kept in store, reserved unto fire against the day of judgment and perdition of ungodly men." This world wide catastrophe from God has never happened before, and according to scoffers it never will. But God's word is sure, and judgment is certain. Therefore, of these things, the Apostle says, we are to be mindful.

II. "Beloved—Be Not Ignorant" (v.8)—Again we ask, left out "of what?" The reply is, "Be not ignorant of this one thing, that one day is with the Lord as a thousand years, and a thousand years as one day." This does not mean that God expands a day to a thousand years, nor does He collapse a thousand years into one day. What is meant is that time is not of any essence to God. He is not bound by a time and space world as we are.

The Apostle explains that God is not slack as some may think, but that He is longsuffering to all mankind. He is "Not willing that any should perish, but that all should come to repentance." (v.9) In other words, God loves every person, and in His love and Grace He sent Christ to die for the sins of everyone. The church has been commissioned to carry this message to all the world. (Matt. 28:19,20) For the past two thousand years the church has done so, though not perfectly. Only God, in His omniscience, knows who the last person will be that accepts God's offer of Salvation. Then Jesus Christ will return for the Christians, as He stated He would. The Christian's response is not to be concerned as to when Christ will return, as much as it is to be ready for it, and in the intervening time, to faithfully continue to carry out our commission, and trust Him as to when.

In v.10,12 the Apostle notes that the "Day of the Lord," the great day of Jehovah, the covenant keeping God will come. (Zechariah 14:9) He will do away with the heavens, the atmospheric and starry heavens and earth, because of Satan's contamination through sin. They will be replaced with "new Heavens and a new earth, wherein dwells righteousness." (v.13)

This is God's everlasting promise to His children. We are to live and reign with Him eternally, and this earth will be part of God's eternal Heaven. He does not desire His children to return to a sin-polluted environment. Therefore, transformed and perfected Christians will be brought back to a perfect pristine world in order to spend eternity. God doesn't want us to be ignorant while we await His return.

III. "Beloved—Be Diligent (Careful) (v.14) Why should we be diligent or careful, and of what? As we await Christ's return, and we have a goal or commission, our diligence is that, "We might be found of Him in serene confidence, free from fears, agitating passions, and moral conflicts." (Amplified Bible)

As we reflect upon our world, we know that fear, guilt, passions, and moral conflicts are all-consuming and everywhere we turn. In Revelation 9:21, we see four consuming elements that drive mankind: 1) murders, 2) drugs, (the word sorceries in the Greek is the word pharmacopoeia, from which we obtain the word pharmacy, or drugs) 3) immorality and 4) thefts. The Bible plainly states that mankind will refuse to give them up. II Timothy 3:1,2 tells us why: mankind is consumed with SELF and its gratification.

In verse 11 we see God's admonition to the Christian in today's world, "Seeing that all these things shall be dissolved, what manner of persons ought you to be in all holy manner of life and Godliness?" The rhetorical question here is plain; God intends us to keep ourselves "unspotted from the world." (James 1:27) In light of God's future judgment, it is apparent how He desires we should live in this wicked world.

IV. "Beloved—Beware" (v.17) Again, we ask the question, "Beware of what?" We are not be led astray of the error of sinful people and thereby fall from our secure position in Christ. There are two thoughts to consider here: first, that we not allow the things of the world—the flesh, and the Devil—to deter us from our spiritual maturity in Christ. Second, that our salvation is not in question as it pertains to our relationship with Christ, but our fellowship with Him may be broken by our selfish ways. See Mark 4:19 as to that which interferes with our spiritual growth.

In I John 2:15-17 we see the infusion of this world's system as a hindrance to Christian maturity. This humanistic philosophy drastically impacts behavior and character development. The Biblical admonition is, don't fall into this system, "But grow in the grace and in the knowledge of our Lord and Savior Jesus CHRIST." (v.18) For the Christian this is the most important aspect of life, coming to spiritual maturity in Christ.

John 1:17 says, "For the law was given by Moses, but grace and truth came by Jesus Christ." In II Corinthians 4:6 we read, "For God who commanded the light to shine out of darkness, has shined in our hearts, to give the light of the knowledge of God in the face of Jesus Christ." What the law of God could not do through the strength of human endeavor, Jesus Christ did by coming into the world. He revealed God to us, through His love and grace. Our response is to refrain from worldly ways and grow in God's grace and in the understanding of Jesus Christ.

Someday my earthly house will fall,
I cannot tell how soon twill be,
But this I know, my all in all,
Has now a place in Heaven for me.

Someday when fades the golden sun,
Beneath the rosy, tinted West,
My blessed Lord will say, "Well done,"
And, I shall enter into rest.

And I shall see Him, face to face,
And, tell the story, saved by grace;
And, I shall see Him face to face,
And, tell the story, saved by grace.
—Victorious Life, Keswick, NJ

Chapter 29

HEAVENLY REWARDS
I Cor. 3:11-15; II Cor. 5:10

Christians will never be judged with regard to their eternal salvation, that is a certainty. But, every Christian will someday be judged according to their works. Salvation is a gift of God, not according to one's works. (Eph. 2:8,9)

The judgment of believer's works will be on the basis of how one has lived for God after becoming a Christian. The result will be either a reward, called a "crown" or a lack of reward. The believer's sins were judged at the cross of Christ; the believer's works will be judged as to how one has utilized his gifts, talents, and resources for the Lord.

We are commended to be ready, so that "When He shall appear, we may be confident, and not be ashamed before Him at His coming." (I John 2:28) Perhaps our sorrow at the loss of reward, may be the tears that God will wipe away. (Rev. 21:4)

I. That Which Leads To A Reward In I Corinthians 4:1-5 we see that being stewards of the mysteries of God prepares us for eternal reward. A mystery in Scripture is not something mysterious, as we might think, but refers to something that in the ages past was hidden from our understanding, and is now revealed by God to us. In this sense our stewardship of the *mystery* is understood in Colossians 1:27 where we see that as God's children we are to proclaim the truth of God, "Which is, Christ in you the hope of glory." Our commission as part of the church, the body of believers, as stated in Matthew 28:19,20 is to proclaim the message of Salvation to all mankind. This was revealed by Christ to the Church when He came the first time. Faithfulness in carrying out our commission prepares us for reward.

As stewards of God's grace, we also are responsible for being trustees of our material possessions—how we use them. The way of the world is to selfishly acquire and use what can be gained. For the Christian there is a Biblical formula as to the gathering and dispensing of one's material wealth. (Matt. 25:14-30; Gal. 6:7; Matt. 6:20; II Cor. 8:12;9:6) Proper utilization of one's material possessions on earth will prepare one for an eternal heavenly reward.

The Christian lives in a self-centered and greedy world. We are commended to do good unto others, and be of help to them, (Gal. 6:2) especially unto the family of believers. (Gal. 6:10) A kind word, even a "cup of cold water," will prepare us for eternal reward.

Persistence in godly living, as a Christian, within an evil environment, will prepare us for eternal blessings and a reward. (Matt. 5:11,12; Luke 6:22,23; II Tim. 2:12)

II. <u>The Time of the Reward</u> In Matthew 16:27 we see that it will come on the day when Christ shall return, and "Then shall He reward everyone according to his works." This is emphasized again in Revelation 22:12.

III. <u>The Nature of the Reward</u> The Bible describes the rewards as *crowns* to be bestowed on the victor. Our responsibility is to run the race of life, keeping our eye on Jesus Christ, and trusting Him for our eternal reward. (Hebrews 12:1,2)

1. <u>An Incorruptible Crown</u> (I Cor. 9:25-27) This is God's reward for those who strive for mastery in the Christian faith. As we meditate on the Word of God, (Joshua 1:8; Ps. 1:2,3) and allow the Holy Spirit to give us wisdom and discernment, (I Cor. 2:14; James 1:5) then our lives come into conformity to God's design for us. Then we will be able to be a good witness for Him. (I Peter 3:14-17)

2. <u>A Crown of Rejoicing</u> (I Thess. 2:19) This reward is for souls we win to the Lord. We are to let the light of the Gospel of Christ shine through us to others, so they may see Christ in us. (Matt. 5:16) A Christ-like life is the best witness, for others are more impressed

by who we are, than by what we say. In Prov. 11:30 it says, "He that winneth souls is wise."

3. A Crown of Glory (I Peter 5:4) This reward is for the shepherds of the flock, who have oversight, but are also to be examples. This primarily refers to the spiritual leaders in the family of God. I believe it also pertains to parents raising their children; to faithful Sunday School teachers who minister to their classes; to anyone who influences others in the things of God's Word. In this sense, each one does shepherding. God is not unmindful of that influence we have in shaping others' character for the Lord Jesus Christ. It, too, will gain the reward. This should be an encouragement to every Christian.

4. The Crown of Life (James 1:12; Rev. 2:10) To those who endure the testings of life and are faithful, God will give a reward. God's children, past and present, have endured many trials and tribulations, even unto death for His name sake, and God is keeping a record.

5. The Crown of Righteousness (II Tim. 4:8) To those who long for and anxiously await His coming, God promises this reward. The anticipation of Christ's return, in this day of increasing wickedness becomes even greater for those who know Him and love His Word. This love knows no bounds.

The Apostle Paul had a fitting conclusion to the understanding of these rewards in II Timothy 2:10-15. He instructs us to, "Give diligence to your exhibit of works before God, that you may be approved of Him, a workman who has no cause for shame, because you have cut in straight lines the truth of His word." What an admonition to us today.

A medical missionary in Africa, many years ago, told of a native to whom he had ministered. He was asked to care for something for the doctor, who was in a hurry to go to a meeting. The native respond by saying, "I'll take your alms, but I won't be your servant." As Christians, do we respond at times, out of selfishness like that man? Or are we mindful of what God has done for us, desiring to love Him, please Him, and serve Him, for in so doing, "Great is our reward."

"Shall I empty handed be, when beside the crystal sea,
I shall stand before the everlasting throne?

Must I have a heart of shame, as I answer to my name,
  With no works that my Redeemer there can own?

When the harvest days are past,
  Shall I hear Him say at last,
Welcome pilgrim, I've prepared for you a place?
  Shall I bring His golden sheaves,
Ripened fruit, not faded leaves,
  When I see my blessed Savior face to face?

When the books are opened wide,
  And, the deeds of all are tried,
May I have a record whiter than the snow?
  When my race on earth is run,
May I hear Him say, "Well done,"
  Take the crown that love immortal doth bestow.

                              —Victorious Life, Keswick, NJ

Chapter 30

THE SEVEN JUDGMENTS

There is a coming day of judgment upon the earth, that will affect all mankind. It is taught in both the Old Testament and the New Testament. It will include Christians, non-Christians, Jews, Gentiles, and all the nations of the world.

Psalm 96:13, Ecclesiastes 12:14, and Hebrews 9:27 speak of a general judgment that will take place at the end of the age. Acts 17:31 declares the certainty of this judgment, by the fact that God raised Jesus from the dead, showing His ultimate power, even over death. John 5:22,23,27 declares Jesus Christ to be the judge. The Bible speaks of seven distinct judgments.

I. The Judgment of Believer's Sins on the Cross of Christ John 12:31; I John 3:8.

The sins of the believer in Jesus Christ were judged by His death, burial, and resurrection. Hebrews 2:14,15 speaks of the fact that Christ came into the world in human form, to meet sin head-on and conquer it. The result was that mankind has been delivered from the bondage of sin and death, eternal and spiritual separation from God.

The result of Christ's coming into the world was God's declaration of righteousness, justification, to every person who makes a commitment to Jesus Christ as Savior and Lord. Romans 3:24 explains that every believer is justified through the redemption that is in Christ Jesus. Romans 5:1,9 notes that one who is justified by faith has peace with God through Jesus Christ. Furthermore, being justified by His blood brings salvation from the judgment to come.

II. The Believer's Self Judgment I Corinthians 11:31.

In the context of one's coming to the communion table there is the necessity of self-judgment. This is a time of evaluation of personal sins that need to be confessed to God, so that any broken fellowship with Him may be restored. This self-judgment avoids chastisement from God.

Chastisement from Him is not condemnation, (I Cor. 11:32) for His chastening is always corrective not vindictive. (Hebrews 12:10,11) God does not chasten non-Christians, only His children, to bring them back into the way of holy living.

III. The Judgment of the Believer's Works II Cor. 5:10.

This is a judgment that takes place in heaven, all believers, when their works as Christians are evaluated. This is a judgment of one's works, not one's sins. Every work of the child of God will be evaluated for reward or loss thereof. (Gal. 6:7; Col. 3:24,25)

In I Corinthians 3:11-15 we read that Christ is our foundation of life. Every child of His builds upon that foundation a superstructure of *gold, silver, or precious stones* or *wood, hay, or stubble*. The text tells us that God has an account of our works and that the day of judgment will declare them. Then everyone will receive a reward or loss of it, but the Christian will be eternally saved, even through the judgment of God's refining fire.

The time of this judgment will be at the return of Christ to take over the world. (I Peter 5:4) Therefore, the admonition to every Christian is, "Whatsoever you do, do it heartily as to the Lord, and not unto mankind." (Col. 3:23)

IV. The Judgment of the Nations at Christ's Return Matthew 25:31-46.

When Christ returns to judge the world, He will judge the nations on the basis of how they treated His people, Israel. Since nations cannot be judged apart from individuals, it will be a judgment of individuals within those nations.

The test is their treatment of Israel during the Tribulation period. In the Matthew passage it speaks of three classes of nations: "Sheep" nations, "Goat" nations, and "My Brethren."

166

V. The Judgment of Israel at Christ's Return Ezekiel 20:33-38.

This is a prophecy of future judgment upon Israel. At issue will be who will enter the promised land for the kingdom blessings.

In Malachi 3:2-5; 4:1,2 it speaks in prophetic tones, that refer ultimately to the Lord Jesus Christ, as the "Sun of Righteousness." He will bring healing to the people of Israel. From Jesus Christ's personal testimony in the New Testament we recognize that only those who believe in Him as their Messiah and Savior will enter into the kingdom blessings. (John 6:26-29)

VI. The Judgment of Angels and Satan After the Millennium Jude 6,7 and Revelation 20:10.

After the thousand year reign of Christ on earth, and Satan's loosing "for a little season," he will be judged, along with all the fallen angels, now demons. (II Peter 2:4)

When Lucifer fell from Heaven, and became Satan before the creation of the earth, (Isa. 14; Ezek. 28) he drew a third part of the angels in heaven. (Rev. 12:4) They threw in their lot with him. There was war in Heaven, and God cast Lucifer and his angels out of Heaven. Those fallen angels became Satan's demons.

They all will be judged for being against God, and will receive eternal damnation in "the lake of fire." (Rev. 20:10 and Matt. 8:29; 25:41)

VII. The Judgment of the Wicked Dead Revelation 20:11-15.

This is the final judgment. It will include every person who has not acknowledged Jesus Christ as Lord and Savior of their lives. This is a judgment that the Bible calls the "second death." It is eternal separation from God, not annihilation. It is called the "lake of Fire," which not only is total separation from the life of God, but will be the torment of eternally unfulfilled desires.

For those who plead their "works" as justification from God's judgment, the "Book of Life" is God's answer. (Rev. 20:15) The way by which one enters into the Book of Life is through a personal commitment to Jesus Christ, and His covering for their sins. Then one's works, which never can measure up for Salvation from sins, will bring reward, as done out of love for Him.

God never created anyone for judgment, but for eternal fellowship with Him. It would be inconsistent with God's attributes to send anyone to eternal damnation. Each person condemns himself to eternal separation from God through his sins. Christ came to redeem every person, (Rom. 8:1-4) so that the judgment of God would not fall on him. (John 6:26-29)

Again, it is the individual who accepts Christ's redemptive work, who has eternal life. To the one who does not accept Christ's sacrifice for his sins, then God has no other alternative but to judge that person to eternal separation from God. For God in His holiness cannot countenance mankind's sin. This is why Christ died for all, to become the way to pay for the sins and eternal destiny of every person.

Breathe on me breath of God, fill me with life anew,
That I may love what thou dost love, and do what thou would do

Breathe on me breath of God, so shall I never die,
But live with thee the perfect life, of thine eternity.
—Victorious Life, Keswick, NJ

Chapter 31

THE TRUMP OF GOD

Date setting for the return of Christ has become commonplace in Christian circles today. Some say the catching away of Christians in not a matter of secret. They claim that the Rapture will be in the middle or end of the Tribulation.

These assertions lead to some inescapable conclusions. The very mention of a mid-trib or post-trib rapture is the same as date setting, since the Bible is explicitly clear as to the time period for the middle and end of the Tribulation. Thus the church is robbed of the blessed hope of Christ's imminent return, since for centuries He has been momentarily expected. The imminency of Christ's return, or lack of it, then ceases to be a sanctifying factor and a motivating element in the lives of Christians.

Much of this controversy is based on the *trumpets* in Scripture, and particularly, The *trump of God*. There are 115 passages in the Bible relative to trumpets. These passages show that there are three kinds, human, angelic, and Divine. Human trumpets were used by Israel to make announcements to the people. Angelic trumpets announced judgments or victory, and Divine trumpets followed the same pattern.

I. The Trump of God and the Last Trump are One and the Same:

Two primary Scriptures speak to this: I Thessalonians 4:15-18 and I Corinthians 15:51,52. Five elements identify these two trumpets: 1) both were written to believers in the church, 2) both discuss the same subject, the resurrection, 3) both describe the same effect on the saints, 4) both hold forth the same hope for living saints, and 5) both passages use this hope as the occasion for comfort and exhortation. (I Thess. 4:18 and I Cor. 15:58)

With this remarkable agreement, there is but one conclusion, they are the same. The *Trump of God* identifies it as to kind—it is a Divine trumpet. The *last trump* identifies it as to order—it is the final trump.

II. The Last Trump of God Points to the First Trump of God:

In order to have Biblical understanding the terminology of Scripture must be followed. The term, "last" means the final or end of things in a series. It may be two or more, such as "the first Adam," and the "Last Adam." (I Cor. 15:45) Thus, the *Trump of God* is last in a series of Divine trumpets. A study of the 115 references to trumpets reveals that just two may be called, *Divine*.

To understand about the *last trump* we must know about the *first trump*. The first mention of the trumpet in Scripture is the trump of God. (Exodus 19:13,16,19; 20:18,19) To confirm the writing concerning the first trump, the writer of Hebrews refers to this. (Hebrews 12: 18,19,26, v.26 speaks of the last trump; see Joel 2:1 with 3:16)

III. The Last Trump Will Announce Resumption and Completion of God's Dealings With Israel Upon the Basis of the Law:

God's plan for Israel's future unfolded with the prophecy of the "Seventy Weeks" in Daniel 9:24-27. The 70th week has not been fulfilled as yet. Faith assumes it will be fulfilled in the future, as the first sixty nine were in the historical past. This *seventieth week* is a week of years, rather than days, and is the future period of the seven years of the great Tribulation. For a differentiation between weeks of days, and weeks of years see Genesis 29:27,28.

The very "Day of the LORD (Jehovah)" will be characterized by the "Last trump of God." (Zephaniah 1:14-16) During this period God will carry to completion His program for Israel under the covenant He made with them, beginning with His unconditional promises to Abraham. God announces the resumption and completion of this covenant by blowing the trumpet, as in the days of old.

IV. The Last Trump Will Cover the Seven Years of Tribulation:

The trumpet of Israel announced God's dealings with Israel over a long period of time. So, the last trump will announce God's dealings with Israel over the seven years of Tribulation. This is why Zephaniah

1:14-16 speaks of "A day of the trumpet" meaning the period of the trumpet.

It also means the announcement of the gathering of Israel from among the nations. (Isaiah 27:13; Matthew 24:31) It means wrath for the rest of the world, (Joel 3:1,2,16 with Hebrews 12:26) and tribulation for the Jews. (Zephaniah 1:4,12)

V. <u>The Last Trump of God Announces the Deliverance of the Saints</u> From the World:

In I Corinthians 15:52, the Apostle Paul uses the sounding of the trump of God to signalize the time when the believers will be raptured. The first trump of God was at Mt. Sinai, with its tremendous impact for Israel. The sounding again will mark the completion of the work of the Church, and renewal of relations with Israel.

At this point, God's administration through the church, the Church age, is finished. God then takes up with His children of Israel, in the final seven years, the great Tribulation, the 70th week of Daniel, before His coming to set up the Kingdom. Hallelujah.

Jesus shall reign where e'er the sun,
    Does His successive journey's run;
His kingdom spreads from shore to shore,
    Till moons shall wax and wane no more.

It may be at morn, when the day is awaking,
    When sunlight through darkness and shadow is breaking;
That Jesus will come in the fullness of glory,
    To receive from the world His own.

O, Lord Jesus how long, how long,
    E'er we shout the glad song,
Christ returneth, Hallelujah! Hallelujah, Amen.
    —Victorious Life, Keswick, NJ

Chapter 32

TOWARD A WORLDVIEW

In a national survey (Barna) it was determined that only 9 percent of Evangelical Christians had a Biblically centered worldview. Barna noted that the primary reason Christians do not act like Jesus is because they do not think like Him. Behavior stems from what we think. Proverbs 23:7 states, "As a person thinks in his heart, so is he." A Biblically centered worldview will provide a foundation for the Christian to both think and act in accordance with that view of life. This chapter has been designed to assist every Christian to formulate his or her own Biblical worldview. These principles are in general, and apply to every Christian. It is the individual's responsibility to apply them specifically to their life, by the help of the Holy Spirit, since we all differ, and God has given to each one differing gifts and abilities. May God grant you grace and wisdom as you read and apply these truths to your life."

The survey also found that those without a Biblical worldview are more likely to accept the ways of the world, than those who have a committed Biblically centered way of life. What is the importance of one needing to have a Biblical worldview, what is it, and what does it mean?

A worldview in general, is one's philosophical view of life that encompasses a person's ideas about life, purpose, understanding, commitment to it, and goals. It is the "track of life" upon which one runs, and becomes the determining factor as to how a person operates their life over the course of one's years. A Christian Biblical worldview is one's commitment to accepting and following Biblical principles as the guide to life in all aspects of daily living. If one is committed to that, then God is the guarantor that there will be fullness of life. (Joshua 1:8; John 10:10)

For thousands of years mankind has been struggling with three ponderous questions that have confounded society in general: where did I come from; why am I here; and, where am I going? Regardless of the many answers that have come from the mind of mankind, the Bible provides God's definitive answer to these three questions. Originally, in the creative act of God in Adam and Eve, He intended them to: 1) enjoy fellowship with Him; (Psalms 8:4) 2) to be a reflection of God's moral character; (Psalms 8:5) 3) to be king over all the creation. (Psalms 8:6) When Adam and Eve sinned by turning from being God-centered to being self-centered, they lost all three purposes that God had for them. Since God's purposes are eternal, He decreed that through the coming of Jesus Christ, restoration would be made possible for mankind to eternally fulfill God's original purpose for His creation.

Since all peoples of the earth are the result of Adam's sin, (Romans 5:12) it has been natural for mankind to consider these three great questions. The brief Biblical answers to them are: We all are, by the creative act of God and by human propagation, the descendents of Adam. We are here to be a reflection of God's moral character, but sin distorted that reality, but through Jesus Christ restoration is possible. In the future all people will stand before God in judgment; those who have acknowledged Jesus Christ as Lord and Savior for their sins will inherit eternal life with Him, and those who have rejected God's offer of eternal life, by rejecting Jesus Christ, will suffer eternal separation from God and be eternally unfulfilled.

In order to adequately answer these questions individually, one must construct a proper worldview. For the Christian, who accepts the Bible as the revealed word of God, the answer to these great questions is formulated through the filter of Biblical principles. It is the safeguard that his worldview fit with God's design for his life. When this is in place, then one can be confident in knowing he will enjoy fullness of life, whatever will come. Furthermore, God will guarantee to the individual that when the end of life comes, that person will be able to say, "I've had a fulfilled life." What more can one say than this?

The foundation of a Biblical worldview is found in seven specific principles in Scripture that define God's basic revelation to mankind, upon which one must commit himself to accepting: 1) the divinity of Jesus Christ, 2) the sovereignty of God over the universe, 3) salvation by faith in Jesus Christ for the remission of sins and the hope of eternal life, 4) the reality of sin and Satan, 5) a Christian witness to the world, 6) the inerrancy of Scripture, and, 7) the return of the Lord Jesus Christ to rule over the world. Granted, there are theological differences of understanding these basic principles, but these need to be accepted at face value. As the Apostle Paul noted, "Now we see through a mirror darkly, now we know in part; but then shall I know." (1 Corinthians 13:12) Though our vision of these elements are often blurred, yet one must trust the Lord for these truths. It is the work of the Holy Spirit to guide us into all truth. (John 16:13) As we submit to his guidance, God directs the thoughts and intents of our lives to conform us to his perfect will.

A Biblical worldview must consider four basic questions: 1) origin of life, 2) meaning in life, 3) morality in behavior, and 4) one's future destiny? To answer these questions from a Biblical perspective the New Testament book of Colossians, which is the philosophical book of the Bible, becomes the Christian's guide to understanding. Given the fact that not only does God desire everyone to become His child, (II Peter 3:9) but God furthermore provides the "track of life" upon which, if one desires to run his life, provides the Biblical worldview to operate life to the full. Therefore, it is important for one to consider what Colossians has to say to us, in answer to these four important questions. By way of introduction, the Apostle prays for the Christian in Colossians 1:9-14, that we "Might be filled with the knowledge of His will in all wisdom and spiritual understanding." He further prays that we might be fit to be partakers of the kingdom of His son, Jesus Christ. A personal Biblical worldview is the process in the life of the Christian toward becoming fit for the kingdom of God. This is accomplished by accepting and understanding Biblical principles, and submitting one's life to the guidance and control of the Holy Spirit, who guides us into all truth.

175

The first Biblical principle relative to the question of the origin of life is answered in Colossians 1:16-18, along with other passages of Scripture. It tells us that all things in the universe were created by God and for God, and that all matter in life is held together by God's power and word. God is the creator and sustainer of life. (Jeremiah 1:5) This is what is termed *Natural Law* over against the theory of evolution, that says that the world and mankind came by chance, which is contradictory to Biblical truth.

For one to embrace a Biblical worldview, it is imperative to accept the Genesis account of creation, "In the beginning, God created the Heaven and the earth." (Genesis 1:1) It is hard to conceive of any Christian not believing in the creative act of God.

The second question of the meaning of life from a Biblical perspective is found in Colossians 2:8-10. The Christian is first warned against the philosophy of the world, which is basically a narcissistic or self-centered view of life. The Apostle Paul notes that this view of meaning in life is after the traditions of worldly philosophers, the elements of the world, and not after Christ. He then goes on to state that in Christ "Dwells all the fullness of the Godhead bodily," in that the human person, Jesus Christ, was the embodiment of the whole of the triune God. (II Corinthians 4:6) He came into the world to reveal God to us, so that we could comprehend God in the person of Jesus Christ. Since God does not dwell in a body, is eternal in being, and incomprehensible to mankind, who is limited, the only way by which one could come to an understanding of God would be through Him becoming one of us, in the person of Jesus Christ,

The Apostle provides the answer to the meaning of life in verse 10, "You are complete in Him, who is the head of all principality and power." Meaning in life and fullness of life comes by one's relationship to God through Jesus Christ, who provides us all that is needed for life itself. In I Thessalonians 5:23 we read, "And, the very God of peace, sanctify you wholly; and I pray God your whole spirit, and soul and body be preserved blameless unto the coming of our Lord Jesus Christ." This is God's commitment to the Christian, which gives meaning to life itself.

Fullness of meaning in life is desirable for every person. The promise Christ has given to the Christian is found in John 10:10, "I am come that you might have life, and that you might have it more abundantly." A Biblically centered worldview in the life of the Christian will bring what Christ promised to reality. In John 15:11, Jesus said, "These things have I spoken unto you, that my joy might remain in you, and that your joy might be full." A Biblical worldview provides the elements that produce fullness of joy in that, "Of Him are you in Christ Jesus, who of God is made unto you, wisdom, and righteousness, and sanctification, and redemption." (I Corinthians 1:30) These are the spiritual elements that produce meaning in life for the Christian.

The third question of morality in behavior and how to handle it, in a Biblical worldview, is found in Colossians 3:1-3, 5-10. The argument by Paul consists of an assumption that since the Christian has now become related to God through a personal commitment to the risen Christ, that one should "Set your mind on things above, not on the earth." (v.2) Why, since we are earth creatures, and live in a mundane world? The Apostle does not mean that we should not be concerned about the normal affairs of everyday life, for that is necessary, but that we should not allow those things to control us, or take first place in our lives. Rather, allow the things of eternity to control us, so that the normal activities of life take their rightful place, through our daily commitment to the control of the Holy Spirit. That is why it states in verse 3, "You are dead, and your life is hid with Christ in God."

With this in mind, verses 5-10 give us a list of things, that one with a Biblically centered worldview should do in daily living, through the control and power of the indwelling Holy Spirit. In verse 10 we are told as Christians to, "put on the new person, in which our life is ever being renewed in knowledge after the likeness of Jesus, who was born of God." In other words, once a person becomes a Christian, the primary thrust of one's life is to become spiritually mature. (II Peter 3:18; I Peter 2:2) Patterning one's life after Christ in all aspects of living, is what God desires for us. Galatians 5:16-25 provides a contrast between the worldly Christian life and the Holy Spirit filled life. Galatians 5:16 commends us to, "Walk by the power of the Spirit, and you will not fulfill the lust of the flesh." Another admonition is found in Ephesians 5:1-9. Commitment to God through the power of the Holy Spirit, helps us not only to grow spiritually, but to also overcome the constant pull of the self-life and worldly attractions.

The final question in constructing a Biblical worldview is what is the future destiny of the Christian who is committed to Jesus Christ? The Apostle Paul's succinct answer is found in Colossians 3:4, "When Christ, who is our life shall appear, then shall you also appear with Him in glory." How is that amplified in understanding? Consider the following passages of Scripture: In John 14:19 Jesus stated, "Because I live, you shall live also," meaning that His resurrection from death would guarantee that every Christian would have eternal life. In I Corinthians 15:20-23; 51-58 there is an amplification of Jesus' declaration of eternal life. It tells the Christian that though physical death may overtake him, someday Jesus Christ will return to earth, to not only raise the Christians who have died, but also transform them into Christ's likeness eternally, with no sickness or death, and live with Him eternally. This is the future hope and destiny for every Christian.

Furthermore, in I John 3:2 we read, "Beloved now are we the children of God, and it does not yet appear what we shall be, but we know that when He appears, we shall be like Him, for we will see Him as He is." Our transitional life which will someday die, will be raised by God's power to eternal life, and transformed into the likeness of the Lord Jesus Christ, Himself. (Philippians 3:20,21) Last, but not least, in Philippians 1:6, the Apostle Paul made a very definitive statement, "I am confident of this very thing, that the Holy Spirit who has begun a good work in you, through regeneration, will bring it to completion at the day of Jesus Christ." What a glorious contemplation and guarantee.

When a Christian desires to formulate one's worldview according to the principles of the Bible, he allows the word of God to dwell in him richly, and meditates and prays for daily wisdom and discernment, through writing the Holy Spirit a "blank check" each day of his life. Then God will guarantee that person to be able to say when one comes to the end of life, "I have had a fulfilled life." What more is one able to ask for than that?

T'is so sweet to trust in Jesus,
    Just to take Him at His word,
Just to rest upon His promise,
    Just to know, "Thus saith the Lord."

Yes, 'tis sweet to trust in Jesus,
    Just from sin and self to cease,
Just from Jesus simply taking,
    Life and rest and joy and peace.

Jesus, Jesus, how I trust Him,
    How I've proved Him o'er and o'er.
Jesus, Jesus, precious Jesus,
    O for grace to trust Him more.

                  —Victorious Life, Keswick, NJ

Chapter 33

THE SEARCH FOR TRUTH

For centuries mankind has been searching for the truth, which has been very elusive, and difficult to know. Truth has been a very subjective element, since a definition of it has been in the minds of philosophers, etc., and mankind really does not know what absolute truth really is. Not only has there been an exhaustive search for truth, and along with that search has been a search for meaning and/or purpose in life. Ancient philosophers posed three questions on this search: where did I come from, why am I here, and where am I going? The search for answers to these questions, are couched in the search for truth. The two concepts are bound together. Therefore, the question is, are we able to know absolute truth, and does it provide an answer to these three questions?

The answer to the question is an unequivocal yes. If so, where then does one find the answers? They are found in the Bible, which is the revelation from the creator God, who formed mankind, and gave him the absolute truthful "Manual" for living a fruitful and full life (John 10:10). The Bible is the only absolute, objective document of the pure truth in the world. It comes not from sinful, subjective human beings, but from a holy God, who created the universe, and all that is in it, and has given mankind a revelation of Himself, to provide us with a roadmap for life, and to find fulfillment, and ultimately enjoy an eternity with Him. We can with absolute confidence accept the principles and precepts of Biblical truth, and confidently apply them to our lives.

For many years, skeptical mankind have attacked the Bible with alleged untruths and misinformation, as well as questioning the Bible's historicity, and categorized it as myth and fables. However, none of these attacks have proven to be true. In fact, just the opposite has occurred through the efforts of Biblical Archaeology. Until two hundred years ago, most people accepted the validity of the Bible, until the age of skepticism arose, to try and undermine the Bible. Around the same time, God opened up the sands of Biblical lands to the science of Archaeology, which has uncovered countless artifacts, that have proven to be true what once was alleged to have been false, concerning factual and historical accounts in the Bible. Never has there ever been an attack on the Bible that has been proven true. Never!

Along with the skepticism of the world against the Bible, there has in recent years come a declension within the Church, as to questioning the absolute truth of the Bible. There has been a so-called accommodation of Biblical principles and precepts, that have lowered the understanding and acceptance of these principles, hopefully to attract people to the Church, and make the Bible more palatable to accept. Much of this change has been in the realm of homosexuality, same sex marriage, abortion, etc. Along with these issues has been an attitude with regard to the Bible, that it is a "living document", that changes with the times. It is alleged that we know more today than the ancients knew, as directed by the Holy Spirit (2 Peter 1:21), so that one is able to rationalize what the Bible teaches in the realm of spirituality, morals, ethics, etc. in order to "accommodate" one's behaviors, etc. to modern day life style, without their conscience bothering them. This is in contradiction to the absolute clear principles of the Bible to us.

In Matthew 28:19, 20, Jesus Christ gave the Church, of which He is the head, its Mission Statement, to go into all the world, and make disciples of Him. For all the following centuries the Church has labored to fulfill Christ's command. If this is His command to us, the question then is, upon what foundation do we carry out this command? There have been many purposes suggested, and short pithy statements have been given, most of which have merit. However, if one looks at the overall concept of the Bible, it may be found in one word, TRUTH. Therefore, the purpose of the mission of the Church of Jesus Christ, must be, "To proclaim the Truth, as revealed by God, in the Bible", for the Church is "The pillar and ground of the truth" (1 Timothy 3:15).

If the mission statement of the Church is to spread the Gospel to all the world, then what is the Gospel? It is the truth, as revealed by God, that is found in the Bible. This truth is what the Church is to proclaim, therefore, its purpose. The most direct indicator of this revelation from God, was stated by Jesus Christ himself, when he said in John 14:6, "I am the way, the truth, and the life, no one comes unto the Father, but through me". This makes Biblical Christianity exclusive, as absolutely stated, and without equivocation or accommodation, as the only true way to eternal life.

In John 17:3, Jesus said, "And this is life eternal, that they might know you, the only true God, and Jesus Christ, whom you have sent". Again, in John 17:17, when speaking of Christians, Jesus said, "Sanctify (i.e. set apart) them through your truth, your word is truth". In John 1:17 it notes that, "Grace and truth came by Jesus Christ". The Bible claims that, "God was made flesh, and He (Jesus) dwelt among us, as the only begotten of the Father, full of grace and truth" (John 1:14). When Jesus was in His ministry, He said, "You shall know the truth, and the truth shall set you free" (John 8:32). Jesus told His disciples that when He returned to Heaven, He would send the Holy Spirit, as His replacement, who would guide them into all truth (John 16:13). The four Gospel accounts repeatedly speak of Jesus Christ, as the only means to eternal life, and that He spoke the absolute truth from God.

In 2 Corinthians 5:19, we read that, "God was in Jesus Christ, reconciling the world unto himself". And, Jesus spoke the truth, so that mankind might know the truth, that would set one free from sin, and give the assured hope of Heaven. This aspect of revealed truth is seen in all the New Testament Epistles. In I Thessalonians 2:13, the Apostle Paul said, "When you received the word of God—you received it not as the word of men, but as it is in truth, the word of God". The Apostle John noted in 2 John 4, that he was rejoicing because he found, "God's children walking in truth". In the two single chapter books of 2nd and 3rd Johns, the word "Truth" is stated twelve times. IN 3rd John 4, the Apostle notes that he has "No greater joy than to hear that my children walk in truth". The truth of which the Apostle speaks, is that the truth of God, as revealed in both Jesus Christ, as well as in God's revealed word to mankind, the Bible. Finally, the Apostle Paul admonishes Christians in 1 Timothy 3:15, to know how to live in the house of God, "Which is the Church (i.e. the body of believing Christians, not the building itself) of the living God, the pillar and ground of the truth".

Mankind, because of his wickedness (Jeremiah 17:9) does not countenance the absolute truth of God. In Romans 1:18, it states that the wrath of God is against all ungodliness of mankind, who, "Suppresses the truth in unrighteousness". In Romans 1:25 God states that the wickedness of mankind has, "Changed the truth of God into a lie". Finally, the Apostle Paul notes that in the last days perilous times will come (2 Timothy 3:1), which is much in evidence today, and Paul further states that at that time, "Mankind will turn away their ears from the truth, and shall be turned aside unto myths". How right the Apostle Paul was, in describing what we see today, not only in the world, but in even some aspects of Christianity.

The mission statement from Christ to the Church, is as much needed today, as ever, and the absolute truth of God, as revealed by Him through Jesus Christ, the Holy Spirit, and the Bible, which is the written word from the living Word, needs to be proclaimed by God's children, to a lost and searching world, both by example as well as by precept. An excellent commendation to Christians is given in Ephesians 5:6, where it says, "For the fruit of the Holy Spirit is in all godliness and righteousness and TRUTH".

Everything that the people of the family God should do, preaching, teaching, evangelism, missionary effort, spiritual growth, etc., should have its foundation in the absolute truth of God's revelation to us, in the Bible.

The Bible stands like a rock undaunted
'Mid the raging storms of time;
Its pages burn with the truth eternal
And they glow with a light sublime.

The Bible stands like a mountain tow'ring
    Far above the works of men;
Its truth by none ever was refuted,
    And destroy it they never can.

The Bible stands and it will forever,
    When the world has passed away;
By inspiration it has been given,
    All its precepts I will obey.

The Bible stands ev'ry test we give it,
    For its Author is divine;
By inspiration it has been given,
    And to prove it and make it mine.

—The Bible Stands
Haldor Lillenas

Chapter 34

A BIBLICAL PHILOSOPHY OF LIFE

A great theologian Dr. B. B. Warfield once said, "Any doctrine in Scripture is established, if only one verse teaches it." II Timothy 1:7 states, "For God has not given us the spirit of fear, but of power, and of love, and of a sound mind." This summarizes God's philosophy to fit mankind's needs. It provides balance in life for all God's children. This Biblical principle is explained and amplified in many places in Scripture, through teaching by the Prophets, and illustrations in the lives of Biblical characters.

I. The Analysis: In order to achieve a balanced view or philosophy of life, God has given us both a mind to think with, and emotions with which to feel and love. The problem is that human beings tend to gravitate to one extreme or the other.

To be overtly *minded* tends toward a cold, analytical, empirical thinking, that may adversely affect those who are more emotional in their makeup. The result is to become acutely logical and critical without much compassion emotionally.

To be overtly *emotional* tends toward acting and reacting with one's feelings and lacking logical thinking, which may result in one vacillating emotionally to *highs* and *lows* in their feelings. This tends to hinder one from thinking rationally in a balanced manner, and constantly keeps the logical thinking person off balance in trying to relate to the emotionally minded person.

God desires His children to be balanced in life, so that He has given us both thinking and feeling for this purpose. The Bible speaks of Jesus Christ as being a *meek and lowly* person. Meekness is not a sense of timidity, but refers to balance in life. Christ was perfectly balanced in His life, with a servanthood attitude. (Matthew 11:29; Mark 10:45) Since Christ is the Christian's model, we should be desirous of emulating Him.

II. The Teaching: II Timothy 1;7 uses four key words that need to be understood in order to grasp the meaning and intent of how we should live.

A. FEAR: There are two words used in Scripture for fear. The one means to have awe or respect for God because of Who He is. (Philippians 2:12) The other word used here refers to being afraid. (Hebrews 13:6) Christians have no cause to fear their heavenly Father. (Hebrews 4:14-16)

B. POWER: God has given the Christian power in order to live CONSTRUCTIVELY. (Matthew 28:18; John 1:12; Ephesians 3:7) This power provides for progressive maturity in life through the Holy Spirit, and His application of the truth of the Bible to our lives.

C. LOVE: Since we are all creatures of emotion, we desire to love and be loved. God, Who is the very essence of love, (I John 4:8-10) desires that we love SACRIFICIALLY. To love in this fashion, is to give of one's self unselfishly for the good of another. This is exemplified in Christ, who gave Himself for us. (John 3:16) Therefore, we ought to love one another. (I John 4:11-21)

D. SOUND MIND: The logical, analytical, empirical thinking that we have, is given by God, in order that we might live REASONABLY. This rational thinking counter balances an irrational world which is contrary to God, and His program for us. (I Corinthians 2:9-14; Colossians 2:8-10)

III. The Application: This balance that we have received from God, provides the Christian with a sense of self-esteem, worth, dignity, and security. It helps to reject fears as well as feelings of inadequacy and inability to act properly. This balance in life is obtained through appropriating God's grace in daily living. It comes through a daily commitment of one's life to the control of the Holy Spirit.

God has promised to supply our needs, (Philippians 4:19) and our resources are the riches of God's grace. (Ephesians 1:7; Romans 11:33) From these assured *bank accounts* the child of God can draw on an inexhaustible supply to meet every need. Our Heavenly Father desires that we trust Him implicitly, (I Peter 5:7; Hebrews 4:16) follow the principles of His word reasonably, (Psalm 119:11) and love one another fervently. (John 13:35; I John 4:18-21)

IV. The Conclusion: This is the formula for a full life (John 10:10) that eliminates fear, and produces a balanced wholeness that brings fulfillment to the child of God.

"Only one life, twill soon be passed;
Only what's done for Christ, will last."

Simply trusting every day,
    Trusting through a stormy way;
Even when my faith is small,
    Trusting Jesus, that is all.

Brightly doth His spirit shine,
    Into this poor heart of mine;
While He leads, I cannot fall,
    Trusting Jesus, that is all.

Singing if my way is clear,
    Praying if the path be drear;
If in danger, on Him call,
    Trusting Jesus, that is all.

Trusting Him while life shall last,
    Trusting Him till earth be past;
Till within the jasper wall,
    Trusting Jesus, that is all.

Trusting as the moments fly,
    Trusting as the days go by;

189

Trusting Him whatever befall,
Trusting Jesus, that is all.

—Victorious Life, Keswick, NJ

Chapter 35

PRINCIPLE VS. PRAGMATISM

Biblical teaching tells us that there are only two personality or character types in the world: one is a God-centered life and the other is a self-centered life. Granted, there are modifications of both types, but essentially there are only these two. Every person has entered the world as a totally self-centered individual, desiring only that which fulfills the self. Any parent who has born children knows the extreme selfishness of a baby. As a child grows and develops, character change comes through learned behavior, at the first through parental guidance, both by precept as well as by parental example, good or bad. As one develops into adulthood, the learned behaviors of childhood, indelibly instilled in that one, from birth to puberty, and which indelibly becomes the primary character of that person, results in being either a self-centered person, or a God-centered individual.

When one becomes a Christian, the Bible notes that the Holy Spirit not only regenerates the believer (Titus 3:5, i.e. spiritual re-birth), and places that one into the family of God (1 Cor. 12:13 through Spirit baptism, not water baptism), but also gives that person both a new nature from God, and also spiritual discernment (1 Cor. 2:14), to learn how to turn from being self-centered to God-centered. The ability to accomplish this as an adult comes form the principles in the Bible, as administered to the person, who opens up both his mind and heart to the Lord (See: John 16:13, 14—the word "glorify" in v.14 means to be re-characterized by the Holy Spirit, into the likeness of Jesus Christ).

Now, as a Christian, in the family of God, through spiritual re-birth, the self-centered nature of the person now has an additional "new nature" within, administered to him by the Holy Spirit. These two natures are diametrically opposed to each other, and in constant conflict. In Romans 7:7-25 and 8:5-10, the Apostle Paul outlines his personal conflict with the two natures in him, and his struggle in life. He also notes the victory his new nature is able to have, through willingly allowing the Holy Spirit to control his life (Note: Rom. 8:6). This transformation in a Christian's life, in turning from being self-centered to God-centered, is a progressive constant daily allowing the Holy Spirit to guide one through studying Scripture and applying it to one's life.

An illustration of the conflict of the two natures within a Christian, is illustrated by two variant philosophies that have beset mankind over the ages, i.e. Principle and Pragmatism. Historically it has its beginnings in ancient desires to have three questions answered as to life itself: where did I come from, why am I here, and where am I going? As mankind has perused the answers to these three questions, generally speaking, the answers have been directed to the self-centeredness of the individual. These questions are still being debated by people today, with no definitive answers. Why? Answer, because of the self-centeredness of every human being, and answers being subjective with every person, to his or her desires for selfish fulfillment. To mankind there are no objective answers, only various definitions depending upon the ego-centeredness of the person.

Is there an objective answer to these questions, outside the realm of human nature, that is absolute, final, and on which can depend and trust? The answer is an unequivocal, yes; it is found in the Bible, which is the manual for living and fullness for life, given to mankind by God who created all things, including the human race. It is a book of divinely inspired principles for living, as well as the answer to the devastation of a self-centered (i.e. ego-centered) life, which no one wants, but is driven by one's selfishness, in contrast to a God-centered life, which produces fullness of life (John 10:10) here and now, as well as beyond this life, into eternity (Titus 3:4-7), by the divine fiat of God, himself.

Principles are fundamental truths upon which our various ideas of life and behaviors are based, as well as the ultimate source of that which is judged to be right and true. The only absolute truths found anywhere in life, are those in God's word, the Bible. These principles not only give answer to the three great questions: 1) We all came from the creative hand of God, 2) We are here to be a reflection of God's righteous character, and to enjoy fellowship with Him, and 3) Someday, when God brings justice and perfect order to this world, the Christians will enjoy the blessings of eternal life with God. On the other hand, Pragmatism is a philosophy, which tests the validity of all concepts by their personal results. In other words, if it works, it's OK. This results from the ego-centeredness of the person, and is subjective (i.e. it's the individual making the decision out of his ego-centeredness, and thereby subject to error).

Biblical principles are ideal, God created, with practical application for all mankind. On the other hand, Pragmatism has its center based on human nature, skewed by sin thereby ego-centered, and subject to error of judgment. Pragmatism is not always wrong. Illustrations: when choosing something which has no moral, ethical, or spiritual component, such as what kind of car to purchase, or the color of the car, a pragmatic choice is fine, but when a moral component is introduced (e.g. stealing, abortion, homosexuality, etc.) and one exercises a pragmatic point of view, then the tendency to selfishness of the individual, is to override the principles of the Bible, and more likely than not, it is wrong to the detriment of the person, and any others whom it may affect. To the person who makes a morally loaded pragmatic choice, it may be alright to him, but detrimentally wrong on principle, as well as to others, and certainly to God's principles.

The only way to properly overcome the selfishness of the human heart and mind, is to have an objective set of absolute principles, totally apart form human intrusion, and those must be Biblical principles (Note: John 17:17 and 8:23). The principles of the Bible, given by God for the benefit of all mankind, are for our ultimate good and fulfillment of life. God guarantees that fullness, when one accepts Biblical principles and lives by those precepts.

It is interesting to note, that all athletic competition is played by a set of objective rules. If each team brought its own rules to the game, it could not be played. The referees make a judgment call, not on what they think, but on what the rule book says. Nor can people interact with each other in society on a moral, ethical, or spiritual frame of reference, without accepting and following a Biblical set of principles. Our country and Constitution was formed on biblical principles, because our founding Fathers, though not all were Christians, nevertheless recognized the truthfulness of Biblical principles, and used them as a foundation, upon which to construct our society as a nation. As a testimony to the validity and worth of them, our Constitution has stood us well over two hundred years, and has been a model for other countries.

It is interesting to note, that our Constitution has come under fire in the past number of years, as Pragmatists have proclaimed it as a "Living Document", that necessarily changes with passing generations. This is set over against those who believe the Constitution is a "strict constructionist" document, that in itself, sets the standard for all time. If it changes with each generation, then we have lost the "game of life" in our country. For not only given is the liberalization of our country, which is going on, it also means that the subjectivism of mankind will rule the day, and Pragmatism will out. It would be comparable to playing an athletic event, by changing the rules of the game being played, depending upon how one side or the other could control the situation. Again, if there is no moral, ethical, or spiritual consideration, and that choice does not impinge upon another person's personhood, then a pragmatic choice may be made.

To illustrate the differences and conflict between the two philosophies, allow me to recount an incidence where a member of the President's cabinet was being questioned by a Senate Committee for confirmation to the position. In response to a question, the person stated that the new Cabinet would make decisions based on a pragmatic understanding, over against the previous administration's idealism. When it comes to administrative choices that have a moral, ethical, or spiritual component, will that help or hinder our country's well being and the people's good?

As Christians, we are seriously desirous of everyone's civil rights as citizens, but when civil rights are meant to include so called rights, that are morally wrong on Biblical principles (e.g. same sex marriages, etc.) then as Christians we have to refer to what the Apostles stated, when the Roman magistrates in their day, ordered them to conform to the law of the land, "We ought to obey God rather than man" (Acts 4:19, 20 and 5:29). As citizens and as Christians we are to obey those who have the rule over us (Romans 13:1, 2; 1 Peter 2:13-15), as well as honoring the personhood and civil rights of every human being, regardless of whether they follow principle or pragmatism. But, when man's law transgresses God's law (i.e. Biblical principles) then the Christian is obliged to follow God's word, as a higher law than that of man.

It is not easy for Christians to live in today's secular world, but one is able to have hope, in that the principles of the Bible state, "He that is in you (i.e. the Holy Spirit), is greater than he that is in the world" (1 John 4:4). So, when the issues of life overwhelm one, as a child of God, remember what is said for our help in Hebrews 4:16 and Philippians 4:5-7. "If God be for us, who can be against us" (Romans 8:31). Doing what is spiritually right, on Biblical principles, is always the correct response and choice.

How firm a foundation, ye saints of the Lord,
Is laid for your faith in His excellent Word!
What more can He say than to you He hath said,
To you who for refuge to Jesus have fled?

"Fear not! I am with thee; O be not dismayed,
For I am thy God and will still give thee aid.
I'll strengthen thee, help thee, and cause thee to stand,
Upheld by My righteous, omnipotent hand."

—How Firm a Foundation
The Living Church

Chapter 36

THE BIBLE AND PSYCHOLOGY

Modern day cognitive is to know or perceive, psychology says, the important motivating aspects of life are what a person thinks, and how one feels. The Bible says, "As a person thinks in his heart, so is he." (Proverbs 23:7) In other words, what one thinks about characterizes him. If one's emphasis is on his feelings, he is characterized by selfishness (Proverbs 3:5,6) and self-centeredness.

Psychology includes the following assumptions regarding mankind:

1) that people are both rational and irrational,
2) that people are as likely to believe a lie as well as the truth,
3) that people are predisposed to be creative in their thinking, as well as irrational and destructive in behavior,
4) that people's thinking is affected by external impressions both rational and irrational, (Media programs appeal to both right and wrong.)
5) that people tend to think, then act, and
6) that behavioral problems can stem from unsubstantiated acts. These assumptions color the way psychology impacts individuals, and counseling procedures.

When we turn to the Bible to see what its principles are relative to mankind's basic character and behaviors, we come to a more penetrating foundation from the God who created all mankind, and who knows absolutely and best as to our makeup. Therefore, since

He is the creator of our minds and how we think, it is imperative that we consider God's "handbook" of life the Bible, to evaluate how one should both think and feel. When one studies the principles of the Bible, which are always an accurate barometer of mankind's thinking as well as a true guide to life, it is easy to understand why the Bible places so much emphasis on the "renewing of your mind." (Romans 12:2)

It is not necessarily activating events that produce rational or irrational behavior, for there is an intervening belief about the event that comes in between.

A ————————→ B ————————→ C
(Event)   (Belief about the event)   (Behavior
or emotions)

The person's "belief" is in control, not the "event" itself; therefore, it isn't the circumstances, but one's belief about the event that produces the behavior or emotion. What one believes, which is typical of one's character, is the dominating factor as to behavior or emotions.

The Christian is commended to have the mind of Christ. (Philippians 2:5) We are instructed to be of the same mind in love toward others. (Romans 12:16) When one's mind is guided by Biblical principles, then any event in life will be processed through a Biblically principled mind. This will then produce the behaviors and emotions that God desires, and brings us to maturity in Christ.

God's salvation includes a new nature, (II Corinthians 5:17) as well as spiritual discernment to understand Biblical principles, (John 16:13; I Corinthians 2:14; Colossians 2:8-10) so that as one goes through life he may experience the wholeness and fullness of cognitive and emotional health.

It is the responsibility of parents, pastors, teachers, and counselors, to educate people on Biblical truth and submission to the control of the Holy Spirit. It is He Who directs the child of God into all truth. (John 16:13) It is the means that God uses to change one's character. In this way individuals will arrive at balance and wholeness for productive living.

O Jesus, I have promised, to serve thee to the end;
    Be thou forever with me, my master and my friend;
I shall not fear the battle, if thou art by my side,
    Nor wander from the pathway, if thou wilt be my guide.

O let me feel me near thee, the world is ever near;
    I see the sights that dazzle the tempting sounds I hear
My foes are ever near me, around me and within;
    But, Jesus draw me nearer, and shield my soul from sin.

O Jesus, thou hast promised, to all who follow thee,
    That where thou art in glory there shall thy servant be
And, Jesus I have promised, to serve thee to the end;
    O give me grace to follow, my master and my friend.

—Hymns for the Family,
Paragon Assoc., Inc.,
Nashville, TN

Chapter 37

BALANCING CHRISTIANITY AND PSYCHOLOGY

There is a growing emphasis today upon combining modern day psychology with Biblical truth This is to the dismay of some, others have great interest in integrating the two. Some believe that trying to integrate the two philosophies or worldviews of life, is to the detriment of Biblical principles. Others feel that though psychology is a humanistic philosophy, Christians can gain a degree of understanding that is able to help them better handle the problems of life.

Though humanistic psychology has its flaws, to eliminate it altogether, is like throwing the baby out with the bathwater. One of the problems with human nature is to turn to one extreme to avoid another. Balance in life is both Biblical and desirable, in order to enjoy the fullness of life.

In order for one to both understand Scripture, as well as the emotional aspect of life, and how Biblical principles can be applied to daily living, it is imperative to be guided by some basic assumptions.

A high view of Scripture does not require that all knowledge must come from the Bible. God has given to all mankind a natural revelation of Himself. (Romans 1:19,20) His perfect revelation to mankind is imperfectly perceived because of sin, yet he does understand some of God's revelation. Even unregenerate people are able to learn God's truth through observing nature. (Psalm 19) It is important for us to communicate the gospel in love to those who do not know God.

Psychological elements of mankind are learned through empirical research and are valid truths, though not stated as such in Scripture. It is not the knowledge gained in itself that causes the problem, but the human philosophy of life in the mind of the individual, in applying that knowledge to life's situations that becomes the problem.

In order to achieve a high degree of Godly understanding, it is imperative to understand Biblical principles. The Bible urges the Christian to have a willing mind for the principles of God's Word, in order to grow in maturity. (Romans 12:1,2; II Corinthians 8:12; I Peter 2:2; II Peter 3:18)

When psychological research, relative to the mental and emotional elements of mankind is explored and applied, it can be checked against the principles of God's Word. If not contrary to them, it may be legitimately utilized. Some maintain that all we need for Godly living is found in the truth of the Bible, and that is so. However, even Christians often "see through a glass darkly." We need not disdain the knowledge that God has allowed mankind to learn. However, it must coincide with God's truth, which supersedes all our understanding.

In God's view, sin is still sin, not a personality problem or an addiction that can be rationalized. One may have a personality problem, which in itself is not sinful, but could cause one to fall into sin, or make one more vulnerable to sinning. Christ told us that out of the heart of mankind comes all forms of sin. (Matthew 15:19) Humanistic psychology often attributes sin to other causes, and rationalizes away the responsibility one has for his own behaviors.

All assertions of unregenerate psychologists are not necessarily untruth. Psychology is an area of valid inquiry where one may learn from the research and insights of non-Christians. Much scientific knowledge that Christians use daily, comes from non-Christian understanding and exploration.

Some argue that scientific research that has produced the physical advantages of labor saving devices which we all use, is one thing—and acceptable. However, when unregenerate and humanistic individuals delve into the mental and emotional aspects of mankind, the application of their reasoning is suspect and must be contrary to the Biblical principles for living. That is why the principles of the

Bible must be clearly understood so we can discern and appreciate the help that psychology is able to provide.

Colossians 2:9 states that, "In Him dwells all the fullness of the Godhead bodily." In numerous ways a psychologist is able to help a Christian become more consciously aware of his needs, and better able to understand himself, and thus more intelligently find his needs supplied in Christ.

Finally, mental and emotional healing can come from psychotherapy, though this is not equivalent to Salvation. Becoming a regenerate person, cares for one's penalty for sin, through the blood of Jesus Christ. Spiritual maturity comes through the work of the Holy Spirit applying the truth of God's Word to life. A Christian psychotherapist can provide both help in the emotional and mental areas of the Christian life, as well as applying the principles of the Bible to those needs.

The Bible states that we are composed of spirit, soul, and body. (I Thessalonians 5:23) The spirit is the life we have in Christ, the soul is our will, emotions, and mind, and our body is the flesh. All three elements interact positively or negatively with each other. To impact one element of our self, is to touch the other two. Therefore, we need to address all three elements simultaneously, in order to come to wholeness of life. Biblical psychotherapy is able to meet the needs of both the spirit and the soul, and medical help is able to meet the needs of the body.

When Christians accept psychology as a valuable tool of human behavior and understanding, one moves into a very delicate area of life. The human personality is complex beyond the total understanding of the most competent theologian or psychologist. The Bible states that we are, "fearfully and wonderfully made." (Psalm 139:14) The Bible provides final truth, as stated in its principles, which may or may not be understood by the Christian, for we are less than perfectly mature.

Thus, when psychology provides insight into human nature and its workings, it behooves the Christian to evaluate that understanding in light of Biblical principles, and not arbitrarily dismiss it. To accept the Bible and reject psychology is just as extreme as to accept psychology and reject the Bible. Balance is needed, and spiritual discernment as to that balance is essential. (I Corinthians 2:9-14 Colossians 2:8-10)

Amid life's busy hurrying throng,
    The gay, the sad, the weak, the strong,
While I am traveling along,
    I want my life to tell for Jesus.

I want to be a beacon light,
    To cheer wayfarers in the night,
And, help them on their way aright,
    I want my life to tell for Jesus.

I want my life with Jesus hid,
    That I may do as He shall bid,
I want to love as Jesus did,
    I want my life to tell for Jesus.

To wealth and fame I would not climb,
    But, I would know God's peace sublime,
And everywhere and all the time,
    I want my life to tell for Jesus.

I want my life to tell for Jesus,
    I want my life to tell for Him;
That everywhere I go, men may His goodness know,
    I want my life to tell for Jesus.

—Hymns for the Family,
Paragon Assoc., Inc.,
Nashville, TN

Chapter 38

THREE HAUNTING FEARS

In a recent nationwide poll it was determined there are three areas of life that haunt people: death, guilt, and lack of purpose in life. These consuming problems are in marked contrast to what God states in Psalm 8:4-6. Mankind was created to reflect the moral character of God, for eternal fellowship with Him, and to enjoy the fullness of life of being custodians over all God's creation. The deception of sin has turned mankind from being God-centered to being self-centered and has caused these threefold fears.

Let us consider the contrast between God's purpose for His creation, and mankind's philosophy of life. Then we shall evaluate a resolution to this conflict, as to how it can be overcome, and the ability to bring one's life into conformity with God's will, so that fullness of life becomes a reality. In John 10:10, Christ noted, "I am come that you might have life, and that you might have it more abundantly." God desires all His children to enjoy life to the full, without these haunting fears plaguing the Christian through life.

In Isaiah 55:8, God says, "For my thoughts are not your thoughts, neither are your ways my ways." The Bible notes that the philosophy of the unregenerate one is after "the tradition of men, after the elements of the world, and not after Christ." (Colossians 2:8) In other words, one's worldview, one's opinion of what constitutes living, is basically self-centered, not God-centered. Therefore, one's philosophy of life is governed and patterned after what the majority think, or what is the trend at the time, not that which the Bible teaches.

This basic philosophy is what produces the fear and guilt, and in reality does not provide for real purpose in life. The reason this is true is that mankind was created to reflect the moral qualities of the creator. When one turns from that, the only alternative is the self. Since one does not have creative life within himself, which comes only from God, one no longer has the resources to deal with the issues of life itself. The end result brings fear of the future and the unknown, as well as purposelessness in life.

Biblical truth for living is quite the opposite. Christ said, "I am the way, the truth, and the life." (John 14:6) The worldly philosophy of life does not satisfy in the long run, but God's way brings life and peace. (Romans 8:6)

God's antidote to these three areas that haunt people, is found in the Bible. The resurrection of Christ, who conquered death, has brought eternal immortality to every Christian. (I Corinthians 15:54-57; II Timothy 1:10; I Peter 1:23) The *sting* of everlasting death, and fear of the future have been removed. Though the child of God may suffer physical death, one need not fear eternal death, because of trusting in Christ's work on their behalf.

For every Christian the guilt of sin can be removed through confession to God. (I John 1:9; Psalm 32) No one needs to have guilt hanging over him, and, once confessed, there is not only forgiveness, but also cleansing. God *wipes the slate clean*, never remembering it again. (Hebrews 10:17)

One of the most persistent designs of Satan against the Christian is to *bug* one with past sins that have been confessed, and God has forgotten. In Philippians 3:13,14 the Apostle Paul stated that he had forgotten those things which were behind, and that he was pressing forward to the mark for the prize of the high calling of God in Christ Jesus. As he went about ministering to the saints, as God's Apostle to them, one can easily believe he could have been overwhelmed with remorse at what he had done to the Christians in the past.

At one time Paul, whose original name was Saul, was an employee of the Roman government putting Christians into prison. After the Lord regenerated him on the Damascus road, (Acts 9) and now as the Apostle Paul, he probably was preaching to some whom he had previously put into prison. It can be easily imagined that he would have a great deal of guilt at what he had once done, as he saw the marks of imprisonment in their faces. Yet with confidence he was able to proclaim God's message to those Philippian Christians. He fully trusted what God had declared in His Word, that Paul's sins were forgiven and forgotten.

There are times in every Christian's life, when past failures and sins are brought up by Satan, to lay a guilt trip on the person. So that one has to tell Satan to *bug off.* For no child of God owes Satan anything, but owes God everything. When God forgives and forgets the confessed sins of His child, it brings peace to the believer, who accepts what a loving heavenly Father has done because, "the blood of Jesus Christ His son, has cleansed us from all sin." (I John 1:7)

In today's world of stress and strain there is no reason to multiply the problems that face us by adding to them the guilt of confessed sins of the past which God has forgotten. If we but follow His guidelines for life, by trusting Him, and relying upon His Word, the Bible, we can be freed from these three haunting fears.

Christ gave us the assuring promise in John 14:27, "Peace I leave with you, my peace I give unto you; not as the world gives, give I unto you. Let not your heart be troubled, neither let it be afraid." Eternal death for the Christian has been conquered, guilt through confessed sin has been wiped out, and God desires us to have purpose of life and fullness through Him. What more can the Christian ask?

When we walk with the Lord, in the light of His Word
    What a glory He sheds on our way.
While we do His good will, He abides with us still,
    And with all who will trust and obey.

Not a shadow can rise, not a cloud in the skies,
    But His smile quickly drives it away.
Not a doubt nor a fear, not a sigh nor a tear,
    Can abide while we trust and obey.

Trust and obey, for there's no other way,
    To be happy in Jesus, but to trust and obey.

—Victorious Life, Keswick, NJ

Chapter 39

SIX EMOTIONAL CAUSES FOR DISEASE

I Thess. 5:23 states that humans are composed of three elements of life: spirit, soul, and body. Our spirit is the life we have from God, our soul is our emotions and will, and our body is the flesh. It is well known that all three elements through transference, either positively or negatively, reinforce each other.

When one element is affected, it affects the other two to some degree, for the majority of organic diseases have a psycho/somatic origin. There are six basic causes for these problems, and there are means that the Christian can employ to offset them, in order to achieve wholeness in life, which is what God would have us to enjoy. In John 10:10 Christ said, "...I am come that you might have life, and that you might have it more abundantly." God desires that every child of His have a full life.

I. FEAR This can be a healthy element; fear of fire, when out of control, fear of unknown, future, death, etc. becomes a problem. God's antidote to uncontrolled fear is His love in and through us. In I John 4:18 it notes that "There is no fear in love; but mature love casts out fear."

Again in II Tim. 1:7, it tells us that "God has not given us the spirit of fear, but of power, and of love, and of a sound mind." Therefore, the Christian has no reason to fear the future or death. In Heb. 13:5,6 we read, "...For He has said, I will never leave you nor forsake you, so that we may boldly say, the Lord is my helper, I will not be afraid.

What can man do to me?" We are commended to, "…approach the throne of grace with confidence, so that we may receive mercy and find grace to help us in our time of need." With these assurances, the Christian is able to overcome fear, by God's power and grace.

II. <u>ANGER/HATRED</u> A healthy and controlled temper. God has given us a temper to energize us productively and is quite normal. But uncontrolled, it is destructive and results in anger. Uncontrolled anger and hatred should not be characteristic of one who is controlled by the Holy Spirit. Only as one submits the self to the Spirit's control is there victory over anger and hatred.

In II Cor. 5:14 we see that it is, "The love of Christ that constrains us," and helps the Christian to handle his temper. It is normal to have a temper which spurs one on constructively, but temper uncontrolled is anger, which is destructive, and may produce hatred as well.

Anger against another is sin. The angry person really hurts himself, for anger burns within and consumes the individual, so that he is unable to think or act properly. God's remedy for this is found in I John 1:9. "If we confess our sins, He is faithful and just to forgive us our sins, and to cleanse us from all unrighteousness." In II Cor. 5:14 we see that it is, "The love of Christ that constrains us" and helps the Christian to handle his temper. In I John 4:16-21 we see again that the love of God within us helps us control our temper. It allows us to project ourself in love to others, rather than in anger. The result is a lessening of tension, stress, and strife, with God's replacement of love toward each other.

Some years ago, a mother brought her teenage daughter to me for counseling. They did not agree with each other and were constantly at odds. The daughter expressed much anger against her mother. When the school year ended, the mother she took her daughter to a mental institution, where she spent the summer. At the end of summer, she came back to counseling with me. I asked the girl about what went on at the institution. She told me they had a large room with pillows and empty garbage cans. When she was angry with her mother, she was to pound the pillows and kick the garbage cans. When her Mother visited, she was, then, to tell her off. I asked her if it had helped, and was their relationship better? She replied that it wasn't. I asked her if I could offer another alternative, to which she answered that I could.

210

I turned to I John 4:7:21 and showed her of the love of the Lord. I explained how if we allow Him to fill our lives, His love rather than anger could flow through us to others. This was new to her. In succeeding sessions, as a Christian mother and daughter allowed the love of the Lord to permeate their lives, it brought healing to their relationship.

III. <u>DEPRESSION</u> In today's world we see much depression, because of the many burdens people are carrying. The transforming power and help of the Holy Spirit in the life of the Christian can overcome this problem. A healthy outlook in life through spiritual exercises, Bible study, prayer, worship, and praising the Lord, as well as proper food, rest, and physical exercise, all are contributing factors to alleviate depression. Chronic depression, which lasts for a period of time, may require professional help and possibly medication for a time. Psalm 139:14 tells us that we are, "fearfully and wonderfully made," a delicately balanced instrument of God's creation. When one gets out of balance, depression can set in.

The transforming power and help of the Holy Spirit in the life of the Christian can overcome this problem. A healthy outlook in life through spiritual exercises like Bible study, prayer, worship, praising the Lord, as well as proper food, rest, physical exercise, all are contributing factors to alleviate depression. Isaiah 61:3 speaks of, "The garment of praise for the spirit of heaviness." Singing melody in our heart, with praise to God, is spiritual medication that can do much. The great hymns of the faith have contributed a great deal to elevating spirits.

Psalm 42:11 provides a therapy that does much to help depression, "Why are you depressed, O my soul? And why are you upset? Hope in God: for I shall yet praise Him, who is the health of my countenance and my God."

One of the best ways to overcome depression is to help someone else. (II Cor. 1:3,4) "Blessed be God—the God of all comfort; who comforts us in all our troubles, so that we can comfort those in any trouble with the comfort we ourselves have received from God."

The Christian ought to be the most optimistic person in the world, because he has the most going for him. (Rom. 8:31) "If God be for us, who can be against us?" The resources the Christian has are found in trusting the Lord, "I can do all things through Christ, who strengthens me." (Phil. 4:13) As humans we are all prone to sadness periodically, but we need not despair; the Lord is our helper, why should we fear?

IV. <u>SELF-CENTEREDNESS (Narcissism)</u> This kind of stress is unbelievable, since it is directed inward and builds up, which creates an ever increasing constriction within the person. The primary sin in the Garden of Eden was Satan's deception of mankind, to get Adam and Eve to turn from being God-centered to being self-centered. This sin not only caused a separation between God and mankind but has been passed down to each of us in a sinful, self-centered, nature.

The result of this turning inward has produced all the problems inherent within mankind. All the wars, oppression, bloodshed, greed and power, stem from the sin of self-centeredness.

God's answer to ego-centeredness is to focus on the Lord Jesus Christ, not only as Savior, but also as Lord and master of one's life. God has given us an empty place in our lives that only He can fill and satisfy. And God desires to do this. But, only as we surrender our lives to the Holy Spirit's control, is He able to bring balance and fulfillment to us.

The Apostle John stated in John 3:30, "He must increase, but I must decrease." Our submission to His control, provides the proper balance in life. This is why Rom. 12:3 states, "...that everyone should not think of himself more highly than he ought to think, but to think in a balanced way, according as God has given to each one a measure of ability." Submission to the Holy Spirit's control brings a healthy balanced ego, with security and fullness of life.

V. <u>LONELINESS</u> It is a well known fact of life that the death rate of lonely people is two to ten times higher and faster from this than from other factors. God created us as social beings, and we enjoy the fruits of fellowship with one another. This, enjoyed with others in Christ, element provides the fullness of life we so much desire.

In the Garden of Eden, God and Adam had sweet fellowship. So, the qualities of God in mankind extend to a continuing desire for friendship with one another. Christian fellowship is both necessary and beneficial; God ordained it. Therefore we have a responsibility to extend ourselves to lonely needy people.

Five times in Scripture the word "Paraclete" is used. It means, "called alongside to help." It is primarily used regarding the Holy Spirit. (John 14:16,26;15:26;16:7; I John 2:1) When Christ told His disciples He was returning to heaven, He promised that He would send the Holy Spirit to, "come alongside of them to help." This is part of the Spirit's responsibility to the Christian. Now, in turn, the Christian is to be a paraclete to fellow Christians, as well as to others in the world. In Gal. 6:2,10, we are admonished to "bear one anothers burdens, and so fulfill the law of God." As we do this, we help overcome the loneliness that some people experience.

VI. <u>STRESS FACTORS FROM OTHER PEOPLE</u> As human beings we are very sensitive to other people, and adversity in relationships causes stress. This can be very debilitating to people already weighed down with burdens.

In Rom. 12:9-21 we are commanded to live peaceably with all, and never allow our differences of opinions to adversely affect our love for one another. In Rom. 12:16 it says we are to be, "of the same mind toward one another." This does not mean that we are to think alike, for God created us all differently. It means we are to love each other, although we think differently. In I John 4:7-21, the Apostle enlightens us as to how to accept others in love as Christ loved us. We should exercise this love, so that we reduce, not create, stress with other people. In this way we are fulfilling the law of God, in ministering grace to others.

In conclusion there are four means by which we are able to overcome these emotional problems: 1) Recognize the healing process available to each Christian by simply trusting the Lord. 2) Teach, as well as learn from others the healing process for our emotions as seen in God's Word. (Eph. 4:23; Phil. 4:6-8) 3) Recognize the sacramental process of healing as seen in James 5:13-16. 4) Learn to care for others by listening to them. (II Cor. 1:3,4 and Heb. 10:24) 5) Integrate the time and space world in which we live with the spiritual world. Ask for His help through the wisdom and discernment of the Holy Spirit. This helps to come to totality and wholeness in life. (Eph. 6:10-18)

Under His wings, what a refuge in sorrow,
How the heart yearningly turns to His rest.
Often, when earth has no balm for my healing,
There I find comfort, and there I am blest.

Under His wings, who from His love can sever?
Under His wings my soul shall abide,
Safely abide forever.

—Victorious Life, Keswick, NJ

Chapter 40

LIFE'S THREE PROBLEMS

Of the many and varied problems that people face, there are three that are foundational to life: 1) The feeling of depression; 2) Worthlessness and low self esteem; and 3) A sense of hopelessness. Much of professional counseling today is consumed in alleviating these needs.

It is interesting to note that most all, if not all of the problems that people face have their answers somewhere in the Bible, woven into the fabric of human relationships, as recounted in God's dealings with mankind. (I Corinthians 10:11) Therefore, it is imperative that one consider what God's Word has to say relative to meeting these concerns.

I. <u>Alleviating Depression:</u> Every person has moments of sadness and so called depression, but when a person has a chronic problem, involutional melancholia, it is time to seek professional help. A Christian counselor knows that in the pathology of depression, the truth of the Bible plays a great part in alleviating the distress. This is not to discount the part proper medication may play in helping the problem, but medication is only a means of immediate help, so that the problems that caused the depression can be worked on, for permanent relief.

The principles of the Bible, when seriously considered and acted upon, provide constant strength in overcoming. (See particularly Isaiah 61:3; Psalm 42:11; and II Corinthians 1:3,4.) Along with God's promises the singing of the great hymns of the faith bring uplifting help to the one who is downcast. Many hymns were written out of the crucible of trials and tribulations, by people who have experienced what sadness and depression brings, yet have triumphed, and written marvelous hymns to that effect. God has used these hymns to strengthen and bless His children, who have been going through similar circumstances.

Then too, prayer is, as the Bible describes, the soul's sincere desire, and to be able to cast one's care on the Lord is most important. (I Peter 5:7; Hebrews 4:16; Psalm 55:22) Worship and fellowship with other Christians is most energizing in helping one to overcome a downcast spirit. (Psalm 27:1-3)

All of the above elements must begin with a sincere acceptance in the mind, that what the Bible says, must be taken at face value, believed, and acted upon, constantly. Then, and only then, can one expect these truths to control the person emotionally. All this must be accepted in the mind, before it filters down to the emotions.

II. Coming to worth and self esteem: Though as humans we are created in the image of God, with a potential to mirror God's moral qualities we often suffer from a sense of worthlessness and low self esteem. Unfortunately, in today's world, undue emphasis is placed on self worth and esteem, in order to bolster the ego-centeredness of the individual. Going from one extreme, low self esteem, to the other extreme, pride, is wrong. It certainly is not the balance that the Bible desires for a person.

Though the Bible warns against pride of self, (Romans 12:3) it also teaches the eternal worth of every individual, and God's desire that Christians have a balanced new life in Christ. When God created Adam and Eve in their sinless estate, they reflected the fullness of God's moral qualities, which gave them self worth and esteem. They recognized this as coming from and dependent upon God.

When they fell into sin, and turned from being God centered to becoming self-centered, their worth and esteem had to come from within themselves, and then they began to have problems. This is why God promised the coming of Jesus Christ, to restore mankind to his original state. When one accepts what God has done for him through His love, the self worth and esteem has its source in God's love and grace. The proper Biblical view of mankind's worth and God's esteem of His creation is found in Ephesians 2:4-7; Titus 3:4-7; John 10:10, 12:26, 13:34, and 14:27.

One's self esteem and worth does not come through ego-centeredness, else it is distorted by selfishness, but through an acceptance of what one is and has through being "In Christ," and the dependency upon Him for worth and acceptance.

III. A life of hope: Hope in life ahead is one of the most motivating factors in one's existence. Whereas hopelessness is the most devastating. The Bible teaches that the only real hope is that which is beyond the grave, eternally. That which we find only in Jesus Christ. (Lamentations 3:21,24,26; Romans 5:2-5, 15:4,13; Colossians 1:5,23,27; Titus 2:13; Hebrews 6:11,18,19; Philippians 1:6)

In the midst of moral and spiritual declension, and the blackness of wickedness in the world, the Christian can rest in the hope of the sovereignty of God. In spite of what we as humans see today, God's program is on track. Our response should not be one of despair, but of trust in Him, and for us to carry on with the responsibilities entrusted to us, resting in His control.

Resignation of despair to the hope we have in God brings true joy in life. The following passages give us cause for hope, that is beyond anything the world can offer: Philippians 1:6; I John 3:2; Romans 12:12; I Peter 1:3; John 14:19. It is comforting and strengthening to realize that God has ordained all things to, "Daily give us all the benefits of life." (Psalm 68:19)

My hope is in the Lord, who gave Himself for me.
    And paid the price of all my sins at Calvary.
For me He died, for me He lives,
    And everlasting light and life He freely gives.

No merit of my own, His anger to suppress,
    My only hope is found in Jesus' righteousness.
For me He died, for me He lives,
    And everlasting light and life He freely gives.

217

And now for me He stands, before the Father's throne,
  He shows His wounded hands, and names me as His own.
For me He died, for me He lives,
  And everlasting light and life He freely gives.

His grace has planned it all, 'tis mine but to believe,
  And recognize His work of love, and Christ receive
For me He died, for me He lives,
  And everlasting light and life He freely gives.

—Victorious Life, Keswick, NJ

Chapter 41

FOUNDATION FOR MARRIAGE

The primary complaint in most marriages is that there is a lack of communication resulting in discord and misunderstanding. Though this is a problem, to be sure, it is the result of the problem, not the root cause. In order to construct a foundation for marriage, based on God given principles, one must first look at the basic problem.

I. The Causes of Marital Discord: The first cause is SELFISHNESS. Since selfishness began with Adam and Eve, and was passed along to all mankind, this problem constantly intrudes into marriage, which leads to division not union. The ego-centeredness in all of us brings problems in every aspect of life.

Second, there is the problem regarding COMMITMENT. The original commitment made in the marriage vows, needs to be reinforced daily on the part of both husband and wife. The selfish tendency in each of us to go our own way, can only be overcome through exercising daily and continuing commitment.

Another problem is that of PRIORITIES. Generally we tend to place our work first, then our family, and finally our responsibility to God. For the Christian these priorities need to be reversed. When God is placed first in our life, the family second, and our work last, then our personal life will be more fulfilling, and God will honor our priorities. (Joshua 1:8; Psalm 1:2; Romans 8:6) Most ministers and Christian workers seek to have their priorities right, but have a tendency to fuse one and three together, so that their wives and families get left out, which is tragic both to them, as well as a poor testimony to their congregation.

Finally, the fourth problem is a lack of TRUST between husband and wife. Trust is the foundation and jewel of marriage. (Proverbs 31:11) Trust is built through the WILL of Agape love. (I Corinthians 13) This type of love is not of the emotional variety, but of a willingness to project one's self to their partner unselfishly, through honesty, truthfulness, integrity, understanding, openness, and encouragement. The combination of the willingness on the part of each, produces a trust that nurtures emotional love and fulfillment that is so satisfying.

Selfishness is a hindrance to building trust, whereas trust can only be nurtured by not only trusting the other, but by being trustworthy of the trust they have received. This takes a commitment of the WILL.

II. Building a Fulfilling, Fruitful, Relationship: There are three basic principles or guidelines to follow in order to have this kind of a marriage relationship.

Since most marriages suffer from a daily, almost imperceptible erosion, there needs to be a RE-COMMITMENT to each other. This means a renewal of trust in each other. It may not be easy, because of the past abuses of trust. But one must first trust the Lord, then their mate. It is also necessary for each to trust the Lord to help them be trustworthy, since each has squandered the original trust that was given to them.

Moreover, it requires a cutting off of past *garbage*, and not *dumping* it on each other every day. Instead each must be committed to work at being trustworthy of the new reservoir of trust they have received. Included must be a willingness to forgive and be forgiven, since a change of habits does not come easy. When one slips back into the old habits, there must be confession and forgiveness, without a casting up of the past such as, "there you go again, I knew it was too good to be true." Rather, reflect upon the time and place where the re-commitment took place, and a trusting in the genuineness of the willingness of the commitment that was made.

Each has a personal responsibility to make the necessary changes, and at the same time, be accepting of the other, realizing the imperfections each has. This takes time to change, as well as trusting and becoming trustworthy.

The next step is to develop the WILL of Agape love. As was noted above, this is the love of will, not emotion. It is a selfless love, willing to give, rather than take. Selfless love, bonds; selfish love divides. Agape love accepts each other, *warts and all*. It produces a reservoir of trust, through daily, positive reinforcement of each other, refraining from criticism and casting up, and never takes one's partner for granted.

The final step is to work on the four "C's" of marriage: 1) A daily COMMITMENT to the one you love; 2) Developing open COMMUNICATION, by accepting each other's thoughts. The ultimate goal of every marriage should be an "emotional nakedness" between husband and wife, without fear of being "attacked." This does not mean they have to think alike. This is far harder than physical nakedness in the bedroom, but far more important. 3) Provide for loving CONFRONTATION. It is not, do you confront, but how? In Proverbs 15:1 it says, "A soft answer turns away anger." 4) Have a willingness to COMPROMISE. Compromising helps us to overcome our bent toward selfishness.

III. Conclusion and Commendation: God has entrusted the leadership of the family to the husband, and therefore it is his responsibility to *set the pace* by example, rather than by precept. (Ephesians 5:25; I Peter 3:7)

When a husband sets a loving pace by example, and treats his wife like a *queen*, then she will have no problem willingly submitting to her husband. She does not want a driver, a bully, or a dictator, but a loving, accepting mate.

Since parents are developing learned behaviors in their children, which they will carry over into adulthood and transfer over to the one whom they marry, it behooves parents to set a proper example before their children. Dr. Shedd, a Christian psychologist, once asked a five year old boy if his daddy loved his mother. The boy proudly answered that he did. Then Dr. Shedd asked him how he knew that? The little fellow said, "When my Daddy comes home at night, and Mommy is in the kitchen getting supper, Daddy comes in and pats Mommy on the fanny; boy does my Daddy love my Mommy." That Father probably never realized that his behaviors made such an indelible impression on his son. And this carries over into most all examples parents display before their impressionable youngsters.

Finally, daily pray that you may be sensitive to meeting your beloved one's needs. There is nothing greater to bind and bond a husband and wife together than a spiritual sensitivity that each has for the other. This produces the Lord's blessing on the relationship that is fulfilling.

Have thine own way, Lord, have thine own way;
　　Thou art the potter, I am the clay;
Mold me and make me, after thy will,
　　While I am waiting, yielded and still.

Have thine own way, Lord, have thine own way,
　　Hold o'er my being, absolute sway.
Filled with thy Spirit, till all shall see,
　　Christ only always, living in me.

—Victorious Life, Keswick, NJ

Chapter 42

DIVORCE AND REMARRIAGE

With the ever-increasing divorce rate in our country, and the percentage of divorces among Christians almost equal to that of the rest of the nation, it is important to consider what God's word says about divorce and re-marriage. Unfortunately there has been a great deal of misunderstanding on the subjects, as well as misconstruction of the Biblical passages that deal with them. We shall look at the Biblical principles in both the Old Testament as well as the New, consider the original language employed, and deal with the texts and contexts from a theological consideration, in relation to basic Biblical truths.

When God created the man, (Adam) he noted that it was not good for him to be alone, so he created a helpmate (Eve). (Genesis 2:18) Later he instructed the man to leave his father and mother and cleave or be glued together to his wife. (Genesis 2:24) God said that what he had joined together in marriage, "Let not man put asunder." (Matthew 19:6) God's design for the marriage of a man and a woman was to be for life until death not divorce separated them. This was God's perfect plan.

However, once sin entered the human race, with all its problems and issues that were basically contrary to God's spiritual plan, divorce, polygamy, and adultery, all became part of human behaviors. Therefore, God's perfect plan for relationship in marriage and the propagation of the human race, was distorted by the reality of what mankind distorted.

God gave Moses and Israel His law, the Ten Commandments, plus over 600 other laws and guidelines for living. By this time the nation of Israel had acquired the behaviors of the nations around them, which were pagan and idolatrous. This included polygamy and divorce. Therefore, God in his graciousness accepted mankind where he found him, and gave strict guidelines concerning divorce and remarriage.

In Deuteronomy 24:1-4 God gave to Moses and Israel instructions regarding the proper thing to do, if a man wanted to separate from his wife. He was to "write her a bill of divorcement" so that "she may go out and be another man's wife." In the polygamous world of the day, if a wife fell out of favor with her husband, the tendency was just to "put her away." This left her in marital limbo. Legally she was still his wife, and if she did marry another man she was guilty of adultery. So, God said a man should do the honorable thing and give his wife a bill of divorcement, so she was free to remarry. The following passages also relate to this concept: Ex. 21:7-11; Deut. 21:10-14; Ezra 10:1-17; Leviticus 22:13.

When the Pharisees confronted Jesus with all this, they asked him if it was lawful for a man to "put away his wife?" (Matthew 19:3) Jesus response was (Matthew 19:4-9) that from the beginning God ordained a man and woman to be together for life, as one flesh. Then he added that "Moses, because of the hardness of your hearts, allowed you to put away your wives: but from the beginning it was not so." (v.8) Then Jesus added that anyone putting away his wife, save for fornication, caused her to commit adultery. (v.9) A bill of divorcement freed the woman, whereas putting away kept her still legally married, but in limbo.

Not only was this the law in Moses' day, as well as in Jesus' day, it is still the law today, as Christ came not to do away with the law, but to fulfill it. (Matthew 5:17) Therefore, the elements of the law, as pertaining to divorce and re-marriage are the same today, as in Jesus' day.

The confusion and misconstruction relative to the right or wrong of divorce and re-marriage concentrates on Matthew 5:32, where in the King James version the word, "divorced" is used. In the Old Testament there are two different Hebrew words for "putting away" (shalach) and "divorce" (keriythuwth). In the New Testament there are two different words for "putting away" (apoluo) and "divorce" (apostasion).

The Jewish law demanding written divorce (Deut. 24:1,2) was largely ignored in Jesus' day, so if a married man married another woman who was "put away," so what? Who was going to object? This is why the Jews confronted Jesus with this issue, trying to trip him up.

Now, comes the problem in Matthew 5:32, as translated by the King James version, where the word in English is "divorce," whereas the Greek word is "apoluo," and should have been translated, "put away." A form of the Greek word, "apoluo" is used by Jesus eleven times in the Gospels, and in every passage He forbade, "putting away" (apoluo). In Matthew 5:32, Jesus reverted to the law of Moses, when He stated that any man marrying a wife who was, "put away" committed adultery. The law was clear, a man giving his wife a "bill of divorcement" (apostasion) freed her to marry again. Jesus affirmed the law of Moses.

The King James translation of Matthew 5:32 is not consistent with the other ten times the word, "apoluo" is used and should be rendered, "put away," instead of "divorce." The American Standard Version of 1901 translates it correctly. However, this correction never caught on with subsequent translations, and in the Christian world this mistake has taken a great toll on couples. Divorce is a gracious privilege by God for couples as a corrective for an intolerable situation. It is not to be used lightly, yet has been often abused.

Often, Malachi 2:16 is referred to in the Old Testament as stating that God is against divorce. However, the word translated, "putting away," is not the Hebrew word for divorce, (keriythuwth) but is the word, "shalach," put away. Thus was Malachi affirming the law of Moses, in stating that God hated *putting away*, not *divorce*. The context of this passage is speaking of Israel's spiritual idolatry with other nations, and thereby *putting* themselves *away* from God and His law, since He had espoused them to Himself. This He hated. Though this is a spiritual relationship, the same word for putting away, *shalach* is used here, as it is in reference to a man putting away his wife. God hated Israel doing this, just as He does a man with his wife.

The next issue with regards to the subject is, can a divorced person ever be a Pastor or a Deacon? In I Timothy 3:2 the Apostle Paul noted that a Pastor must be, "the husband of one wife." Paul was an Apostle and a Pharisee Jew, who knew the Law of Moses, as well as Jesus' teaching on divorce and remarriage. He knew fully well the different Greek words for "putting away" and "divorce." He also knew that in his day the culture allowed for plural wives, etc. So, when he addressed the qualifications of a Pastor or a Deacon, he stated that they must be the husband of one wife, and only one at a time. Despite the serious abuse of the divorce law, (Deuteronomy 24:1-4) it was still valid, as it is today. Divorce is a radical solution to an insurmountable marital problem. Divorce declared the legal end to a marriage, thereby precluding any charge of adultery or bigamy, should either party marry again.

In I Corinthians 7:10-29, the Apostle Paul amplifies the husband and wife relationship with its problems. He provides some pointers as to how one should act and react in the marital relationship, with its issues. He admonishes the believing spouse to stay with the unbelieving, if they be pleased to dwell with each other. For, he notes, the believing spouse sanctifies, is a holy setting apart, a model of Christian behavior to the unbelieving spouse, the unbeliever, which may lead to their salvation.

In verse 15 he says that if the unbeliever leaves, the believing spouse is to let them go, for he says, "A brother or sister is not under bondage in such cases, but God has called us to peace." I believe here is where Paul would call into account the Law of Moses (Deut. 24:1-4) to cover this situation. On the other hand, Paul may be using the term unbeliever, in the sense that the person is a Christian, but an "unbeliever" in the sense that the one no longer believes in nor is committed to the vows of marriage they once took. The conclusion would be the same; the Christian believing spouse is to allow the Christian partner, who no longer subscribes to their marriage vows to leave. Peace and a Christian testimony is far more important for the individuals, the children, and the Christian testimony, than remaining together just because the law says they should.

A final word by the Apostle Paul is in I Corinthians 7:28, where in speaking to those who have been divorced, he says, "But, and if you marry, you have not sinned." Again, here is an implicit acknowledgment of Moses' law as stated in Deuteronomy 24:1-4.

In considering this issue, one needs to consider God's point of view, as to His Holiness in relation to mankind's sinfulness, even the sinfulness of God's children. The Bible teaches that God is perfect, that His principles in the Bible are perfect, and that is what He desires of His children. However as idealistic as God is, He is also very realistic. He takes us where He finds us, which is far less than perfect, and elevates us to Himself in the person of Jesus Christ. In I John 2:1 we see in one verse both the ideal of God and the real, "My little children, these things write I unto you, that you sin not." That is God's ideal for we who are His children. But, that is unattainable in this life, so the conjunction, "And" in the verse ties the last half with the first half, "And, if anyone sin, we have an advocate, a defender, with the Father, Jesus Christ the righteous." That is the realistic view that God has of us.

When this Theological concept of Biblical principles is applied to divorce and re-marriage, it is evident that as God created man and woman to be one flesh, until death parts them, that is not necessarily the realistic way in which human life operates. Therefore, God, in His graciousness and love, has provided a means whereby sinful, selfish, human beings do not have to be tied together in a destructive marital situation, but are able by God's allowances and grace, bring closure to the situation through divorce, and if so desirous, may remarry by God's love and grace.

God is both a God of justice, but just as well a God of love and grace. He accepts us as sinners, and by faith raises us up to be with Christ in Heavenly places, (Ephesians 1:3) as well as carrying for our "Downsittings and uprisings," (Psalms 139:2) and is a loving, gracious Father. (Psalms 86:15; Jeremiah 9:23,24) As the Apostle Paul well said in Romans 11:33, "0 the depths of the riches both of the wisdom and knowledge of God! How unsearchable are His judgments, and His ways past finding out!"

In the cross of Christ I glory,
Towering o'er the wrecks of time;

All the light of sacred story,
Gathers round His head sublime.

When the woes of life o'ertake me,
Hopes deceive and fears annoy,
Never shall the cross forsake me:
Lo! it glows with peace and joy.

When the sun of bliss is beaming,
Light and love upon my way,
From the cross the radiance streaming,
Adds more luster to the day.

Bane and blessing, pain and pleasure,
By the cross are sanctified;
Peace is there that knows no measure,
Joys that through all time abide.

—Victorious Life, Keswick, NJ

Chapter 43

TOWARD A BALANCED VIEW OF SEX

When God created Adam and Eve, he infused within them a normal desire for sexual relations. (Gen. 1:22; 2:25) God saw that this was good. It was His idea for sex to be enjoyed, as well as for propagation of the race. All of sexual enjoyment was to be within the confines of marriage. Furthermore, God placed no prohibition on whatever sexual desires or fantasies, within the marriage bounds a couple desired to do. (Heb. 13:5) Therefore, the greatest emotional drive, next to eating, was to be indulged in to the fullest, without any prohibition whatsoever.

When sin entered the human race through the fall of Adam and Eve, they turned from being God-centered to becoming self-centered. Not only has the bottom line of sin, selfishness, adversely affected the whole human race, but it has caused all the problems of the world of mankind, through the centuries. Since the family unit, ordained by God to be the foundation of society, has been adversely affected by the sin of selfishness, it has left its scar on the God-ordained delightfulness of sexual relations between husband and wife. Consequently, what many couples ardently desire in a fulfilling sexual life in marriage, has become an almost insurmountable barrier between them. Their selfishness causes a diminishing of sexual relations, and sets up barriers between them. Real, intimate friendship and communication breaks down.

In order for a couple to enter into the joys of a fulfilling sexual life in marriage, they need to realize that God ordained it. They need to understand how God created them sexually, and how each desires to have the other one meet his or her needs sexually, without prohibition. Only in this way will each one have their sexual needs fulfilled.

Selfishness, on the part of the man, demands that his wife submit to his sexual desires. But, this is not God's way, for in Eph. 5:21 it states that each is to submit to the other. Furthermore, in Eph. 5:25 the husband is admonished to love and to willfully project himself to meet the needs of his wife, just like Christ loved the church and gave Himself for it. However, the selfish husband, driven by passion, presses himself upon his wife, so that she not only is turned off, but ultimately despises her husband. He creates this within her, by selfishly coming to a climax before she is ready, by lack of tenderness, by uncleanliness, by demands when she is tired, or by not treating her. He is somewhat like a hungry man, who sits down to eat his meal, and without regard to manners, plunges in with his hands and fills his stomach, while ignoring others at the table. This not only repels the others at the table, it shows him up for what kind of a person he really is. So, many a man treats his wife this way, in the confines of their bedroom where no one else sees him. It is no wonder that many a wife secretly despises her husband.

It is the husband's responsibility to lead his wife, to set a proper course by example before her. This is the way God ordained the marriage relationship. If he leads like the man at the dinner table, then he has only himself to blame that she is turned off, sexually, by his advances. As a loving husband sets a good example before his wife, he will not only love her emotionally, but also willfully. We will work at trying to understand her and meet her needs. Then she has a responsibility to project herself to meet his needs. Since God created the woman for the man, (I Cor. 11:9) He has given her a desire to do just that. When a woman turns aside from meeting her husband's needs then she does not give of herself intimately to her husband, and thus feels cut off from doing the very thing God ordained her to do.

There is no person who is either oversexed or undersexed, there is no basic element of being a frigid wife, and there is no person who is devoid of being capable of enjoying a full and free sexual life. True, there may be medical reasons for experiencing the above, but under normal conditions God has given us the capability of a full enjoyment of a sexual relationship. It is the selfishness of mankind, both male and female, that has created these abnormalities, and for whatever reason(s) any of the above are an inhibiting factor to a sexual life within marriage they need to be addressed, corrected and guided toward the enjoyment that each desires.

Many of the problems within the sexual side of marriage are due to misconceptions as to what is proper in the sexual relationship. In Heb. 13:5, it says, "marriage is honorable in all, and the bed undefiled." God's principles are stated plainly and clearly. This simply means that within the bonds of marriage, anything sexually that a husband and wife wish to do, is perfectly acceptable in God's sight. The only prohibition is that one should not selfishly impose his or her sexual fantasies on the other one in a selfish way that would hurt or offend their partner. There is nothing wrong with various positions in sex, nor is there anything wrong with oral sex, or a wife desiring to seduce her husband, or engaging in sex in a swimming pool, or taking showers together. If both enjoy these pleasures God gives His approval.

One of the great differences between a man and a woman, is that a man is turned on by sexual sight, and a woman is turned on by gentle touch and feel. She desires to snuggle and be held, to be caressed and feel secure in the strong arms of her husband. When a man projects himself to meet his wife's needs in this way, it may result in sexual intercourse, but then again, it may only go that far on a given occasion. A giving, loving husband is sensitive to what his wife desires at that point, and does not selfishly press himself upon her.

For a wife to meet her husbands needs, she realizes that her body, with its voluptuousness, means much to him. He enjoys being titillated by her seductiveness. He enjoys seeing her in various stages of undress, and provocatively being enticed by her in this way. This too would have its approval by God between husband and wife.

In my counseling of dysfunctional marriages over the years, I have realized how great an impact the sexual area of life has in the relationship. I would even go so far as to say that the behaviors between husband and wife are directly proportional to their sexual life. If the husband has been sensitive, loving, and given to meeting his wife's needs, she will in turn meet his primary need, which is much sex. If he has not met her needs, she will be turned off by him, and if she does give in to his sexual demands, it is only because of duty, not desire. The conclusion is that the marriage disintegrates, communication breaks down, anger, hostility, and lack of trust sets in, and ultimately bitterness. Most of the husbands I see feel that their sexual life is seriously deficient; most wives do not trust their husbands. When this impasse comes about, their marriage is in serious difficulty.

The only way to correct this great need is to realize how important that sex is for each other to be totally open and free in all your other relationships; keep it a top priority! Those beginning marriage should understand, through counseling, how each is constructed and how to project one's self to meet the other one's needs, and forego these problems. To those who are married, and through lack of understanding or selfishness have come into a dysfunctional marriage, they should get professional assistance, and come to counseling with an open mind, and a willingness to correct their behaviors, as well as project themselves to meet each others needs. (I Cor. 7:1-16)

Love divine, all loves excelling,
   Joy of Heaven to earth come down,
Fix in us thy humble dwelling,
   All thy faithful mercies crown.
Jesus, thou art all compassion,
   Pure unbounded love thou art;
Visit us with thy salvation,
   Enter every trembling heart.

Breathe, O breathe thy loving Spirit,
   Into every troubled breast;
Let us all in thee inherit,
   Let us find that promised rest.
Take away our bent to sinning,
   Alpha and Omega be,
End of faith, as its beginning,
   Set our hearts at liberty.

Come, Almighty to deliver,
    Let us all thy life receive,
Suddenly return and never,
    Never more thy temples leave.
Thee we would be always blessing,
    Serve thee as thy hosts above,
Pray and praise thee without ceasing,
    Glory in thy perfect love.

Finish then thy new creation,
    Pure and spotless let us be;
Let us see thy great salvation,
    Perfectly restored in thee.
Changed from glory into glory,
    'Til in Heaven we take our place,
'Til we cast our crowns before thee,
    Lost in wonder, love, and praise.
                        —Victorious Life, Keswick, NJ

Chapter 44

DON'T SQUEEZE THE BALLOON

Reflecting on the joys of childhood often brings to mind the fun of playing with a balloon. Squeezing an inflated one could produce interesting shapes, some of which stayed, while others would remain only if the fingers were kept in place. Sometimes the rubber would stretch in such a way that if the air was let out, the rubber was permanently stretched in a rather grotesque fashion.

In an analogous manner, life itself is somewhat similar to the balloon. A person is molded and shaped as one grows and expands their horizons. There are many and varied forces tugging, pulling, squeezing—all trying to shape or misshape one's life. Let us consider how one may evaluate their life, then compare that to the Biblical principles, and finally the ministry of the Holy Spirit recharacterizing the Christian's life to become more Christ-like in the maturing process.

When my children were growing up I told them that the books they read, the television they watched, and the company they kept, all contributed to molding their character, for good or evil. For every Christian this may be helpful or harmful, depending on the many facets of life to which one is exposed and subjected and to which one listens.

From birth to death, one is never immune to external forces which constantly bombard us. We have an internal response that accepts or rejects these intrusions. Therefore, what one meditates on and continuously thinks about, is that which shapes the character and molds one's life.

Psalm 1:2 tells us that the truly fulfilled person is the one whose, "Delight is in the law of the Lord, and in His law does he meditate day and night." The Psalmist goes on to state the result, "He shall be like a tree planted...that brings forth fruit,...and whatsoever he does will prosper." (v.3) Every person desires fulfillment in life, and Christ noted in John 10:10 that, "I am come that you might have life, and that you might have it more abundantly." To experience that kind of life, the Christian must follow the principles of the Bible, then God guarantees success and prosperity.

When Joshua led the children of Israel into the Promised land, God told him, "This book of the law shall not depart out of your mouth; but you shall meditate, go over and over it, day and night, that you may observe to do according to all that is written therein; for then you will make your way _prosperous_, and then you will have _good success_." (Joshua 1:8) Prosperity and success is desired by everyone. For the Christian, these two elements must be obtained by following Biblical principles, not the ways of the world.

Furthermore, Romans 8:6 it tells us that "To be fleshly minded or self-centered brings death, but to be spiritually minded, set on God's principles, is life and peace." The conflict in the development of one's character, revolves around the WILL, as to whether one follows God's way or the self-centered way. There are many people just existing, a living death and not enjoying the fullness of life. They have allowed the world to mold and shape them, rather than the truth of the Bible. It is no wonder they are not enjoying life and peace.

The finest thing a person is able to say, when they come to the end of life is, "I have had a fulfilled life." Whereas, the saddest comment one's life is, "I wish I had it to do over again." It seems only reasonable to accept the guarantee of God—follow His way—so that we can enjoy the fullest life possible.

Recharacterization of life through the transforming work of the Holy Spirit—bringing the Christian into conformity with God's way—is the manner by which this is accomplished. It must begin by a willful desire to submit one's life to Holy Spirit's control. In a sense this means writing the Holy Spirit a "blank check" for each day, and allowing Him to teach, guide, and control one's activities, thoughts, and decisions.

In John 16:13,14, Christ pointed out that when the Holy Spirit would come that "He will guide you into all the truth," and that "He will glorify me." The result is that the Christian's character will exhibit, "the fruit of the Spirit." (Galatians 5:22-24)

To try to be Christ-like in behavior by suppressing anger, hostility, and bitterness, is to, ultimately, *squeeze the balloon*, and distort one's life. It will probably bring emotional and even physical disaster to one's life. The God-designed way is to confess, rather than suppress, one's sin. That will bring forgiveness, healing, and cleansing, (I John 1:9) and allow the Holy Spirit to mature the child of God.

Submission of one's will to the recharacterization of life by the Holy Spirit, through the Word of God, (Romans 12:2) is for the individual to become more Christ-like, (II Corinthians 3:18) and is God's admonition to every Christian for fullness of life, and maturation as His child. (Philippians 2:5; Ephesians 5:18; II Corinthians 4:6)

When a person allows the Holy Spirit of God to shape and mold his life, the result is not a warped, devastating life as the world shapes a person, but a wholeness and fullness that produces a fruitful and satisfying life, enduring for eternity.

O to be like thee, blessed Redeemer,
    This is my constant longing and prayer.
Gladly, I'll forfeit all of earth's treasures,
    Jesus, thy perfect likeness to wear.

O to be like thee, full of compassion,
    Loving, forgiving, tender and kind.
Helping the helpless, cheering the fainting,
    Fit me for life and heaven above.

O to be like thee, O to be like thee,
    Blessed redeemer, pure as thou art.
Come in thy sweetness, come in thy fullness,
    Stamp thine own image deep in my heart.
        —Victorious Life, Keswick, NJ

Chapter 45

"SO - AS"

As human beings we constantly and consistently are in need of guidelines to help us toward wholeness in life. Externally, we have laws in society, and internally we have values, principles and priorities, all of which give us guidelines and direction for life. The question then is, what guidelines do we follow, and where do they come from, in order to provide us with resources to insure that we have a full life?

God also desires that we enjoy fullness of life, for Jesus Himself said, "I am come that you might have life, and that you might have it more abundantly." (John 10:10) In Psalm 119, there are six admonitions specified by, "So - As," in order to be a guide in life according to God's directive for the Christian. When we follow them, He guarantees an abundant life.

I. Psalm 119:11 - So - As Not to Sin: The inability to measure up to what God desires of us, constitutes sin, as He evaluates it. Since God is a perfect being, His Word the Bible, produces perfect principles. However, though we are unable to measure up to God Himself, He is also realistic in that He accepts us where He finds us, and through Christ and the Holy Spirit we enjoy a perfect position in Him, as His children. At the same time through the principles of the Bible, we are progressively being conformed to His Word and will for us. For further understanding of this concept, see chapter 23—The Threefold Elements of Sanctification.

Hiding God's Word in our heart, learning the Biblical principles helps us to become molded in character into the likeness of the Lord Jesus Christ. This is a return to the "image" or "glory" of God in us, which is a transformation into the moral qualities of God. The result is that we become more mature as His children, and thereby the pull of sin weakens in us as we seek to know Him intimately.

II. Psalm 119:18 - So - As To Behold the Wonders of God's Law: God's revealed word, the Bible, provides the principles and guidelines for living a full life. Then it is the work of the Holy Spirit to apply the principles individually, according to the person's maturation process. This differs with every Christian.

In Romans 12:2, where it tells us how to do this, it says, "Be not conformed to this world, the lust of the self life, the pull of the world, and the designs of Satan against us, but be transformed by the transformation of your WILL, that in so doing you may prove God's will for your life, which is good, acceptable to Him, and perfect." As we willfully allow the Holy Spirit to transform our character behaviors, we become more Christ-like. (II Corinthians 3:18) We will enjoy increasing discernment in spiritual things. (II Corinthians 2:9-14)

Psalm 19:7 tells us, "The law of the Lord is perfect, reviving the soul. The statutes of the Lord are trustworthy, making wise the simple." When Christ stated, "Take my yoke upon you, for my yoke is easy, and my burden is light." (Matthew 11:28-30) He meant that God's parameters for the Christian were meant to free him up. Not to bind one. For the committed Christian, this is all too true, by experience.

III. Psalm 119:89 - So - As To Be Able To Be Settled In Life: The foundations of the truth of God's Word provides a surety upon which one is able to fashion his life. God's Word is "settled in heaven," therefore it is absolute, final, and is that upon which the Christian can depend. In Matthew 24:35 Christ tells us, "Heaven and earth shall pass away, but my words shall not pass away."

Therefore, we can depend absolutely upon the eternal truth of the Bible, over against the relativity of our world's system. It is reassuring to know that one can trust the truths of God's Word rather than our world of today, where nothing is certain or secure.

IV. Psalm 119:97-98 - So - As To Provide Wisdom For Life: As a child of God grows in the grace and knowledge of Jesus Christ, one gains a greater degree of wisdom, the God given ability to apply the principles of life to daily decisions. (II Peter 3:18)

There are two ways of gaining knowledge: Intellectual and Experiential. In Philippians 3:8 the knowledge spoken of here is intellectual, an understanding of the truth of Christ Jesus. In Philippians 3:10 there is the experiential, the experience of being a living sacrifice for Jesus Christ. God uses both in the life of the Christian to *flesh* us out to fullness of maturity. Just as every science course in school has both the classroom learning, the intellectual, and the laboratory learning, or experiential, so that a complete knowledge can be gained of the subject. God uses both areas of learning for our completeness.

The intellectual points to the mind. The experiential strikes the emotions. In order to become a well rounded whole person, God is concerned with both elements of our development. The Bible teaches us intellectually. It is the work of the Holy Spirit to teach us experientially. Together, we have it all, in order to become a mature Christian, and be a testimony to the world.

V. Psalm 119:105 - So - As To provide Light Upon The Pathway of Life: When walking through life, it gives one assurance to know there is light upon the pathway. The Christian doesn't have to stumble or grope, for God's Word provides the light of understanding and wisdom. Proverbs 1:7 tells us that, "The fear or the respect of God for who He is, is the beginning of wisdom." Proverbs 4:18 states, "But the path of the just one is as a shining light, that shineth more and more unto the perfect day." Proverbs 9:10 it tells us, "The knowledge of the holy is understanding."

James 1:5 promises us wisdom from God to those who lack it. There are three relevant words used in Scripture: 1) Knowledge - this is the acquiring of facts, which comes through study. (Proverbs 18:15) 2) Understanding - is the comprehension of the facts one has acquired, (Proverbs 2:6) and 3) Wisdom - is the application of what one knows and understands to life's situations. For this the Christian needs the light of God's wisdom to properly navigate through the problems of life. (Proverbs 3:13)

VI. Psalm 119:133 - So - As To Not Have A Sinful Spirit In Life: Anything that is contrary to God's moral attributes is sin. In order for the child of God to understand what offends God's holiness, there are

241

three specific words used in Scripture, to help guide us. They are found in Psalm 32:1,2 and 51:1,2. The first is the word: 1) <u>Iniquity</u> - this refers to one's basic sin nature, which we all received from our common father, Adam. It is the self-centeredness of every person, which is in opposition to being God-centered. Out of this nature comes the two basic acts of sin, which are: 2) <u>Sin</u> - this more restricted word for sin, refers to one falling short or not measuring up to God's behaviors for the Christian. It is like an arrow being aimed at the target, and not making it, but falling to the ground. King David fell short as God's king over Israel. He did not measure up to the position God had given him. 3) <u>Transgression</u> - this means going against God's principles, and doing what the self desires. It is somewhat analogous to the hunter going over the farmer's fence, when it is posted against hunting. King David went against God's commandments, in that he coveted another man's wife, committed adultery with her, and killed her husband so he could have her.

As seen in David's testimony in both Psalm 32 and 51, he acknowledged his sin, and God forgave him. The joy of his salvation was returned to him, and God even called him, "A man after my own heart." (Acts 13:22) This shows God's unconditional grace to His children. Oh, if we Christians would only have as much grace and forgiveness for one another, as God does toward His children. The truth and acceptance of God's Word gives us a right spirit. We will not want to continue sinning against Him. (I John 1:9)

<u>Conclusion</u>: In Psalm 19:14, David said, "Let the words of my mouth, and the meditations of my heart, be acceptable in thy sight, 0 Lord, my strength, and my redeemer." Again in Psalm 19:13, he asked God to keep him from "presumptuous sins." We dare not presume upon the Grace of God. Therefore, God's Word helps us to have a right spirit before Him, so we do not continue in sin. The joy of the Lord in the life of the Christian is characterized as we follow His guidance in our daily living. <u>SO - AS</u> to arrive at a mature fullness of His life in us.

Jesus, I am resting in the joy of what thou art;
    I am finding out the greatness of thy loving heart.
Thou hast bid me gaze upon thee, and thy beauty fills my soul,
    For by thy transforming power, thou hast made me whole.

Ever lift thy face upon me, as I work and wait for thee;
    Resting neath thy smile, Lord Jesus, earth's dark shadows flee.
Brightness of my Father's glory sunshine of my Father's face
    Keep me ever trusting, resting, fill me with thy grace.

—Victorious Life, Keswick, NJ

Chapter 46

FEAR NOT, FRET NOT, FAINT NOT

In today's world there are many problems that produce fear and guilt in the lives of people. The resulting stress becomes at times, unbearable, and may ultimately lead to emotional breakdowns and physical problems. The Creator of our bodies never intended for mankind to live under these kinds of problems, for which we were never created.

In Psalm 139:14 we read "For I am fearfully and wonderfully made." The whole of an individual is a wonderfully complex structure. But not suited for the stresses to which we are subjected. The body has marvelous recuperative powers, yet undue and prolonged stress is harmful. The Bible provides a threefold formula to help us overcome the problems of life. Problems of which we may have little or no control, so that we are able to handle life itself.

I. Fear Not, But Trust: The following passages all speak to the child of God, in promises that help us overcome fear. (Luke 12:32; Psalm 27:3, 48:14; Isaiah 41:10, 58:11; Hebrews 13:5,6) The reason the Christian need not fear is that God is sovereign and in control. This is a simple, but reassuring fact. (I Chronicles 29:11,12; Psalm 10:16, 22:28, 24:1, 115:3; Isaiah 40:15-23) Therefore, we should TRUST our heavenly Father, which helps to alleviate any fear or apprehension.

II. Timothy 1:7 points out that, "God has not given us the spirit of fear, but of power, and of love, and of a sound mind." The spirit of fear comes from Satan using it to neutralize our Christian living, and keep us down. God has given us the spirit of power to live constructively. The spirit of love to live sacrificially. And a sound mind to live reasonably. I John 4:18 states that mature love casts out fear. When our love for Christ is being strengthened and matured, then fear decreases.

III. Fret Not: Much of the fear in society today comes because of evil and wickedness, and those who promote it. God's Word tells us to fret not because of evildoers. (Psalm 37:1,7; Proverbs 24:19) This does not mean that we should be blind to evil, nor that we don't need to stand up for good, but that we have no need to worry or get bent out of shape because of it.

Remember, God is in control, and He sees all the evil that is going on in the world. In Psalm 7:11 it says that, "God is angry with the wicked every day." I Peter 3:12 says, "The face of the Lord is against them that do evil." In Daniel 4:17, 25, 35, 37 the prophet Daniel pointed out the sovereignty of God over the kingdoms of mankind. It is comforting to understand these truths in dark days of wickedness among the peoples of the world.

IV. Faint Not: At times it seems as if, "right is on the scaffold, and wrong is on the throne." Reality is not that way, though it may seem that way. This is why God says to us, faint not. In Galatians 6:9 we are told, "Be not weary in well doing, for in due season we shall reap, if we faint not." Other passages speak to this concept. (II Corinthians 4:16 and Isaiah 40:28,31)

Our responsibility is to keep on following the pathway of righteousness, trust our Heavenly Father and "Cast all your cares on Him for He cares for you." (Psalm 37:3; Proverbs 3:5,6; I Peter 5:7)

These three admonitions are not glib panaceas for a troubled heart, they are God's principles and promises for today's stressful and complex living. These are promises the Christian can bank on. Know they are backed up by the "Word of God, which lives and abides forever." (I Peter 1:23)

My hope is built on nothing less,
    Than Jesus' blood and righteousness;
I dare not trust the sweetest frame,
    But wholly lean on Jesus' name.

246

His oath, His covenant, His blood,
    Support me in the whelming flood;
When all around my soul gives way,
    He then is all my hope and stay.

On Christ the solid rock I stand;
    All other ground is sinking sand,
All other ground is sinking sand.
            —Victorious Life, Keswick, NJ

Chapter 47

A WEEKEND FOR REFLECTION UPON A LIFE OF RELATIONSHIP

The fast pace of life, with all its responsibilities is not conducive to building an intimate husband and wife relationship. In order for a husband and wife to provide a foundation of life that is both productive as well as mutually fulfilling, it is imperative they spend a working weekend together, away from all the responsibilities of life.

They need to retreat to a motel away from where they live, and evaluate their lives: individually, together, and in their family relationships. They need to work out their worldviews, priorities of life, what their life principles are, their relationship and responsibilities to their children, and to each other, including common interests. They need to think through each of these areas, and how they are intertwined. If a couple will dedicate themselves to this task, and will faithfully confront these areas, then apply their conclusions, the results will be manifold in fulfillment to every person in the family.

Since the Bible is the standard guide of God's revelation to mankind as to how to live, there are certain basic principles that act as a general foundational guide upon which Christians can erect the superstructure of their lives. The primary principle is found in Romans 12:1,2, "I implore you brothers, by the fact that God has with held His judgment from you, and instead has given to you of His grace, that you present your bodies as a living sacrifice, dedicated unto Him and acceptable unto God, for this is only reasonable. And be not conformed to this world, but be transformed by the renewing of your WILL, so that you are able to prove what is that GOOD, and ACCEPTABLE, and PERFECT will of God for you." Conformation to the world is basically living a self-centered life, with all of its problems and lack of ultimate fulfillment. Being transformed by an act of one's will to the control of the Holy Spirit and through guidance of God's word in the Bible, is to assure one of fulfillment in life which every person desires, and for which God created us. (John 10:10) If a couple commit themselves to that basic philosophy and principle, then God is the guarantor that they will enjoy the intended fullness of their marriage and family.

Everyone has a worldview. The boy riding his bicycle has one, though if you asked him what it was he probably wouldn't know what you were asking him, nor could he articulate it if you explained. Nevertheless, he not only has one, but is actively pursuing it in his life. What is this worldview you ask, and in what way do all people live by it? A worldview is people's idea or philosophy of life as they evaluate it, how it motivates them through life and the decision making process, and the guide and parameter that gives direction to them. This is all encompassing for it not only differs with each individual, but is the pattern that molds their entire life. A worldview is ultimately important for every person, and is necessary for one to think through, since it is the guide through life.

When a couple is married they bring to that union two different worldviews. Their friendship, common interests and philosophy of life become the framework upon which they relate and desire to marry. The commonality of their individual worldviews or the divergence, is that which produces harmony or dissonance between them. Therefore, it is imperative that before they marry they think through their worldviews. If they have been married for sometime they must take time to reflect, refine, and coordinate their worldview, if they haven't already done so. It is imperative to break out some time together, just to enjoy the love God pours out on them and to share time with Him, and each other. Amos 3:3 says, "Can two walk together except they be agreed?" Obviously the answer is, no. God did not make us to think alike, and no husband and wife will ever agree upon everything, since our backgrounds differ. It is not, do we think alike, but, do we have a unified worldview, so that we are able to resolve situations from a common foundation even though we all have differences of opinion.

A worldview encompasses goals, principles, behaviors, attitudes, desires, objectives, accomplishments, ethics, morals, and all that goes into life itself. It is necessary to evaluate these areas, and come to conclusions as to how to operate. In marriage, in order to have harmony and progression, a couple must have similarity in their worldviews. Otherwise, it won't be long after the wedding that the divergence of two worldviews will produce major differences in application to decisions. The result is that soon each will be going their own way. This certainly is not productive to building a relationship and fulfillment.

One aspect of life that bonds a couple together is having similar interests. This does not mean that everything they do or desire must be held in common, but a majority of interests should be of such similarity that they would enhance bonding. A couple would do well to list on paper, individually, what each enjoys doing as to work, play, cultural desires, etc., and then compare notes. When that is done, they will each realize there are areas of interest that have not been communicated before. It opens up doors that otherwise may have never been opened. After they have established expectations for involvement together in agreed areas, then each one is free to pursue avenues of interest themselves. When the majority of time is spent on common interests, individual interests pursued will be more delightful and without undue stress.

Part of the problems that individuals face in life which causes continuing irritation is that of priorities. In order to enjoy an orderly fulfilled life it is important to have right priorities. For a couple to have mixed priorities is to have a constantly confused and disordered marriage. This produces mixed signals that each gives to the other. The result is anger and frustration, since they are at cross purposes, and then each one fails to have their priorities executed in the way they figure they should be. For the Christian the Biblical order of priorities should be, God first, the family second, and work third. Usually, the man has business first, the family second, and God gets the left overs, if any. Many pastors have the proper order, but unfortunately tend to fuse the first and third, God and their ministry are one and the same, so that the family gets left out, which is why many pastors' families have anger against their husband and father's ministry.

Because of the press of life today to get ahead, it causes many families to place work for material gain ahead of everything, thus putting undo stress on the family and certainly on our devotion to God. This is why a couple needs time together to sort out their priorities, put them in proper Biblical order, have a common understanding, and determine to carry them out regardless of what the world's pressures that are brought to bear on them. With a united front, and with God's blessing, they can't miss in life. In I Samuel 2:30 God says, "…them that honor me, I will honor, and they that despise me will be lightly esteemed." Right priorities faithfully placed and implemented in the family life will not only bring blessing and bonding to a couple, but an important added blessing of modeling excellent learned behaviors before their children, who will then find it easier to have right priorities in their adult life, and with the one whom they eventually will marry.

Most couples, when they marry, do not know the basic principles of marriage. They are so filled with emotional love that there is a tendency to gloss over the realities of life. They believe their love will carry them through. This lasts for a while, until the selfish realities of life emerge, and consequently the divisions that are born out of that self-centeredness. It is imperative for a couple to know and understand the basic principles of marriage. There are many good Christian books to assist in the knowledge of these principles, and I would recommend Dr. Ed Wheat's book, "Love Life" as a premier book on the subject.

If a couple really desires to enhance their relationship and enjoy fullness of marriage, it is imperative to know the principles and then to be committed to putting them into operation. Properly understood and carried out, these principles along with the other elements outlined above will all work together to produce a loving, and fulfilling relationship that will endure, "until death do us part."

If the couple have children who are old enough to have observed their parents behavior, and thereby incorporated their parents learned behaviors into their own lives, it is important for the couple to explain to their children what they have done over their weekend of marital work, so that the children know and understand any significant changes in the lives of their parents. This is important, for children tend to be impacted by parents life styles, and in adulthood reflect in their own behaviors what they picked up from parents in their childhood. They then transfer over to their spouse those behaviors from childhood and the family of origin. Children are resilient enough to be able to handle and accommodate in their lives, any significant changes for the better that they see in their parents behaviors. There is an old saying, which is true, that example is greater than precept, and parents inter action between each other has an impact on children such as to model their behavior significantly.

In John 10:10 Christ said, "I am come that you may have life, and that you may have it more abundantly." God created all of His children to enjoy an abundant life. In order to have that we must follow Biblical principles, and then God will see to it that our lives are fulfilled. Marriage, which has been ordained of God, is one of the greatest elements that God has created for our fulfillment. Properly administered it will do just that, but improperly lived, marriage can be a living hell. One's spouse is either one's greatest asset or one's greatest liability. And, it is incumbent on each spouse to see to it that the other one's needs are met, thereby assuring that each one will have their own needs met. I don't care how poor a person's work is, if they have a good marriage they are able to handle their job. Also, I don't care how good a job a person has, or the money they make, if they have a poor marriage, it adversely affects their job. Therefore, it seems reasonable that one put time and effort into their marriage relationship. In order to enjoy that for which God created us to enjoy companionship for fulfillment, as well as for procreation of the race.

A good marriage that lasts for a lifetime takes constant work and monitoring. Only by understanding a Biblical worldview, enjoying common interests, having God-honoring priorities, knowing, understanding, and putting into operation the principles of marriage, and modeling good relationships before one's children, can any couple have a blessed life of fulfilled companionship that ministers to each one's needs.

As a fitting conclusion to the principles and concepts that have been developed in the chapters of this book, consider the delights of the verses of this great hymn of the faith, "Like A River Glorious"

Like a river glorious is God's perfect peace,
Over all victorious in its bright increase.
Perfect yet it floweth, fuller every day,
Perfect yet it groweth deeper all the way.

Stayed upon Jehovah, hearts are fully blest,
Finding as He promised, perfect peace and rest.

Every joy or trial, falleth from above,
Traced upon our dial, by the Sun of love.
We may trust Him fully, all for us to do;
They who trust Him wholly, find Him wholly true.

Stayed upon Jehovah, hearts are fully blest,
Finding as He promised, perfect peace and rest.

—Victorious Life, Keswick, NJ

Chapter 48

BASIC PRINCIPLES FOR CHRISTIANS IN TODAY'S WORLD

Since the world in which we live today, is in a constant state of declension, spiritually, morally, and ethically, along with declining principles and moral relativism rather than any absolutes, it is imperative that Christians become knowledgeable as to basic Biblical guidelines for living in this wicked world. It is also important that these principles be instilled in our children, for their future (Deuteronomy 11:18,19; 32:46).

Of first importance is that Christians are in the world, but not of the world (John 17:14,16). Granted, every Christian lives in society, and works in the world, but our spiritual life is related to Jesus Christ and the Biblical principles of spiritual truth, that guide, motivate, and bless us. Our worldview is quite different than that of the person who is not a child of God.

Our service and contribution in the world, is to let our light shine for Jesus Christ, to proclaim the truth of eternal life, and to make disciples for the Lord (Matthew 28:19,20). In truth, we are to be God centered in our behaviors, rather than self centered as are people of the world, so that others see Jesus Christ in us. Our worldview (i.e. the track of life upon which we run our life) comes from the principles in the Bible, which are given for our welfare and fullness of life (John 10:10), as we employ them in our daily living.

255

Christians should not live by the ways of the world, even though there is a strong pull from the world to conform (Colossians 2:8-13), but to be open to Biblical principles for spiritual growth and guidance (Joshua 1:8; Psalms 1:2,3; Romans 8:6). When the Christian follows God directed influences on his life, then God promises fullness of life.

Second, the whole world system is in the hands of the wicked one (1 John 5:19), but has been condemned by God (1 John 2:17), and Jesus Christ came into the world to judge Satan (1 John 3:8; John 12:31). The moment God, in His omnipotence raised Jesus from the dead, it forever sealed the doom of Satan. Since then, he has been living on "borrowed time", awaiting the day of God's eternal punishment of him, and all unsaved people.

Therefore, though it may seem to Christians, that "right is on the scaffold, and wrong is on the throne", we should not be discouraged, at what we see transpiring and swirling downward in this world, God is still sovereign and on the throne, and we are able to take heart for, all is well, and with God, one is a majority. As Christians live and work in the world, we must reject the ways of the world and keep our mind and heart on God and Biblical principles, in spite of what we see transpiring today.

The third principle and mission for the Christian in today's world, is to realize that we are not here to improve the world, nor even try to bring in the kingdom, but to help bring salvation to individuals out of this world. Christians have been criticized by worldly, ungodly elements as trying to establish a "Theocratic Kingdom of God" here on the earth. This has been fueled in the past by moral political elements, but it has no Biblical foundation. Today, there is a movement, even among evangelical believers, that our mission is to help evolve the world into God's ultimate kingdom. This also is farthest from the truth, and has no Biblical foundation.

One may rightly ask, what is God's purpose through Biblical Christianity, in today's world? The answer is plainly seen in Acts 15:13-18, where Peter was preaching, noting that God was concerned with taking from the people of the world, a people for His name. In other words, the Apostles recognized their mission was to proclaim the truth of salvation to all the world. Peter added that, God would rebuild the "Temple", which had fallen, in that the Jewish nation had not carried out their mission from God, which Solomon well knew (See: 1 Kings 8:41-43), and spiritually speaking the Temple had been abandoned. Therefore, God would raise up a spiritual habitation for Himself, from believing people, both Gentiles and Jews, who would carry the message of salvation to all the world. Over the past two thousand years, this has been accomplished by the "Church", (i.e. the body of Christian believers) through the indwelling Holy Spirit. Peter also added, "So, that the rest of mankind may seek the Lord". This is the primary service and ministry that Christians are to employ today.

Fourthly, though Christians are citizens of their country, we are all primarily citizens of Heaven. We are just, "Passing through". In Philippians 3:20 we read, "For our citizenship is in Heaven, from which we also eagerly wait for a Savior, the Lord Jesus Christ" (NASB). In 1 Peter 2:11 we are told, "I urge you as aliens and strangers to abstain from fleshly lusts which wage war against your soul" (NASB).

Since every Christian has two natures within himself: a self centered nature, desirous of doing selfish things, and a new nature from God unto salvation of eternal life, and by the regeneration of the indwelling Holy Spirit, which nature cannot sin, there is a constant conflict within the person, of these two opposite natures, each vying for control. The only way by which a Christian can gain control of his spiritual life, is through a daily commitment to the Holy Spirit for control. This helps to live a balanced life, as a Christian in the world, by being both a good citizen of one's country, as well as living a God centered life, as an eternal citizen of Heaven. A good illustration of this conflict, and how to overcome the worldly pull, is to read the personal struggle the Apostle Paul had, as told by him in Romans 7 and 8.

Another element in our dual citizenship, earthly and Heavenly, is seen in the conflict the Apostles had with Roman authorities. In Romans 13: 1 we are admonished to obey the powers that be, for they are ordained of God. But this doesn't always obtain. In Acts 4:18-21 we note the Apostles were called into question of their behavior by the magistrate, and in Acts 5;25-29 Peter said, "We ought to obey God, rather than men". Was this a contradiction of Biblical principles? No, generally speaking, as citizens of our country we do have a responsibility to obey the law, but when man's law is contradictory to God's law, then, as Christians, we must obey the higher authority, God. Our right and privilege as God's child, is that we are able to pray and ask Him for divine wisdom (James 1:5; 3:17).

Fifth, as spiritual soldiers of the Lord, one should not be entangled with the affairs of this world (2 Timothy 2:4). Again, we may ask ourselves, does this mean we should not enter the arena of local affairs as a citizen, or vote, or run for public office, or even enlist as a member of the armed forces? To go this far in believing this is what the verse says, is a stretch. As a Christian, committed to serving the Lord, it does not mean we are to be a hermit in the world. Rather, we are to be salt and light in the world, regardless of our occupation, or commitment to our state or country.

Balance in the Christian life is an important concept. A Christian's commitment to the Lordship of Jesus Christ, is paramount in life. But, this does not mean we are to isolate ourselves from normal responsibilities as a citizen of our country. What is important is to not allow our normal daily activities to consume us, to the minimizing of our responsibility to the first and foremost commitment in serving the Lord. For example, if one desires to enter politics, he must remember to serve that position as a Christian, and vote on Biblical principles, and not be swayed by ungodly reasoning. If he feels that is too much, or that he is being led along by the world to compromise his convictions, or that the world of politics is consuming him, then it may be best for him to abstain. This principle can be applied to most anything. Because when one crosses the line from controlling it, to it controlling him, then it is time to consider one's ways, as a committed Christian, and thereby abstain.

Sixth, as Ambassadors for the Lord, we should represent the TRUTH to the world. Spiritually speaking, as Ambassadors for the Lord, in this world (2 Corinthians 5:20), we are representatives to unsaved people for the Lord. This is where our commission is apparent, since we are to spread the good news that Christ came to reconcile all to God, through His love and what He did on the cross for every person. Our Ambassadorship is to proclaim this truth. In John 14:6 Jesus said, "I am the way, the truth, and the life: no one comes unto the Father, but through me".

In this day and age, the truth is very hard to come by, since relativism and rationalization has become the order of the day. For the Christian there is only one place, and by one standard, where the truth is absolutely told, and that is the Bible. It has stood the test of time, never found wanting, though allegations of myth and fable have been lodged against, but never proven. Over two thousand years, by countless numbers of Christians who have given their lives for its truth, as well as by Archaeology that has uncovered countless number of facts and figures of Biblical history and corroborated all that has been revealed, the truth of the Bible has stood true to the test.

The Kingdom of God is not for this world today. Someday, when Jesus Christ returns to this world, He will set up a kingdom of absolute righteousness, which will last for eternity. All of God's children will be citizens of that kingdom. Today, as Christians, we are Ambassadors of that future kingdom, and as such we are to proclaim the truth of God, as revealed in the Bible, to any and who will hear, and commit themselves to Jesus Christ, as Lord and Savior, and thereby enter that coming kingdom.

When Jesus stood before Pilate, he asked Jesus if He was the King of the Jews? Jesus acknowledged that, but stated that, "My kingdom was not of this realm" (John 18:36). In other words, though He came as King of the Jews, yet His kingdom was a Heavenly kingdom, not an earthly one. This is why, we as Ambassadors of His kingdom, are not desirous of setting up a "Theocratic Kingdom" here on earth, as some would accuse us. Our Ambassadorship is of a higher plane and quality. It is a spiritual kingdom, ruled over by God Himself (1 Corinthians 15:22-28).

Finally, politics, by its very nature, tends to become corrupt, and therefore Christians should be careful of its corrupting influence, should they seek to enter. In 1 John 5:19 it says that, "...the whole world lies in the lap of the wicked one". Satan is the prince of the power of the air (Ephesians 2:2), and certainly he exercises great authority and power over the governments of the world. This has been noted throughout history. The Christian should be wary of becoming bound up in the world of politics.

An excellent admonition is found in 2 Corinthians 6:17,18 and 7:1, where it says, "Therefore, come out from their midst and be separate says the Lord, and do not touch what is unclean; and I will welcome you, and I will be a Father unto you,...says the Lord Almighty. Therefore, having these promises, let us cleanse ourselves from all defilement of flesh and spirit, maturing holiness in the fear of God". Not only is this admonition confined to politics, but is certainly applicable to every aspect of life. As we reflect upon these seven principles of the Christian life, it is easily seen that God desires every child of His, to ponder each and every one of them, and to apply them daily to our lives. Since everything is not absolutely "black and white", and there are degrees of variation in some aspects, it behooves every Christian to ask of God, divine daily wisdom to know how to make the right choices, since all choices have consequences, and our personal lives, as well as our testimony for Him, are at stake. We need to navigate through the shoals of life, but Biblical principles, applied through us by the power of the Holy Spirit. Then, with confidence we can live in the world, and with joy serve our blessed Lord and Savior, Jesus Christ.

Living for Jesus a life that is true,
　　Striving to please Him in all that I do,
Yielding allegiance, glad-hearted and free,
　　This is the pathway of blessing for me.

Living for Jesus who died in my place,
　　Bearing on Calv'ry my sin and disgrace,
Such love constrains me to answer His call,
　　Follow His leading and give Him my all.

Living for Jesus thro' earth's little while,
　　My dearest treasure, the light of His smile,
Seeking the lost ones He died to redeem,
　　Bringing the weary to find rest in Him.

—Living For Jesus
T.O. Chisholm and C. Harold Lowden

Chapter 49

THE CHRISTIAN'S RESPONSE TO TODAY'S PROBLEMS

A Christian may ask, what is God's purpose in today's world, given the monumental problems we face, and why doesn't God do something about it? Why is God seemingly silent in the kingdom of mankind, and when will He bring it all into judgment? Fortunately the Bible has very specific answers to these questions. It remains for us to search them out.

God's ultimate purpose in the world, has been and still is, to bring all of mankind into reconciliation with Him. In Acts 15:14-17, the Apostle James states that, "God at the first did visit the nations of the world, to take out of them a people for His name...that the remnant of mankind might seek after the Lord." In I Timothy 2:4 we see that God, "Will have all mankind to be saved, and come to a knowledge of the truth." Also, in II Peter 3:9 we read that God, "Is longsuffering to mankind, not willing that any should perish, but that all should come to repentance."

The reason God is longsuffering, and it may seem to us forever, is answered in Romans 2:4, where we read, "Do you show contempt for the riches of God's kindness, tolerance and patience, not realizing that God's kindness leads you toward repentance?" In other words, God's day of grace to all mankind is still operative, in order to give the opportunity for people to accept Jesus Christ as their personal savior from sin, and have the assurance of eternal life. Though sin is rampant, because of the intransigent self will of mankind, God is still gracious to give us an opportunity to trust Him. Aren't you glad that God didn't conclude all in judgment just before you became a Christian? However, His day of Grace will someday conclude, and His day of judgment will commence. (Hebrews 9:27) We don't know when the shift will come, but it behooves all mankind to get ready.

This separation of God's creation of mankind began in the garden of Eden, when Adam and Eve listened to the voice of Satan, and turned from being God centered to becoming self-centered, by eating of the forbidden fruit, as God had commanded. (Gen. 3:3) Since God created mankind for three reasons: fellowship with Him, for mankind to be a reflection of God's holiness, and to place mankind over the rest of the creation as "king." (Psalm 8:4-6) He now began the process of providing for restoration and reconciliation to all of the creation. Therefore, we have the first prophetic announcement of Scripture in Genesis 3:15, where God noted that the sin which Satan perpetrated in Adam, and from him to the whole human race, (Romans 5:12) would cause God's Son, Jesus Christ, to come to earth and die for the sins of the world. But, in His death and resurrection He would crush forever the power of Satan over all mankind.

The sin nature of Adam was passed to all mankind, (Rom. 5:12) and out of that sin nature comes personal sin, for which each is responsible. Christ died to save mankind from both his sin nature, as well as his personal sin. The sin nature is automatically cared for in Christ's work, for God does not hold one responsible for that which he cannot help, but one's personal sin, for which each is responsible, requires personal commitment. (John 3:16-18,36; 6:28,29)

God's ultimate purpose is the restoration of mankind unto Himself. God's Holiness without proper sacrifice for sins, would not allow Him to accept the restoration of mankind. The way by which God's Holiness could remain unsullied, and at the same time extend His love and grace to all, was to send Jesus Christ into the world and make sacrifice of Himself for our sins, and thereby we are able to be reconciled to God through accepting Christ's work in our behalf. (II Corinthians 5:14-19; Galatians 3:24)

The story of the Bible is the recounting of two lines of revelation in order to accomplish God's purpose: 1) the people of God in the Old

Testament, Israel as His chosen ones, and 2) the Church of God in the New Testament; Christians today.

I. <u>The Old Testament</u>: In the Old Testament God's purpose was fulfilled through Israel and the Theocracy, the rule of God. First, He chose Abraham and told him He would make a great nation through him. (Genesis 12:1-3) Why God chose him as well as Israel is only understood as seen in Deuteronomy 7:6-8, where Moses said God chose them "Because the Lord loved you."

God's purpose in choosing Israel was for them to disseminate the revelation of Himself to all the world. Israel was to be God's channel of revelation. Solomon, the king, recognized this national responsibility, as noted in his dedicatory prayer of the Temple in Jerusalem. (I Kings 8:41-43) In order for God to have a relationship with Israel He ordained the Priestly system, and chose the tribe of Levi to be the tribe of Priests, as mediators between Israel and God. He also used a group of Prophets to become God's mouthpiece of revelation of Himself to Israel.

The problem in this was the inability of Israel to live up to the covenant God made with them. It rested on the ten commandments God gave to them, and their ratifying of it at Mt. Sinai. (Exodus 20:1-7; 24:7) The continuing history of Israel from Sinai to the time of Samuel, about 400 years, was that of falling into sin, repentance, and God's deliverance.

Finally, at the time of Samuel's reign, the Priests and Prophets only governed by the direct hand of God, that is the Theocracy. Israel moved from being a Theocracy to a Monarchy, the rule of man. All this was predicted by God, when He gave to Moses what is written in Deuteronomy 17:14-20, four hundred years before. The corruptness of the priestly system as seen in I Samuel 2:22; 8:3-5 caused the leaders of Israel to demand a king. God told Samuel they had not rejected him, but they had rejected God's rule over them. Thus, began the reign of human kings over Israel starting with Saul. The seeds of this corruption were sown upon entering the land when they disobeyed God's command to drive the Canaanites out of the land, to not intermarry with them, and to not worship their idols. (Judges 3:1-8) The downward trend continued until 586 B.C. when Nebucadnezzar destroyed Jerusalem, and carried the Jews away captive, until 1948 a.d. when the new nation of Israel was established.

God chose them to be His channel through whom He would reveal Himself to the world, Israel was instead lifted up with pride, and cloistered His revelation to themselves. (Romans 2:17-29) Then when Jesus came hundreds of years later, as their Messiah and to save them from their sins, they rejected Him. (John 1:11) In II Corinthians 3:14-16 it states they had spiritual blindness because of their sin of pride, etc.

II. The New Testament: At the outset of Jesus' ministry He preached the Kingdom of Heaven to Israel alone, (Matthew 10:5-7) because as their Messiah, He had come to bring in the Kingdom, as promised by God. However, the kingdom Israel desired was a political restoration of the kingdom they had under David, whereas the kingdom promised by Jesus was a spiritual kingdom, which would care for their sins. Then would come the political restoration. The spiritual blindness of Israel kept them from accepting the offer of Jesus. Had He restored the political kingdom again, it too would have eventually failed for the same reason the first one did, that is, because of Israel's sins.

When Jesus perceived His rejection by Israel, He began to teach His Disciples a new concept, the Church. (Matthew 16:13-18) This was never mentioned in the Old Testament. He pointed out that the Church would be empowered to do what Israel had failed to do, disseminate God's revelation to the world. The difference would be the empowerment of the Holy Spirit. (John 14:16-26; 16:7-14) In I Corinthians 2:9-14 it is seen as to why the unregenerate person cannot understand spiritual things, and why the Christian is able to. This is why the Church has succeeded, even though not perfectly.

Christ gave the Church its commission, (Matthew 28:19,20) as well as the ability to carry it out through the power of the Holy Spirit. This has been the Church's primary role until today. Our responsibility is not to judge what we see in the world, but to be faithful in carrying out the commission. (I Cor. 4:1-5) We are not to get caught up in the ways of the world as did Israel.

III. Today's Application: Given today's world, with the sin we see, in contrast to our commission, how should the Christian respond?

Christ anticipated this dilemma, when He gave the parable of the wheat and the tares. (Matthew 13:10-13,24-30) Just as weeds far outgain the grain, so wickedness seems to prosper more than righteousness. In the parable the Disciples asked Christ about tearing out the weeds, and He replied that the two would grow together until the harvest, then the farmer would separate the grain from the weeds. So, as today, both righteousness and wickedness are prospering, the coming of God in judgment will separate the righteous from the unrighteous. God is sovereign and someday He will judge the world. (Hebrews 9:27) Our responsibility to carry out the commission, and leave the judging to Him. (I Corinthians 4:1-5)

The Christian's response should be: 1) Accept the basic, absolute truth of Scripture. We all start with basic assumptions, and to believe the Bible as foundational, is to begin with the right assumption. (Psalm 119:89, 97, 98, 105) 2) Believe in the sovereignty of God. (Isaiah 46:9,11; Psalm 10:16; 33:11; 103:19) 3) Accept the resources of the Holy Spirit to help give you wisdom, power, grace, discernment, etc. (James 1:5; I Corinthians 2:14) 4) Recognize the ultimate judgment of God on the world. (Romans 3:19; John 5:21-27; II Corinthians 5:10)

Remember, "For God has not given us the spirit of fear, but of POWER to live constructively, of LOVE to live sacrificially and of a SOUND MIND to live reasonably." (II Timothy 17)

Up Calvary's mountain, one dreadful morn,
    Walked Christ, my Savior, weary and worn;
Facing for sinners, death on the cross,
    That He might save them from endless loss.

"Father, forgive them!" thus did He pray,
    Even while His life blood flowed fast away;
Praying for sinners while in such woe,
    No one but Jesus ever loved us so.

O, how I love Him, Savior and friend,
    How can my praises ever find end!
Through years unnumbered on Heaven's shore,
    My tongue shall praise Him, forevermore.

Blessed Redeemer, precious Redeemer!
    Seems now I see Him on Calvary's tree;
Wounded and bleeding, for sinners pleading,
    Blind and unheeding, dying for me.

—Hymns for the Family,
Paragon Assoc., Inc.,
Nashville, TN

BIBLIOGRAPHY FOR SUPPLEMENTAL UNDERSTANDING

1. Baxter, Sidlow — The Strategic Grasp of the Bible Kregel Publications

2. Chafer, L.S. — Major Bible Themes Zondervan Publishing House

3. Colson, Charles — Kingdoms In Conflict Zondervan Publishing House

4. Lewis, C.S. — Mere Christianity Macmillian Publishing Co.

5. McClain, Alva — The Greatness of the Kingdom Zondervan Publishing House

6. MacDonald, Wm. — Believers Bible Commentary - Old Testament Thomas Nelson Pub.

7. MacDonald, Wm. — Believers Bible Commentary - New Testament A and O Publishers, Wichita, Kan.

8. MacDonald, Gordan — Ordering Your Private World Thomas Nelson Pub.

9. Ryrie, Charles — Balancing The Christian Life Moody Press

10. Schaeffer, Francis — How Should We Then Live? Fleming Revell Co.

11. Tenney, Merrill — New Testament Survey Eerdman Pub. Co.

12. Tozer, A.W. — The Knowledge of the Holy Back to the Bible Broadcast

13. Vander Lugt, Herbert — The Book In Review Radio Bible Class